STATES

MY 19,000-MILE

OF

DETOUR TO FIND DIRECTION →

CONFUSION

paul jury

▲adamsmedia

Avon, Massachusetts

Author's Note: The events in this book are generally based on real experiences, though some names and details were changed to protect privacy, or because the author couldn't remember exactly how every conversation went on a seven-week road trip.

Published by
Adams Media, a division of F+W Media, Inc.
57 Littlefield Street, Avon, MA 02322. U.S.A.
www.adamsmedia.com

ISBN 10: 1-4405-1278-7
ISBN 13: 978-1-4405-1278-0
eISBN 10: 1-4405-2484-X
eISBN 13: 978-1-4405-2484-4

Printed in the United States of America.

10   9   8   7   6   5   4   3   2   1

Library of Congress Cataloging-in-Publication Data
is available from the publisher.

Maps © iStockphoto/Glory Robinson

This book is available at quantity discounts for bulk purchases.
For information, please call 1-800-289-0963.

To Mom & Dad, for making this possible.
And to JD, for making it legible.

ACKNOWLEDGMENTS

The adventure of this book began with one person and his dumb idea, but grew to include so many more people and their much-smarter ideas. To these folks, I give my deepest and warmest thanks:

To Jodi Hildebrand and Anne Walls, for pointing me in the right direction.

To Laney Katz Becker, Brendan O'Neill, Jennifer Hornsby, and Wendy Simard, for seeing the potential in this wacky lark, and helping develop it into a "real book."

To everyone who read chunks and gave much-needed criticism and much-encouraging praise, particularly Kasey, JD, Mom, Dad, Mark, and Alex, who isn't really as surly as he comes off in the story.

To Sarah, for being such an important part of my learning process.

And especially to all the friends, family, and people of America, who shared their stories, couches, and lives with me. Without you, this trip would have been just a lot of lonely driving.

CONTENTS

Prologue MINNESOTA → ix
Forty-Eight AAA Maps

Chapter 1 ALASKA & HAWAII → 1
The Greatest Dumb Idea I Ever Had

Chapter 2 IOWA → 9
The Birth of a Pusher

Chapter 3 MISSOURI → 19
Swimming with Snakes

Chapter 4 ARKANSAS → 29
Beers with Ex-Cons

Chapter 5 TENNESSEE → 35
A Case Against Sleeping in Your Car in the Summer in the South

Chapter 6 KENTUCKY → 37
Marijuana Cheez-Its Baggage

Chapter 7 INDIANA → 43
Union Happy Hour

Chapter 8 ILLINOIS → 48
Choose Your Own Adventure

Chapter 9 WISCONSIN → 54
Sarah vs. the Brat-Eaters

Chapter 10 MICHIGAN → 60
Tony the Tiger Must Die

Chapter 11 OHIO → 65
Mennonites in Hollywood

Chapter 12 WEST VIRGINIA → 69
Editing Quicksand

Chapter 13 PENNSYLVANIA → 76
Directionless

Chapter 14 NEW JERSEY → 81
Drinks with a Rabbi

Chapter 15 NEW YORK → 86
The Longest Island

Chapter 16 CONNECTICUT → 93
The Show-Home Disaster

Chapter 17 RHODE ISLAND → 99
Rule #3

Chapter 18 NEW HAMPSHIRE → 102
The Chairman Is Sick

Chapter 19 VERMONT → 109
Tree Blood & the One-Armed Waitress

Chapter 20 MAINE → 114
A Musical in Maine

Chapter 21 MASSACHUSETTS → 119
Car Pranks

Chapter 22 DELAWARE → 124
Late-Night Outlets

Chapter 23 MARYLAND/D.C. → 128
Capital of the Universe

Chapter 24 **VIRGINIA** → 134
King of the Lonely Road

Chapter 25 **NORTH CAROLINA** → 138
Trolley Fight

Chapter 26 **SOUTH CAROLINA** → 144
Alone & Sick in the Imposter

Chapter 27 **GEORGIA** → 148
Beers in High School

Chapter 28 **FLORIDA** → 157
The Jellyfish Cop

Chapter 29 **ALABAMA** → 164
Nukes & Fishing

Chapter 30 **MISSISSIPPI** → 170
The Waffle Heir

Chapter 31 **LOUISIANA** → 175
The Food 'n Bait 'n Pet 'n Explosives Store

Chapter 32 **TEXAS** → 182
Ryadum, Sheadumbaum Heeah!

Chapter 33 **OKLAHOMA** → 187
Little Beauty

Chapter 34 **KANSAS** → 194
Children of the Corn Maze

Chapter 35 **NEBRASKA** → 199
Tornado Girl

Chapter 36 **SOUTH DAKOTA** → 204
The Spacemobile Lives

Chapter 37 **NORTH DAKOTA** → 216
Gemstones & Dinosaur Bones

Chapter 38 **MONTANA** → 220
The Spacemobile Dies

Chapter 39 **IDAHO** → 228
Rabbit Chasing

Chapter 40 **OREGON** → 235
Damn Hippies

Chapter 41 **WASHINGTON** → 238
Revenge of the Sprint Mentality

Chapter 42 **WYOMING** → 243
Cowboy Country

Chapter 43 **UTAH** → 255
Cougar Junk

Chapter 44 **NEVADA** → 262
Rule #0

Chapter 45 **CALIFORNIA** → 266
Letting Go

Chapter 46 **ARIZONA** → 275
"This Place Ain't Safe!"

Chapter 47 **NEW MEXICO** → 280
Four Corners, Forty-Eight States

Chapter 48 **COLORADO** → 284
The Odds

Epilogue **CALIFORNIA 2** → 289
The Next Adventure

PROLOGUE
MINNESOTA

Forty-Eight AAA Maps

The sun had finally poked through the clouds the day I marched into my local AAA branch, located in a strip mall near my parents' house in South Minneapolis. The kindly, heavyset clerk had taken root behind a desk reading a two-foot-tall U.S. road atlas. He wore cargo shorts and a faithfully logoed AAA shirt.

Seeing me, he set down the atlas and jumped up. "Welcome!" he said, in that excessively pleasant manner that means you're either from Minnesota or about to ask for money. "What can I do for you?"

"I'm planning a trip," I said. "*Outside* the state," I quickly added, stopping a podgy hand from reaching into a bin of pamphlets covered with enticing phrases like "Mall of America" and "Paul Bunyan Land."

The clerk nodded and headed toward a dusty shelf lined with piles of small, folded maps, placed there for the rare occasion when a Minnesotan actually wanted to leave Minnesota. "Goin' to Wisconsin?"

"Well, yeah," I said. "And some other places."

"Iowa? The Dakotas? Don't tell me you're goin' to both Dakotas!"

"It's . . . kind of a big trip."

"Sounds like it!" he exclaimed. "Well, I think we got maps for just about every state! Which ones do ya need?"

I paused, wondering if anybody had ever asked for this in an AAA branch before.

"Um . . . all of them?"

The clerk stared at me. His brow furrowed. Minnesotans always help each other. Still, that was a lot of maps to move.

Slowly, cautiously, his eyes settled on the pristine road atlas he'd been reading.

"Maybe I better just give you this instead."

CHAPTER 1

ALASKA & HAWAII

The Greatest Dumb Idea I Ever Had

I'd always done what was expected of me. I got good grades. I went to college. I once tried to stay all night in the closed campus library, only to be chased around at 5 A.M. by Turkish cleaning ladies, but other than that, I followed the rules. I knew that if I stuck to The Plan, Great Things awaited me.

And on a bright, cloudless day in June of 2002, I did it. Wearing a graduation cap with a fake price tag I'd attached that read "$120,000," I graduated from Northwestern University. My parents chuckled at my little joke, and secretly felt ill. My degrees were an ill-advised combination of film and psychology, but it didn't matter: I was ready for Great Things.

Unfortunately, Great Things couldn't give a crap.

"Hire me!" I told every person I interviewed with. "I'm an Ambitious College Graduate!"

"The economy's bad," every interviewer told me. "We just laid off all of last year's Ambitious College Graduates."

All my econ and engineering friends were picked up in gold-plated limos and carted off to cushy jobs, where they would wear monocles and guffaw at the proletariat. I, on the other hand, packed half my belongings into my parents' van, threw the other half out the window into the apartment courtyard (as was the college tradition), and headed home to Minnesota to move back in with my folks.

I'd thought that once I got to college, the "what am I going to do with my life" thing would just sort of figure itself out, but here I was, graduated and still staring up at the old *Sports Illustrated for Kids* posters in my childhood room. I loved creative work, and figured I could be a video and film editor at one of the Twin Cities' post-production or advertising companies, but none were hiring. I know this because I called every single one.

While I waited for call-backs, I found odd jobs: as the skinniest bouncer in all of downtown Minneapolis, as a part-time house painter, and as a freelance web designer, which in 2002 was like getting a job as a deck hand on a sinking ship.

After three months, I finally landed an editing gig. You always find *something*, after all, if you job-hunt six hours every day for long enough. It just might not be what you expected. My job was a graveyard shift gig for a local news company, editing stock footage to go along with anchors' stories about the new puppy-sweater line that was sweeping the nation. I was paid $11 an hour.

But it was work, and I had to start somewhere. I kept my weekend job at the bar, where a bouncer who day-lighted as a mortician and I would joke that we had found the only three industries impervious to economic downturn: news, booze, and death. We would chuckle, then look down at the ground as waves of soul-crushing depression washed over us.

We turned out to be wrong, of course: a month later, my news company went out of business and laid everyone off. The puppy-sweater story had not been the Pulitzer Prize winner we'd all been hoping for.

My college girlfriend, Sarah, had begun her first year of law school in Chicago, and I realized I would be a terrible boyfriend if I didn't at least *look* for work in the Windy City. And so I looked, found something, and in January of 2003 moved in with Sarah in her studio apartment downtown because I couldn't afford my own place. My job in Chicago was running errands and fetching coffee for the editors at a commercial post-production house, sixty hours a week, for a little less than minimum wage.

After three months, they let me go.

It wasn't the layoffs. I knew it was partly bad luck, and that if I kept at it, I'd eventually find work that would stick. Besides, I was a Minnesota Protestant: taking pleasure in struggle and self-sacrifice was what we *did*.

No, it wasn't the layoffs. It was that things weren't turning out as I had expected.

Editing wasn't what I'd hoped. It was creative work, sure (minus the coffee fetching), but I felt my creativity was building toward someone *else*'s Gatorade commercials, someone *else*'s puppy-sweater videos. It was a creativity that was good for some, but maybe not for me.

My entire life, I'd been heading for a mysterious prize I imagined would be waiting after I graduated college. And now here I was, and all I'd found was an array of new, terrifying feelings. Directionlessness. Uncertainty. Confusion.

My dad owned a small employee-satisfaction survey company and had subtly conveyed that I could always work for him, and maybe take over the business someday. But I had no particular enthusiasm or talent for the work, and I didn't want to be the guy whose dad got him the job. Sarah generously suggested living with her, rent-free, until I figured things out, but the only thing worse than being eighty grand in debt and sponging off your parents is being eighty grand in debt and sponging off your girlfriend. My grandmother told me that whatever I did, it'd better be close enough to Minneapolis that I could come play cribbage with her every Friday night.

I'd always had the answers, on bubble-sheets, on nine different college applications, but now I was left with one giant question: *Now what?*

I'd always been a planner. But my plans had run out.

I walked outside Sarah's apartment one foggy morning, past the place where the Route 66 sign at Michigan Avenue marks the beginning of the old road. I liked creative things, didn't I? Well, I needed a hell of a creative plan to get myself out of this.

And that's when I hatched the greatest plan of all: leave it all behind, borrow my parents' beat-up turquoise '93 Volkswagen Eurovan, and drive to all forty-eight contiguous United States.

It's possible I had been drinking.

Something in me came alive at the idea. Here was my chance to find direction! Here was my chance to do something grand, something amazing, something I could tell my grandkids about someday, as a partial explanation for why my student loans still weren't paid off. Here was also the side benefit of showing up all my tech friends, who by now had paid off their loans and were swimming around in Scrooge McDuck money bins.

At first, I wished there were a way to drive to all fifty states. But driving to Hawaii would require some kind of massive bridge across the Pacific, an idea that gave me the tingles but seemed unfeasible, even for a downturned economy's ambitious and desperate contractors. There *is* a massive bridge to Alaska: it's called Canada. But though I could theoretically have made my journey a *forty-nine*-state Roadtrip, if there's one thing more boring than driving across the ocean for three days, it's driving across Canada. Sorry, Canada. This is a book about America.

I couldn't drive around forever, of course: the meager $3,000 I had squirreled away from my random jobs somewhat restricted exactly *how* grand my something grand could be. I settled on the nice, orderly goal of forty-eight days. According to my calculations, this would give me just enough time and money to experience every state without starving to death. Probably. Also, the Forty-Eight-States-in-Forty-Eight-Days angle made the whole trip even more epic, somehow—and it added a nice element of symmetry that satiated my anal, Type-A side.

Along with everything else, here was a chance to be the rugged adventurer I'd always wanted to be. I would be one of those go-with-the-flow, life-loving mavericks who were etched on the covers of romance novels, my conspicuously open shirt blowing in a sultry southern breeze. I pictured myself in the Ozark wilderness, living off the land, ripping grizzly bears in half, looking like the Brawny paper-towel guy.

The problem was, I wasn't that guy. I was the guy who stayed in Friday nights working on draft twelve of his college essays while his buddies were making beer bongs. I had once packed fifteen people into the Eurovan (which we nicknamed the Spacemobile, for reasons I'll get to in a minute) and skipped fourth period to go to McDonald's, but that was only because there was a McNugget special. I'd certainly never done anything like this.

I was also a heavy perpetrator of what I called the Sprint Mentality. When some folks go jogging, they take it slow, enjoying the exercise and scenery as they run. When I went jogging, I dashed as fast as I could, trampling over anything that got in the way. My goal was to get the run over with and move on to the next thing. But where had sprinting gotten me? Back home, directionless, cleaning toilets for my rent. Maybe it was time that I stopped sprinting and tried strolling.

I made some Roadtrip Rules to try to keep my old self at bay:

Rule #1: No Interstates. Our country has a well-designed and extremely efficient interstate system. I wanted no part of it. A person can hop on I-90 in Boston and drive straight to Seattle, without seeing a thing or talking to a soul. I would stick to the smaller highways and local streets, because the true heart of America is not 3,000 asphalt miles of Chevron/Arby's/Sbarro's. The true heart of America lies in its small towns, down its back roads, and in the questionable lunch specials of its local restaurants. This was the America I wanted to see.

Rule #2: No Speeding. It seemed like I'd get more out of the back roads and small towns if I wasn't going 90 miles an hour. Also, my advanced case of Sprint Mentality had resulted in four speeding tickets in the past four years, and if I got another, the friendly folks at the Minnesota DMV had politely informed me that they would revoke my license. This did not seem like a good step toward completing the Roadtrip.

Rule #3: No Going Back. If I got lost, too bad—I couldn't retrace my steps. I had to find a new way. (This would really come back to bite me in Long Island.)

And finally . . .

Rule #4: Do Something Interesting in Every State. Whether it took an hour or a day, whether it was a famous landmark or a scrape of mischief I got myself into, I would try to cull at least one story from each of our United States.

It was ambitious. Possibly too ambitious. But I was determined. I was a pusher, after all. After a few drafts, I came up with the following route:

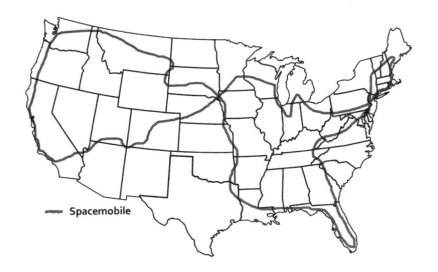

— Spacemobile

At an estimated 12,000 miles, it was a clean, efficient way to accomplish the completely messy mission of driving to every state. I was particularly excited about the Miami-to-Seattle leg: I figured there weren't too many people in South Beach with a "Space Needle or Bust!" sign in their window.

I packed a cooler full of peanut butter, jelly, and bread (after gas, I only had about $400 to spend on food for the entire trip). The dozen or so sets of clothes I owned would have to do; I'd either find washing machines along the way or just quadruple-wear my undies. I crammed everything into a few crates and suitcases, added an airtight bag for the dirties, and prayed it would be enough.

Then panic hit. *What if I had a breakdown? What if I ran out of gas in the middle of nowhere? What if I got kidnapped and was lugged to a cabin in the woods to be used as a sex dummy by demented yokels?* I always had a wild imagination about things like this. My old drama teacher, Ms. Arasim, used to say that having courage didn't mean having no fear— that was fearlessness, and only movie characters were fearless. "Fear Forward!" she drilled into us. Having courage meant being scared as shit, but doing it anyway. (Okay, those weren't her exact words to our sixth-grade class, but you get the idea.)

I swallowed my fear and finished my packing with my new two-foot-tall road atlas, cell phone, and laptop; I wanted to blog about the trip as I went, to share with family and friends the stories I collected, and to let them know I hadn't been abducted by biker gangs.

I couldn't wait. I'd visit everything I'd always wanted to see. I'd visit everyone I knew, everywhere, and sleep in my car the rest of the time—I certainly didn't have enough money to stay in hotels every night, even crappy ones. And on the way, I hoped I'd find where I was supposed to go next.

On a bright, cloudless day in July of 2003, I hugged my parents good-bye and drove away from everything I knew, waving a big middle finger at everything anyone had ever expected of me. Some people graduate from college and get jobs. Other people try to drive to all forty-eight states in a broke-ass Eurovan.

If I was meant to move to back to Chicago and be with my girl-friend, seven weeks alone on the road would show me. If I was meant to return to Minnesota and run my dad's business, two months of subsisting solely off sandwiches made from wholesale peanut butter and Wonder Bread would convince me. If I was going to pee my pants and run home after two states, I guess I'd learn that, too. And if there was something else out there I was meant to do . . . well, I was going to find it. In the meantime, I had some adventures to experience. Forty-eight of them, to be exact.

Remember that license-plate game you played on trips as a kid, where you tried to spot plates from as many states as you could?

Buddy, I *was* the license-plate game.

CHAPTER 2
IOWA

The Birth of a Pusher

One state in, and my trip was already off to a bad start.

First, I had no Spacemobile. My family had nicknamed our 1993 Volkswagen Eurovan "Spacemobile" for two reasons. First, it had the most interior room of any minivan on the market; one more cubic inch and it would be considered a conversion van, or maybe a bus, or a congressional district. The other reason we called it the Spacemobile was because, well, it looked like a Mars Probe. The van was bulky and boxy and seemed like it should be picking up alien droppings instead of school kids. To this day I don't know why my parents picked the color they did; perhaps Volkswagen had an exclusive deal with whatever paint company makes Ass-Ugly Teal, and that was the only color the van came in.

Unfortunately, if the exterior of the Spacemobile had been designed by NASA, the engine had been designed by a gang of mentally handicapped gorillas. To go along with its industry-leading roominess, the Spacemobile also broke down more than any other vehicle in its class, and had suffered yet another meltdown a mere two days before I was scheduled to begin the Roadtrip. The dealer said it might take them a week to do the repairs, because apparently all parts for a '93 Eurovan engine have to be hand-sculpted out of tinfoil and flown in from Berlin.

My parents felt awful. It would have been easy for them to pawn off their degenerate van for me to ride into the ground, but they didn't want to delay my life's big adventure. So they let me use their other car.

My parents' other vehicle was a black Ford Taurus, for which my youngest brother, Alex, had somehow talked them into getting vanity plates that read BIG JURY. It was maybe the greatest ruse Alex ever pulled: at 6'2" and 290 pounds, my "little" brother certainly merited the title, but he rarely drove the car. More often, it was my dad's ride to work, and I think he always felt a little weird driving to business meetings in a car that looked like it belonged to a vaguely litigious pimp.

My mom said they'd call me as soon as the Spacemobile was fixed. She and my dad were heading to eastern Wisconsin the following weekend for a family reunion, and we agreed that if I could arrange to be in the area then, we'd swap cars. It's possible it was all an elaborate ploy to get me to hang out with my grandmother.

But starting the Roadtrip with the Taurus—even if just for a few states—wasn't the same. Sure, the Taurus was inarguably more reliable and gas-efficient, but as far as living accommodations went . . . .

"Mom," I argued. "I'm going to be sleeping on the side of the road. How sketchy am I going to look in a black Ford Taurus with partially tinted windows and vanity plates?"

"Paul," she reminded me, "you're going to be sleeping on the side of the road. You're going to look sketchy no matter what car you're in."

She had a point.

I suppose there's nothing wrong with road-tripping in a sleek, trustworthy black Ford Taurus. It's just that my heart lay in the

German bowels of the blue Eurovan. It was simply a bigger, more ridiculous car. And more ridiculous cars are always more likely to lead to wacky adventures.

In any case, I had no choice, unless I wanted to wait a week or kick a hole in the bottom of the Spacemobile and pedal it Flintstones style for 12,000 miles around the country. As Roadtrip Rule #3 decreed, there was no going back, only finding a new way.

And so, I embarked on my quest in a black Ford Taurus, which I bitterly dubbed the Imposter, and clung to the hope that I would soon be riding high in the aqua throne of my Spacemobile. It was a little disappointing, but I was about to learn my first Roadtrip lesson: the road you planned isn't the only road that can lead to adventure.

Not having the Spacemobile required a rather significant route alteration. If I was to get this trip done in forty-eight days, I couldn't very well waste six of them crawling from Minneapolis to eastern Wisconsin, so I revised my route to dip down and pick up some of the breadbasket states before rolling back up to Appleton the following weekend.

Thus, my revised plan:

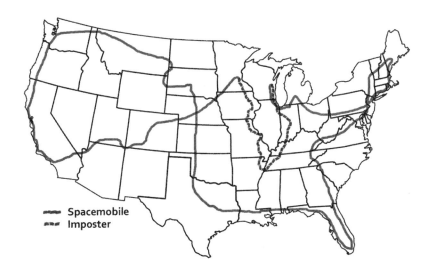

━━ **Spacemobile**
━ ━ **Imposter**

Already, my map was beginning to look like it had been drawn by a sugar-crazed three-year-old with muscle spasms.

To make matters worse, the last-minute Imposter switch had pushed back my departure into Minneapolis rush hour, and I fought traffic all the way out of the Twin Cities. By 10 at night I'd barely made it into Iowa, where I was driving around in exasperated circles trying to find the Field of Dreams. Signs for the attraction were less than clear, and my road atlas was not quite as detailed in small areas as I'd hoped. That's what happens when you try to cram forty-eight states' worth of maps into one book, and you're way too broke to afford GPS.

I felt the Sprint Mentality rising. This wasn't the first time baseball had caused my temper to flair.

When I was seven, a girl named Bridget Walters hit into the first-ever pitching-machine double play and lost the championship game for my second-grade team. I ran off the diamond into a grove of trees, tears brimming, hoping I could just disappear like the ghosts in the movie. But I didn't, and my dad didn't turn up in spirit form to play catch with me. Instead, he came and put his arm on my shoulder, and told me that sometimes in life, people would let me down. I told him that Bridget Walters needed to die. He told me I needed to stop thinking that way, or I wasn't getting any ice cream.

My dad was passing on something grander about life right then, but I was too young to understand. All I knew was that I needed to win, and I vowed to never let anybody or anything come between my goals and me ever again.

This over-competitiveness served me well in other championship games, and on standardized tests. Bridget Walters did not die, though she soon made it up to me by throwing up chicken-noodle soup in the cafeteria in front of the entire second-grade class. But there were times, terrible times, when the world simply refused to comply with my will. Times like tonight, when I found myself driving furiously through the corn, chasing yet another insignificant baseball target.

What was I doing? Racing around in the dark near Dyersville, Iowa, searching for the Field of Dreams just so I could sleep in my car near a cornfield? The competitive bent dies hard.

I whizzed passed a little restaurant that seemed to be built right into somebody's living room. The sign outside read "Pizza—Food!" I considered stopping to investigate: wasn't pizza classified as food in Iowa? Was the condition of their pizza so questionable as to require the qualifying "food" tacked onto the end? Or was it food *for* pizzas to eat? I pictured a huge, snarling pie hopping around, gobbling up smaller, terrified pizzas. But I didn't stop. It's hard to slam on your brakes on an impulse, even on a secondary highway.

So far, my trip felt neither like a leisurely stroll nor a wacky adventure. I drove on into the darkness, wondering worriedly what might lie ahead.

Finally I found the locked gate to the field. The Field of Dreams was closed at 11 P.M., so I pulled the Imposter to the shoulder of the tiny highway about a hundred yards away. I would sleep right there for the night, and see the field in the morning. Okay. This felt a little more like it.

I parked the car close to the stalks and climbed out. Stretched my legs. Brushed my teeth with water from one of the bottles I'd brought and spat into the corn. There wasn't a sound or light around for miles, except the Imposter's tiny dome light and the soft ding of the ignition bell. Suddenly I realized I'd never done this before. I looked at my black car in the black road in the black night. This was going to be my bedroom for the next seven weeks.

There are at least three things that suck about sleeping in a car, all of which hit me within about sixty seconds of lying down in the Imposter's passenger seat.

1. **It's not comfortable.** Turns out, most car seats don't recline all the way (especially when your back seat is loaded with seven weeks' worth of junk). So when you're over six feet tall, the lying-down

situation isn't exactly Sealy Posturepedic. You can't close all the windows, lest you suffocate in your sleep. You can't leave the heat or A.C. on, lest you kill your battery by morning. So whatever temperature it is outside is what temperature you're going to be. All night.

2. **You're on display.** When you sleep in a cavernous monstrosity like the Spacemobile, you can simply crawl into the back, and with enough blankets, nobody can even tell you're there. In a car, however, you're lying inches from a window where any weirdoes of the night can come up and have a peek at you. No matter how you try to cover up, you feel like you're taking a nap in a store window, in plain view of any serial killers. Or more likely, you're at risk of being viewed as a serial killer yourself.

3. **It's scary.** I'll admit it. Besides the whole new set of strange sounds and dangers you face every night, sleeping in a car off small highways puts you in the perfect overlap of busy versus not-busy risks. That is to say, the road you're probably parked a few feet from carries just enough traffic for you to be slammed into by an errant semi truck, but not so much traffic that any homicidal maniac wouldn't have plenty of time to hold a rag over your mouth and carefully slice you into pieces.

Most of these concerns, of course, are somewhat alleviated if you can find a rest stop. But most rest stops are on interstates, and as Rule #1 dictated, I wasn't taking interstates. I was taking county roads and small, abandoned highways. Every night, I realized with a chill, would mean finding a new, unwelcoming place to sleep.

I lay wide awake through most of the first night of my Roadtrip. *What had I gotten myself into?* The night plays tricks on the imagination, I knew, and many of my fears were groundless. But some of them weren't. After all, there are 6 million car accidents in America every year. By driving constantly for the next forty-eight days, I was greatly increasing my changes of being one of them. There are also

18,000 million murders every year in this great country of ours. Over the next seven weeks I would be in the same state as every single murderer.

Somewhere around 5 A.M., I startled from fitful half-slumber to see a man carrying hedge-clippers float silently in front of the car, staring at me as he passed. I nearly laid rubber all the way back to Minneapolis.

I awoke at 8 A.M. to discover that I hadn't slept next to the Field of Dreams after all, but instead next to just another regular cornfield, with no particular baseball diamond or distinction. The real Field of Dreams was a quarter-mile down the road. Shockingly, most corn-fields in Iowa look basically alike.

Partly because of my long history with baseball, the Field of Dreams was the one thing in Iowa that I had always wanted to see. But when I arrived at the famed field, I realized that "if you build it, they will come" applies also to the field's tourism campaign: there were roughly 300 hyperactive little kids swarming the field, throwing balls at each other's heads and running in and out of the corn, wondering why they didn't vanish. The site consisted of the field, a few placards about the movie, and little else. James Earl Jones and Kevin Costner weren't around to sign autographs. I spent a few minutes gazing out over the scene, rubbing the knots out of my neck. Then I moved on, a childhood dream unsatisfyingly checked off my list.

I plowed south through the endless carpet of more Iowa corn, trying to put my first night behind me and refocus. I was still alive. I could do better. And I had two important people to see before I left Iowa: my girlfriend Sarah's parents.

Sarah and I met the day after 9/11. It was the beginning of my senior year at Northwestern, and my buddies and I had just moved into our new cheap (dumpy) college apartment when the tragedy struck. After numbly watching the newscasts for a day and a half, I didn't know what else to do besides go back to painting my room, which badly needed renovation, since the previous owner had apparently used the room primarily as a murder basement. Sarah was friends with one of my roommates, and she came over to find me shirtless after a whole summer of working at a Los Angeles gym—yet another odd job I'd had, which paid the bills while I interned for a film company. She was beautiful. I was tan, as in shape as I get, and covered in paint. Everyone was feeling very emotional. It was, as they say, on.

For both of us, it was our first serious relationship. I had somehow gotten through the teen "Do you want to go out with me? Yes/No/Maybe" years firmly in the No and Maybe categories, and Sarah was the first girl I'd dated for longer than a few months. Sarah, on the other hand, had had plenty of date offers but had elected to be choosy, which made it all the more puzzling that she ended up with me. I suppose I was pretty good about bringing her flowers, and once on an early date I sent her on a poem-based treasure hunt around campus that ended in a picnic in a rose garden. She was lucky she found the place, given my horrendous clues, but somehow they convinced her to stick around.

Sarah and I would lie for hours in my room, staring up at the huge U.S. map I had on my wall, talking about the places we would go someday. Each state was painted one of five colors, and we'd giggle about which color team would win when the inevitable State War someday broke out. It's possible we were both overly biased toward our own states' teams, but one thing was for certain: the Pink Team (or Team Sucky State), with West Virginia, Oklahoma, North Dakota, Delaware, and Wisconsin, was definitely going to lose. We also agreed that Texas had been waiting for a war like this to break out for years.

Now I was checking off colored states on a new map and leaving Sarah back in Chicago, alone. After we both graduated, Sarah had immediately started law school. I had done . . . well, the exact opposite. She knew what her career was for the next forty years. I was looking for the next place to get gas.

I stopped at Sarah's parents' farm in Wayland, Iowa, to pick up a painting to deliver to her. Wayland is a tiny town, but Sarah's mother ran a successful travel agency there and was the kind of woman who lived on a farm but traveled the world and collected fine paintings. Sarah's father had been a successful farmer, but a health condition had forced him out of the fields when Sarah was still young. Sarah had a sister but no brothers, and the influence of a kind but infirm father and a strong and successful mother had left her the sort of girl who braves a top-ten law school but was afraid of thunder. I found it an adorable combination.

She was five foot two, fit, with piercing blue eyes. I was over six feet, but somehow we fit perfectly together. We were both planners. She was a good cook; I was stupendous at eating. She was the safe, comfortable girlfriend. Which is why it was so frustrating that something was bugging me.

The previous year had been hard, with her studying around the clock as a first-year law student and me working around the clock as a news editor/errand-runner/waste of human tissue. To buttress my runner job in the Windy City, I found weekend work as an office building security guard, which is like being a bouncer at a bar where nobody ever goes, and where you have to wear a bad suit.

I lived with Sarah but barely saw her. I liked my girlfriend, but my heart wasn't into living in Chicago. What I wanted was to go on my Roadtrip. Sarah once caught me marking off days on my calendar until I could leave—apparently girlfriends don't like it when you do this.

The day I left Sarah's place to start making arrangements for the Roadtrip, she cried. She did this a lot, whenever I did something crappy to her, or whenever *Friends* was over. So of course I cried, too. Some couples yell and throw things when times get tough; we were like a couple of blubbering mothers watching the end of *Sophie's Choice*.

"Will you be able to call me," she asked, "from all those little highways?"

"Of course I will. It's America, not the Amazon."

"I don't want to be a burden to you on your Roadtrip."

"Of course you won't be. You're my girlfriend, not a load of manure."

I always had a way with metaphors around her.

As I helped Sarah's mother in Iowa cram a huge covered painting into what little storage room I had left in the Imposter—completely losing the use of my rearview mirror—the word "burden" burrowed into my head. If anything, wasn't *I* being the burden to *her*? After all, I was the one celebrating our two-year anniversary with a forty-eight-day vacation away from her. I knew she didn't love my Roadtrip. But I knew she loved me.

I had yet to tell Sarah I loved her. It's possible that I felt the same way as she did, but I'd been careful not to use those words until I was sure. And being sure about anything was hard when I didn't even know what time zone I'd be in next week. So I didn't let myself be in love. One more reason why I was a terrible boyfriend.

On my way out of Wayland I passed a wedding. The bride and groom skipped out of the yawning door of a tiny white wooden church, identical to millions of other white wooden churches on the corners of small-town America. A dozen family members and friends showered the pair with confetti that twittered down like dying butterflies. The happy couple didn't look a day over 20. This was the part of the country where the marriage bug catches early, and some people are ready to settle down at age 23. I was starting to think I wasn't one of those people.

Making the person you're with—and care deeply for—your first priority should never be a burden. So why—even if only a little bit—did it still feel like one?

I headed south, still struggling to keep my speed down and resist the tempting blue and red interstate signs inviting me to take the fast way out of Iowa. Nobody said this Roadtrip was going to be easy. Not any part of it.

CHAPTER 3

MISSOURI

Swimming with Snakes

I crossed the border between Iowa and Missouri around dusk, on the type of teensy highway you'd expect of the border between Iowa and Missouri. I immediately came across a hundred people in a dirt field, shooting off fireworks in their own little state-border Fourth of July. The fact that it was now the eighth of July did not seem to faze them; this seemed like a part of the country where holiday dates are observed only approximately—perhaps rural Missoura has its own Independence Day, never mind what them sneaky politicians say.

I recognized what was happening: Missouri had legal fireworks, and communist Iowa did not, so Iowans came down across the state line to sit in the backs of pickup trucks and drink beer from Styrofoam coolers while red and blue explosions lit up the dusty summer sky. Growing up in Minneapolis we'd made a similar yearly drive thirty miles east to Hudson, Wisconsin (chief export: bottle rockets), save for the couple of years when Governor Jesse "The Body" Ventura succeeded in his primary office objective of legalizing fireworks for the Land of 10,000 Lakes. That was a special and dangerous time for the children of Minnesota. I remember driving down the street that first year as a little street kid held up his baggy jeans with one hand and shot fireballs out of a Roman Candle with the other, as he chased another kid in and out of traffic. Fireworks didn't stay legal in Minnesota for very long after that. Rumor has it a lot of little kids burned their eyeballs out that summer.

It seems odd that in this country you can drive past a certain sign and suddenly do things that would get you arrested on the other side of that sign. I guess it's a reminder that not so long ago, the "United States" was simply that: a bunch of different states, united in democracy but not 100 percent sure that they would always get along. And each state reserved the right to bail on the others if they didn't agree about certain things. Like speed limits. Or slavery.

Other than the colorful welcoming party, the scenery didn't change much as I passed down into east-central Missouri. The quality of the cornfields seemed to degrade slightly, but that might have been an effect of the darkness. Or who knows, Missouri corn really might be worse.

I aimed for the distant St. Louis, connecting the dots from one tiny town to another, each with its own curious combination of beat-up, timeless local gas stations. Abel Sneed's Iowa Gas might sit right next to a Subway or a Wal-Mart, where corporate progress had infiltrated and begun to erase the past.

I stopped for gas at Sneed's and stepped out of the car, realizing it was already about ten degrees hotter than it had been at the Field of Dreams. I was starting to question whether doing this trip in the middle of the summer was such a bright idea. The air was heavy with humidity, like a swamp. It was also heavy with bugs. There were swarms of them everywhere: on the lights, on my windshield, and in my mouth when I opened it to tell the station attendant his card swiper wasn't working. Maybe "Bible Belt" refers not so much to the popularity of the Good Book in these parts, but to the biblical-plague level of insects.

Monotonous landscapes, unbearable climate, Subways that are only open until 9 P.M. . . . Why would anyone want to live here? Maybe the locals who hadn't traveled enough to know there was anything else out there.

It was midnight before I arrived at my college friend Craig's apartment in St. Louis, irritable from the sore butt and tried patience that come with thirteen hours of roads with stop signs and wildly fluctuating speed limits. I still hated being late for anything. But Craig didn't seem to mind, and my annoyance was assuaged by cheap beers on his roof deck and a lengthy discussion of the merits of giant fighting robots. It wasn't *that* long since we'd been in college.

The next day Craig gave me a tour around St. Louis and the Wash. U. campus, where he was a med student. Sophisticated and modern, St. Louis seemed like a far cry from the dusty small towns I'd sped through the previous night. But I guess that's how every state is—those with the gumption to do so move to the big city and build skyscrapers, and everyone else stays contentedly in the country and yells at fireworks.

Craig, a biochem major in college, was now in some kind of absurd MD/master's program in which they awarded him a full scholarship plus an annual stipend to stay in school for eight more years. When I asked him why he didn't merely settle for the six-year pain of *regular* med school, Craig responded that what he eventually wanted to do was work on a cancer cure, and this would allow him to get a jump-start on his research. This was insane. Craig was twenty-three and was already *curing cancer.* And getting paid for it. Two years ago Craig and I had been living in the same crappy dorm, drinking even crappier beer. Now Craig was the epitome of the path you're supposed to take, and I was perched on the slippery slope that led down toward the Guy Who Lives in a Van by the River.

The next morning I said goodbye to Craig. I was well rested from a driving break, a day of normal food, and two—count 'em *two*— nights on a couch. But I was anxious to get moving again. It felt like a cop-out, sleeping in Craig's air-conditioned apartment. I hadn't even experienced any real adventures yet, besides being a dreadful pansy during my first night at the Field of Dreams. Whatever my road was, I needed to get back on it.

It wasn't long before I was back in small-town Missouri, seeing signs that said things like "*Jesus saves, and you can too at Hinckley Hardware!*" I cracked the window and a hot blast of air slapped my face. I breathed a sigh of relief and inhaled three mosquitoes. I was back in the muggy Crotch of Nowhere, also known as southern Missouri. My bravado was rejuvenated. I was tough. I was ready. I was down for whatever adventure the road wanted to throw at me.

Little did I know how much I was about to regret those words.

There is a lot of traveling on a two-month road trip, but little of it can be considered exercise. There is, of course, the infinite low-resistance leg-press known as the gas pedal, and I was ever-so-slightly concerned that, by the end of my trip, my right calf would be twice as big as my left, but even this small workout is attenuated by a little device called cruise control. So to keep my muscles from atrophying, I planned to speckle every state or two with a pair of my favorite middle-of-nowhere athletic activities: running, and swimming in mountain streams.

The purpose of the running was threefold. First, I really needed to break up the monotony of driving; 12,000 miles seems fine and dandy on paper, but I wasn't even through three states yet and I already wanted to shoot myself in the face. Second, jogging would help me train for a little 26.2-mile race I hoped to take on once the Roadtrip was over. Yes, I was running my first marathon, and I, Mr. Type A, thought I needed to dominate said marathon. And third, running would let me see the nooks and crannies of America. If driving down a small town's main road is a magnifying glass, jogging through its alleys and backyards is a high-powered microscope. It's also a good way to get the sheriff called on you.

The purpose of swimming in mountain streams was also three-fold. First, I would need to cool off after the aforementioned jogs, which would all be taking place in midsummer. Second, I hadn't really accounted for bathing on my trip, save for the occasional days when I'd be staying with someone I knew, and swimming was as close to showering as I was going to get. And the third reason? I guess swimming in mountain streams just seemed like a really Thoreauvian, nature-man thing to do.

Missouri isn't much for mountains, so I had to take what I could get. And what I could get in southern Missouri was Lake Wappapello, a murky lake/campground/boat launch. (Yes, accurately describing it requires a lot of slashes.)

Lake Wappapello wasn't far from the Arkansas border, but it *was* far from the nearest town, and was basically empty except for a few sweaty people who inexplicably wanted to camp in the boonies in the middle of a heat wave. But the grounds had some hiking paths that were good for jogging and some water that was . . . well, I won't say it was *good* for swimming, but technically it was liquid. Lake Wappapello would have to do.

The Missouri humidity limited my run to an excruciating four miles, and it wasn't until I was done that I got a good view of the lake. I quickly changed my mind about the swim. Lake Wappapello was roughly the color of chocolate pudding and exuded a smell that fell somewhere between "oil spill" and "compost heap." But all was not lost: the campground *did* feature a breezy little dock/boat launch/fuel station (again, slashes are needed), and I really needed to cool off. I grabbed my laptop, locked the rest of my possessions securely in the Imposter, and settled down on the end of the dock to update my blog. There was no cell reception, but at least I could write.

How my car keys ended up at the bottom of Lake Wappapello is hard to say, exactly. It seems my quality pair of red running shorts did not come equipped with quality pockets, because somehow they managed to regurgitate my Imposter keys halfway down the dock. I gaped in horror as I watched them bounce—in slow-motion—from slat to slat, before disappearing into the mucky water below with a sickening gurgle.

It was my only set of keys. The nearest locksmith or auto shop was probably 100 miles away, and who knew how long it would take to get another key made? It appeared I would be getting my swim after all.

Okay, no problem, I thought to myself. *I'll go up to the campground office and see if they have any goggles I can borrow. I'm sure the water can't be that murky all the way down, and it can't be more than a couple feet deep under the dock.* I was feeling pretty swell about my solution as I entered the office.

The gaunt, wild-eyed old man behind the gift shop counter sported bright white hair to match his white moustache. He almost looked like a tall, skinny Albert Einstein, if Einstein had been insane and worked at a campground in Missouri.

Politely, I asked him if he had any advice for fishing things out of his lake.

"Nope, nope, sure don't!" he said, rocking back and forth in his chair.

"Oh," I said, not anticipating quite that unhelpful a response. "Well, do you have any goggles?"

He stood slowly, grabbed a pair of cheap children's goggles from the wall, and plopped them on the counter. "Got these," he offered. "Three dollars!"

I peered at them. They were about three sizes too small for my head, and I seriously doubted that the one-centimeter plastic seal would keep the filthy water out of my eyes.

"Got anything else?"

"Nope, nope, sure don't!" he said. "Three dollars!"

I explained to him that all my money was in my wallet, which was locked in the car, but I would pay him after I found my keys. He just stared at me. This wasn't good enough. He wanted collateral.

"Like what?" I asked. I wasn't even wearing a shirt.

His eyes fell on my laptop.

I rolled my eyes and handed him my computer. Apparently this guy wasn't interested in being tremendously helpful.

"So how deep's the lake, before I try this?"

"Oh, I dunno . . . I reckon a couple inches to about six feet under the middle part o' the dock, where all them frayed cables is at."

Frayed cables. Lovely. And the "middle part o' the dock" was precisely where my keys were. Not good news, but I might as well get to it. I didn't exactly have much choice.

"Uh, all right," I said, turning for the door. "Anything else I should know before I jump in?"

"Uh, nope, nope. Jus' watch out for the snakes!"

I froze. Now, I don't have any particular aversion to snakes, at least not in an Indiana Jones kind of way. Not that I particularly *like* snakes—the idea of huge water snakes, one of God's creepiest creatures, slithering around my ankles as I treaded through the muck was definitely not a pleasant one. But given a choice between snakes and being stranded in southern Missouri?

Everything was still cool; I could handle it. Besides, was this guy even serious? There couldn't *really* be snakes in this random lake in southern Missouri. At least not snakes that could hurt me.

"What, like poisonous snakes?" I asked, with a smirk.

"Why, yup, yup, sure are. I saw some pokin' their heads up around the dock the other day."

Everything was no longer cool.

Poisonous snakes? Are there really poisonous snakes in America? This isn't the Amazon. The white-haired guy was staring at me, straight-faced. *On the other hand, I have heard of water moccasins. 'Moccasin' is a Native American word, isn't it?*

I couldn't believe that the etymology of the word "moccasin" was going to be a factor in whether or not I was about to die in a lake

My panic continued. *And the Southwest! Don't they have poisonous rattlesnakes in the Southwest?*

I suddenly found myself wishing I'd watched more Discovery Channel growing up.

Snakes or no snakes, I was now stuck picturing myself being bitten by swimming, venomous reptiles while I sifted fruitlessly through mucky crap trying to find my invisible car keys. This was already going to be a needle-in-a-haystack job, only now the haystack had snakes in it.

But what could I do? I weighed my options:

1. Brave the snakes. I hoped they didn't like the taste of white meat.
2. Break into and hotwire the Imposter, and then somehow get a new key made in the nearest town, 100 miles away in Arkansas. I didn't know how to do any of this.
3. . . . ? I didn't even know what option three would be. Have the car towed to a locksmith? There wasn't one for 100 miles. And the money I had in the car would barely be enough to cover the $3 goggles, to say nothing of a $300 tow job.

I tried to sound stoic as I faced the white-haired guy. "If I'm not back in twenty minutes, can you . . . come look for me or something?"

"I got a pocket-knife. I can cut an X!"

I froze again. "What?"

"Ain't that what you're supposed to do? Cut an X where the bite is?"

This had officially become the worst thing ever.

"Yeah, uh, I'm leaving now. Thanks for the help."

"Oh," he chuckled. "I didn't really help ya that much!"

Some people graduate from college and get jobs. Other people dive into muddy, snake-filled lakes to find their car keys.

I stripped to my boxers and gazed down from the dock. I had never been so freaked out to jump in a lake. I recalled the words of Ms. Arasim: *It's okay to be afraid of something, as long as you do it anyway.* Somehow I highly doubted this was what Ms. Arasim had in mind. But this trip was supposed to be about adventure, right? I took a deep breath.

Fear forward.

I jumped in.

The horrible squishing feeling I experienced as my feet plunged six inches deep into mushy lake bottom sent me scrambling halfway back up onto the dock. I envisioned baby snake eggs and protective snake mothers recoiling at this attack on their homes and preparing a counterattack, and I clung to the underside of the dock for a full minute. But I'd come this far. I slipped on the children's goggles, let go, and sank underwater.

Barely controlling my panic, I paddled down to the bottom and tried to get a look around. The goggles were completely useless. The water was about as translucent as root beer, and rushed right past the worthless seal into my eyes. I couldn't even see the front lens of the goggles, much less the bottom of the lake. I tossed the goggles back up onto the dock—I would have to do this blind. I was still facing a needle in a snake-filled haystack. Only now I was blindfolded. And I had to hold my breath.

Under normal circumstances I can't hold my breath for terribly long, and I can hold it for even less time when I'm completely wigging out. I would dive down and sift blindly through the sticky bottom for about six seconds before my leg would brush against one of the frayed cables—or worse, a snake-head-sized bubble would ooze from the bottom, tickle up my leg and into my boxers—and I would promptly lose my mind and scramble gasping to the surface. Each time I dove, I could cover only a few square feet—probably the same few square feet—and I had no idea whether I was making progress or burying my keys deeper in the muck. I was panicked, discouraged, smelly from the lake, and getting absolutely nowhere.

After about ten minutes of this misery, I discovered a better method. If I held on to the dock, I could sift through the mud with my feet and keep my upturned mouth barely above water. This meant removing my sandals, which I had kept on to protect me from the serpents of the deep, but by this point I figured I was a goner anyway.

I shed the sandals and sifted frantically with my feet through the muck like a hopeless, armless gold-miner . . . and prayed.

Yes, I prayed. I've always thought that in a world full of suffering, there must be tons of people with problems a lot bigger than mine, so I've tried not to bother God with frivolous requests for help on math quizzes or good luck on the upcoming blackjack hand. But that day I prayed. I prayed for the snakes to have mercy on me and that, by some utter miracle, my digging toes would strike gold.

Heaven must have felt bad about denying me the Spacemobile, because a miracle happened. My feet touched something small and hard and somehow, by some grace, a guy who regularly loses his cell phone in his own pockets was able to find a set of car keys under a cable in some mud at the bottom of an opaque lake. I dove down and wrapped my fingers around my salvation.

I must have launched out of the water Flipper-style and landed in a victory dance on the dock, judging by the way the few other people at the campground gawked at me. I didn't care. I ran to the Imposter, unlocked it, grabbed my wallet, and charged up to the office. The white-haired old guy nearly fell out of his chair as I—a shirtless, soaking, ecstatic, muddy mess—whipped open the door, slammed a $10 bill down on the counter, grabbed my laptop, held up my keys, and proclaimed, "Screw the snakes, screw you, keep the change, I'm out of here!"

I only spent a total of about twenty minutes in mucky Lake Wappapello, but the boxers I swam in reeked like toxic ass. I threw them out the window and rode commando for a few miles before fishing another pair from my laundry bag. And that's how I got the heck out of Missouri: dripping with muddy water, radiating stink, looking frightening enough to scare children. But my prayers had been answered. I was on the road again.

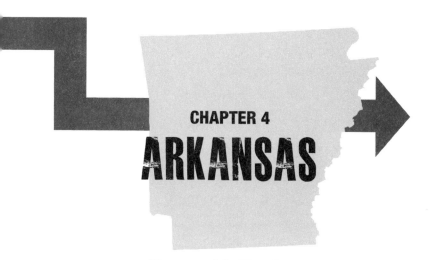

CHAPTER 4

ARKANSAS

Beers with Ex-Cons

I plowed on from Missouri into Arkansas with one mission: to find a bar. And not just any bar—I wanted to appropriately celebrate my victory over the poisonous water snakes of Wappapello with the trashiest bar I could find. Also, I smelled way too bad to go to a normal bar, and I wasn't willing to risk another swim to clean myself up.

And I needed an electrical outlet. The Imposter's cigarette lighter didn't work because Alex had once jammed a carrot into it, and I needed a place to plug in my phone and computer. Leave it to me to remain technology dependent even in the most rustic of circumstances.

Arkansas is the birthplace of John Grisham, Bill Clinton, and Wal-Mart (and the hundreds of thousands of jobs that have come with it). Arkansas even played key roles in the Texas Revolution and the Mexican-American War, given its key location halfway between Mexico and the U.S. capital. Clearly, Arkansas is a state of many cultural boasting points. The bar I went to was not one of them.

The Nic Nac Bar and Grill, located in the bad part of West Memphis (assuming there's a "good" part of West Memphis), was truthfully only the *second*-trashiest bar I could find. First prize went to a decaying shack in the middle of a swamp called the L.E. Social Club, which might have been a KKK meeting house, except that it had a Pabst Blue Ribbon sign in the window. Or who knows, perhaps PBR is the official beverage of the Klan. Anyway, the L.E. Social Club was closed. I was disappointed.

But not to worry, the Nic Nac was plenty trashy. Upon entering the quaint little tavern, I was immediately struck by two things: (1) The only form of decoration was about fifty blank CDs suspended from the ceiling by three-foot pieces of string, and (2) The woman tending bar wasn't wearing any shoes. It seemed like the kind of place my mother would have wanted me to avoid, but I was still drunk on adventure. And hey, if I could jump into a snake-filled river, I could brave a CD cave to get a beer.

The CDs commanded my attention as I took a seat at the bar. There they were, hanging down right above head-level, rotating slowly and reflectively like tiny two-dimensional disco balls. I imagined they had been ostentatiously hung there at a time when CDs were more valuable (back before you could buy 100 of them at Best Buy for ten bucks) in an antiquated exhibition of wealth, the way one might wallpaper one's outhouse with Confederate dollars. Perhaps these dangling discs were once the envy of all West Memphis bars.

I was interrupted from my CD-gazing trance by the barefoot bartender, who pushed a coaster underneath my nose and smiled warmly. "What can I get you, sweetheart?" she asked in a soft twang. She was young—probably Sarah's age, and not bad looking. Then I noticed that a lack of shoes was not this woman's only salient feature; she was also heavy with child. I couldn't help but think of the expression "barefoot and pregnant," though I'd never thought of this term being applied to bartenders. I fought my gut-ward glance and asked what beers they had on tap. "Just Bud Light, sweetie," she smiled back. "It's a dollar twenty-five a glass." I was pleased—about the price, mostly, but also about how nice she was. I couldn't help but imagine that perhaps it was that sweet smile and cheap beer that had helped get her pregnant in the first place.

My Bud Light came in a red plastic party cup (not that I expected more), and after it came several others, each served with a smile, as I settled into my new favorite bar.

The barefoot bartender and I had been the sole occupants of the Nic Nac, but after a couple of beers two other customers stumbled in. Both were in their thirties, and both sported jeans and flannel shirts, in July in Arkansas. They sat down next to me at the bar. Rusty and Jeff were their names, and after a bit of conversation I learned that until recently, they had been cellmates at the local prison. Jeff had gotten out a few months ago, and Rusty had been released earlier that day, and they had agreed to meet at the Nic Nac for their reunion. So they were celebrating, too. We all clinked our party cups, though somehow their occasion seemed a bit more potent than mine.

Rusty and Jeff were not hardened felons. Rusty, whose closely shaved head was offset by a heavy beard, as if his hair had migrated, had done nine months for being caught with a bunch of marijuana in his trunk. I was about to learn that how much jail time you served was as much a product of what legal counsel you had—and how much you back-talked the judge—as it was of what crime you'd actually committed.

"I guess I've always been a bit of a revolut'nary," Rusty said, smoking a damp cigarette and swirling his party cup around as if it contained fine wine. "I realize that my worldview may not be fully appreciated in my lifetime. But someday, society will understand, as I do, that there's a bigger morality beyond our fleeting laws."

"What did your lawyer say about that?" I asked.

"I don't need no thievin' lawyer," Rusty replied emphatically, ashing on the floor, "And I told that fat judge the same thing. I can represent my own self just fine, thank you very much."

The American justice system was starting to make a little more sense to me.

Jeff, a boyish young man with a bowl cut who'd done a few months for a bar fight that had gotten out of hand, was a bit more penitent.

"I'm sorry about what I done," he said. "America's been good to me, and I feel like I let 'er down. This is the number one most freest country in the world—you can do just 'bout anything you like in this great land of ours. 'Cept hit someone in the neck with a tire iron, apparently."

"Actually," said Rusty, correcting his friend. "I did a lot of reading while I was away. Turns out America has the most laws of any country. We also got the most people in prison. So if you wanna think of freedom in terms of not taking people's freedom away, and not making rules about what they can and can't do, America's the *least* free country in the world."

"You're only saying that because you were jus' in jail," said Jeff.

Rusty was unmoved. "Well, it's true. Look it up."

Jeff took a big drink. "I'm not sure I'd wanna live in a country with the *least* laws and prisoners," he pondered. "I bet a lot of stuff's legal in El Salvador, but I wouldn't wanna party there."

"I'm just sayin'. You and I jus' ate up a lot of tax dollars, and we never did nothin' except try to get a little buzz on, and crack a no-good sonofabitch what was comin' to him."

I ordered us another $3.75 round, while the pregnant bartender cleaned our red party cups to be reused.

Presently, the owner of the Nic Nac limped in, toeing open the creaky screen door and carrying several boxes of paper plates for the coming week's lunch specials. She was a hardened woman in her forties, with whiskery hair and pretty but weathered features, like a moderately attractive scarecrow.

"I think I'll save up some money and move to Uruguay," pontificated Rusty, as the owner set the plates down on the bar and took up a stern tone with the bartender. "I hear they're a little more lenient about restrictin' folks' freedom."

"You sound like a hippie," said Jeff.

"Hey." said Rusty, suddenly serious. "I ain't no goddamn hippie."

The owner, Marcy, introduced herself to me, the only new face at the bar, and invited me outside for a smoke while my laptop charged on a barstool. For a while, she puffed her Marlboro and said nothing. Then she gestured down the main strip of road that passed the Nic Nac.

"New fancy bar opened up 'cross town," she said with a frown. "All the regulars are probably there." Then she sized me up. "Where you say you were from again?"

"Minnesota," I said. She nodded, gravely. I probably wasn't going to be a good source of referrals.

She gestured to another bar, next door. Amazingly, it looked even more run-down than the Nic Nac.

"That there's the Pig 'N Poke," she said. I wondered briefly if the name meant that they served barbeque, or if it was a jab at the clientele's physical appearances and promiscuity.

"They used to be our biggest competition, 'afore this new bar. But Pig 'N Poke's low-class." I detected a trace of spite in her voice. "Place is filled with hookers. And not classy hookers, neither; we're talking real low-life, blowjob-for-a-quarter hookers."

Marcy spat in the dirt. I wasn't sure what the going rate for blowjobs in West Memphis was, but a quarter sounded pretty cheap. Secretly I cursed myself for not spotting the Pig 'N Poke first.

"But we're beatin' 'em!" she said proudly. "They're about to go under. We'd be doin' real good," then her mood soured again, "if it wasn't for that new bar 'cross town."

I was just three states from home and here were people tackling life quite differently than I was. But they seemed content. Except about the jail part.

I said goodbye to my new friends and left a massive tip. Somehow it's easier to boldly throw money around when you're tipping on $1.25 Bud Lights. I climbed into the Imposter before too many party cups of beer rendered me unable to drive. As it was, I was feeling a little woozy behind the wheel, but I wasn't going far. Besides, between weed-trunks and tire-irons, I figured the cops in West Memphis probably had bigger things to deal with tonight than me.

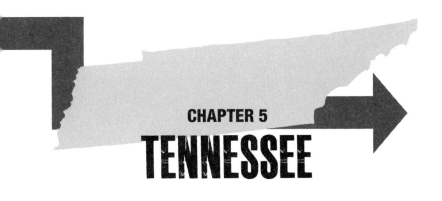

CHAPTER 5

TENNESSEE

A Case Against Sleeping in Your Car in the Summer in the South

I awoke that next morning in the corner of a Shell station parking lot in west Memphis, Tennessee (not to be confused with West Memphis, Arkansas, though the probability of having drinks with ex-convicts is about the same in both places), and immediately learned two new lessons about sleeping in cars:

1. It's easier to do when you're a little drunk.
2. Doing it in a black car in the summer in the South is a terrible idea.

I was now realizing the full downside of beginning my trip in July. It was already about 100 degrees in the Imposter by 8:30 A.M., when I kicked into consciousness, drenched in sweat. The matter wasn't helped by the fact that only one window was open, only a crack, due to my policy of trying not to be butchered in my sleep.

But the heat wasn't what woke me. It was a gas-station attendant's rapping on the Imposter window. He was an elderly black man with a kindly but worn face that looked like it had partly melted from too many years in the Tennessee sun. I jolted awake, afraid for a moment that I was blocking a gas pump or was parked on top of someone's dog. But the attendant's eyes were more full of concern than reprimand. I rolled down the window.

"You alive?" he said.

I *thought* I was alive. A Shell station in west Memphis didn't seem like a very good heaven, although it was a bit mundane to be hell. But I could also see why the attendant's question didn't seem like a joke: my shirt was absolutely soaked in sweat, and I was having trouble peeling myself off the passenger seat pleather. Thanks to a particularly transient set of friends and relatives, I had places to crash in roughly twenty states, but that still left many more vacant nights. I would have to get a little smarter about this whole sleeping-in-a-car thing.

Then I noticed the small group of other employees and customers that had gathered outside the store, all gawking in my direction. Now the attendant's question *really* didn't seem like a joke. Perhaps this wasn't the first time someone had had an automotive slumber party in Shell's parking lot. Maybe last time the outcome had been different.

The attendant was still staring at me, and I realized I hadn't responded. "Yeah," my parched throat croaked. "Still alive."

"Oh," he said, and turned toward the group. "He's alive!"

The group reacted with a mixture of relief and—could it be?—disappointment. The attendant shuffled off without another word about my sleeping in their parking lot. It could have been the heat, but I swear I detected a speck of defeat in his voice. And it could have been the heat, but I swear I saw money change hands.

They were betting on whether or not I had died.

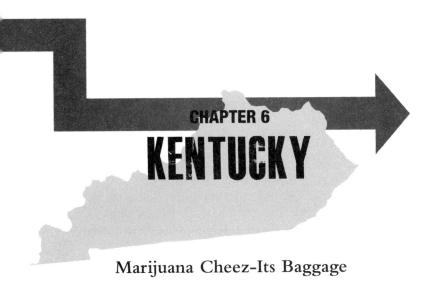

CHAPTER 6
KENTUCKY

Marijuana Cheez-Its Baggage

Gravel scattered from the tires of the Imposter as I flew across the Tennessee border into Kentucky. I was on the closest thing to a road I could find after becoming incredibly turned around somewhere near Paris, Tennessee (home of the Eiffel Tower of bourbon bottles). But neither the vision-blurring vibrations of the forgotten roadway nor the lack of any signs directing me back to the highway could smother my good cheer. I was amped from the madness of the previous twenty-four hours, pumping Whitesnake's "Here I Go Again on My Own" from the upbeat end of my nineties CD collection. I had survived my first real adventure.

I'd opted to skip Graceland, in Tennessee, and Mammoth Caves, in Kentucky. I wasn't really a fan of Elvis or underground geology, and I kind of pictured Graceland as absolutely crawling with Elvis impersonators, like a honky-tonk world in a *Where's Waldo?* book. The idea kind of creeped me out. Besides, I was due up in Indianapolis to visit my friend J.J., and beyond Indy, the Spacemobile was calling from

Wisconsin. I would have to skip a few things if I was going to do this in forty-eight days.

I dug out my cell phone, freshly charged from the Nic Nac. Both Sarah and my mother had made me promise to check in every few days so they'd know I hadn't been eaten by bears, and I was excited to trumpet the glories of my snake swim. But my phone returned only a roaming signal. Cell reception, I was starting to realize, is not quite as ubiquitous in this country as one might think. Even in these high-wired days, there are still a lot of dead pockets around the U.S., and I was systematically driving through every one of them. You know that red and gray coverage map Verizon gives you when you walk into their store? They say it's pretty accurate. I would be the judge of that.

At last I got through. Neither Sarah nor my mother was overjoyed to hear that I had nearly killed myself on Day Three, but they couldn't dampen my glory. I considered celebrating with a stop at a fast-food restaurant until I remembered my budget, and my timetable. Three PBJs would have to do.

I beat on my steering wheel while Whitesnake tried to out-scream their own guitars and flew over a hill—and found myself directly in the sights of a Kentucky Highway Patrol car and its radar gun. I slammed on the brakes and most likely gaped in horror as I rolled past the cop, which is the clearest way to admit that yes, I'm probably speeding.

What the hell was I doing? I was already four tickets deep, and I was racing across Kentucky, risking losing my license—just five states into forty-eight.

I looked with dread into the rearview mirror, but no lights were following me. If I had been speeding, the cop had decided not to bother. I finally exhaled and gripped the wheel with both hands, vowing to drive as old-lady-like as possible from that point on. I was suddenly feeling a lot less brazen. The first ticket of my illustrious speeding career had been in Kentucky. It was the first of many, but it was definitely the most traumatic, and not just, as they say, because you always remember your first time.

It was college spring break, and my friends Charlie and Jeff had convinced me and our friend Elizabeth to drive to Miami for a week at the beach. Well, three days at the beach, anyway—the first and last three days of our nine vacation days would be spent making the lengthy and foolish drive from Minneapolis to Miami and back.

"Aren't there any closer beaches?" I asked when Charlie and Jeff presented their proposal.

"Not like these beaches," said Charlie. "Warm water, hot women . . . I'm gonna get so sunburned that I cry."

"It'll be easy," said Jeff. "We'll take the Spacemobile and drive around the clock. We'll take turns catching Zs in the back, like a sleeper car. Charlie and I will pay for gas."

I was lured. By the free gas, of course, but I also couldn't resist a chance to exploit the Spacemobile's fold-out bed. Jeff would turn out to be wrong on all three accounts, of course: the drive would not be easy, the two of them would not pay for the gas, and there would be little sleeping, with Charlie and Jeff in the front blasting Daft Punk while the Spacemobile jostled recklessly down the highway as I lay horrified in the back. But the plans were set.

To prepare for the trip, we packed swimsuits, a tent for camping, and half a pound of marijuana. My friends were in a weed phase, you see, though not far enough into it to know that half a pound is way more pot than three people can smoke in a week.

I was not in a weed phase. I was in a phase of being very worried about my friends' being in a weed phase, and so it was only with great reluctance that I agreed to let them bring their ganja brick along in the Spacemobile, on the condition that they hide it in the farthest nether-regions of the van, in the bottom of a Cheez-Its box, in a grocery bag, next to some incense (to throw off the dogs). Charlie and Jeff insisted I was being paranoid, but that's probably because they were high.

So you can imagine my horror when I was pulled over in Kentucky for my first-ever speeding infraction, with nothing separating me from going to jail for trafficking a dealer-level amount of weed but a thin layer of cheesy, delicious crackers.

The cop sauntered up to my window, asked for my license, and glanced around at us: an extremely nervous guy in the driver's seat, a slightly nervous girl riding shotgun, and two surprisingly relaxed guys eating Cheez-Its in the back seat. I was already picturing the phone call I'd make to my parents asking them to bail me out of jail in Kentucky, and how they'd respond that, no, they wouldn't bail me out of jail in Kentucky, and that I could rot there, for all they cared.

"What about my college fund?" I would plead from the police station payphone, as large, drooling inmates eyed me salaciously. "Can you at least wire it to me so I can bail myself out?"

"Already divided up between your brothers," my dad would reply coldly. "It's best you just start moving on. Your mother is already looking at adoption photos to replace you."

In hindsight, it was probably the most mundane speeding ticket ever written. There were, of course, no dogs, no jail, no parents disowning me. But at the time, it took me twenty-five minutes to return to a normal pulse rate. In fact, my graciously accepting the $180 fine and sycophantically asking the cop if there was anything else I could do for him probably made him *more* suspicious. But I couldn't help it. It was the kind of person I was.

I never smuggled weed again, but Kentucky was only the beginning of my speeding-ticket binge. A year later, I'd gotten two of them within twenty minutes of each other on the way back to Chicago from a Las Vegas trip. I'd just finished receiving a ticket for flying through a small town in Iowa when I crossed into Illinois, got distracted watching some road construction, and got tagged with a second ticket after I missed the "Slow to 35 mph" sign.

Upon hearing my story, the second cop regarded me with a vague, sickened look, the way he might regard a slimy cockroach crawling across his dinner plate.

"Is there anyone else in the car who can drive?" he asked.

Most states, as you may know, have programs that allow you to scrub speeding tickets off your record with traffic school. But all of my first three tickets were out of state, so the traffic-school trick didn't—or at least I thought it didn't—apply. The fourth citation, in Minnesota (for racing too fast from one job to another), had occurred a few months before the Roadtrip, but the ticket got lost in the shuffle of my moving in and out of Sarah's place, conceiving the Roadtrip, and generally coming unglued. The night before the Field of Dreams, in a last-ditch effort to give myself some speeding breathing room, I found it and stayed up all night plowing through an online traffic course and e-mailed in the exam results. But the deadline to erase the ticket had already passed, and here I sat with four tickets on my record. Everyone said I was stupid for even bothering to try to wipe that last ticket from my record, but I couldn't help it. It was the kind of person I was.

The problem wasn't that I was a rule breaker, obviously. The problem was that speeding just seemed like a really silly rule to me. Sure, there had to be some laws controlling traffic, but why would you take $180 of my hard-earned bouncer money for going 57 mph on an empty road, but not 55?

There was always some objective, some next destination that I wanted to get to just a little faster than the law allowed. Here in northern Kentucky, it was Indianapolis, and then the Spacemobile, and then eventually all the other states. I passed a spectacular old Kentucky mansion, the kind you'd imagine a young belle in a ten-foot-diameter dress traipsing out of, carrying a parasol. I didn't stop. The mansion came up without warning, behind a grove of trees, and by the time I saw it I was already whizzing past, watching it in the rearview. I could have stopped to see if there was a tour. Or tried to figure out the history of the old place. Or at least get kicked off the grounds for trespassing. But I didn't. And then it was gone.

I drove on, something amiss. I tried to justify. *The mansion was probably closed, anyway. J.J.'s expecting me. I have to skip a few things if I'm going to do this in forty-eight days.* But these were all excuses. Really, I was too focused on the road ahead. And then, abruptly, I was out of Kentucky.

What was my "something interesting" in Kentucky? Entering the state on a dirt road? *Not* stopping at a mansion? Pining about the *last* time I'd zipped through Kentucky? The Bluegrass State didn't deserve that. Maybe doing something interesting in every state is hard. The first three days of my Roadtrip had already brought more changes of plans than I'd ever anticipated, but maybe some habits would take a little longer to change.

I downgraded the song to Whitesnake's "Too Many Tears," wallowed in self-pity, and drove on toward the next goal.

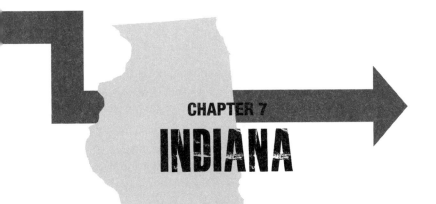

CHAPTER 7

INDIANA

Union Happy Hour

In high school, before I had ever dated anybody, I asked my dad if he thought my mom was perfect. "Of course not," he answered, thankful to have a non-precalculus-related question for once. "Nobody's perfect." He meant that nobody was perfect in the literal sense. But I was getting at something else. "I mean," I persisted, "is she perfect for you?"

He thought about it for a second. "Well, I can't say we never argue, because you've seen us. And is every little detail about her exactly as I would build it? Probably not. Probably not every little detail about me is exactly what she would build, either." My dad has been known to forget his children's names and belch complete sentences in public, so I suspected this was true.

"But yeah," he finished. "She's basically perfect."

I thought about this on the long drive up through Tennessee and Kentucky on my way to Indianapolis. It seemed to me that if you're searching for the person to spend the rest of your life with, you shouldn't have to settle for just anybody. Heck, call me an optimist, but I figured you should be able to find somebody pretty great. Even at age 23 I had a vague inkling that it was dangerous to hold out for "absolutely perfect"—you don't want life to slip by while you're waiting for a white knight or sleeping beauty who doesn't exist. But let's say every person has ten traits they're looking for in someone. There are 6 billion people in the world; shouldn't you be able to find someone with at least nine of them? Nine out of ten. Basically perfect. As long as ten isn't the deal breaker.

I had my list of ten things. Intelligence. Good in a room full of strangers. Attractive. And so on. I know this is a stereotypically female thing to do, but sue me, I'm a list maker—I was in the process of systematically checking off all forty-eight states, after all. Sarah hit most of the items on my list, no problem. She was smart. She was friendly. I was definitely attracted to her. She even had blue eyes—a soft spot of mine. Yet there were still a few things I didn't quite know about.

For instance, she had to fit well with my family. Don't get me wrong, Sarah *got along* with my family: she was a sweet girl, and my family was from Minnesota, so they liked almost everybody. As for fitting, though . . . Sarah had a 90-pound sister who was majoring in playing the marimba at an obscure arts school in Orange County. I had a 290-pound brother who routinely put his head through people's torsos on football fields in New England. Once, while visiting me for Thanksgiving, Sarah had fainted for no reason in our kitchen. She was just fragile like that. My brother Mark's response to this? "People actually *do* that? How's she ever going to give birth to your twelve-pound baby?"

We hadn't dated long enough outside college for family compatibility to be accurately gauged, but I wondered. Was there someone else out there who had all of Sarah's good traits but wouldn't be snapped in two if my brother gave her a hug? Might some other girl be just as cute, and also more okay with my self-finding Roadtrip? Was Sarah not perfect? Was that what was bugging me?

In any case, I needed some time to think. And time was something I had plenty of, as I drove up through Tennessee and Kentucky on my way to Indianapolis and Chicago, Sarah's painting still crowding up the backseat of the Imposter.

Indianapolis, the "Crossroads of America," is at the intersection of about nine major U.S. highways, which means accessing its downtown without taking any interstates is like getting to the ocean without stepping on any sand. But my sophomore-year roommate, J.J., lived there, and I had once helped scoop J.J.'s puke out of a hall drinking fountain after a bad night of drinking. That kind of experience really bonds two people.

The first thing I did upon arriving at J.J.'s apartment that night was dash upstairs and take a flying leap onto his toilet. This challenge of bathrooms, I admit, was another thing I had somehow not anticipated. Number One wasn't so hard: as a guy, the world was my urinal. But Number Two was trickier, at least at night, since any place with a public bathroom on a small highway was closed by 9 P.M., and my nighttime accommodations (the Imposter) weren't exactly a spacious hotel room. And no matter how bad I had to go, there's something wrong—on many levels—with pooping on the Field of Dreams.

Abusing J.J.'s plumbing (it was also the first bathing I'd done since St. Louis, unless you count Lake Wappapello, and I certainly don't) hardly constituted an adventure in Indiana. So we headed out for drinks to Monument Circle in downtown Indy, the center of roads in the city that is the center of roads.

J.J. was one of those students who went about college the responsible way. At Northwestern, instead of frittering away his degree making videos about God dunking basketballs on people, he had earned two separate bachelor's degrees—in mechanical and manufacturing engineering—with the same frenzy of overachievement that had

Paul Jury

landed him his current job making jet engines at Rolls-Royce Allison. Oh, and he'd thrown in a third major—economics—just for kicks. I could only imagine what they paid him. At least cancer-curing Craig was still in med school and poor like me. A year out of college, J.J. was already a manager at his plant and had forty people working under him: union folks, Indy lifters, much like the people who now rolled their souped-up cars around Monument Circle.

J.J. and I were sitting on a bar patio, sipping blue-collar beers while heavy traffic circled the towering Civil War monument in the middle of downtown. Most nights, J.J. told me, the city's elite came out to honor their fallen forefathers by cruising the Circle in tricked-out Mustangs. This had been happening all night: guys in nice (loud) cars would drive around and around, making an impressive (loud) show for the women and other pedestrians on the sidewalk, who would yell and whistle back. It was like a noise-pollution mating dance. J.J. spotted someone he recognized from the plant and offered to introduce me. I politely declined.

"So," I finally yelled over the engine-revving and country bass, as a bright red truck with wheels as big as cable spools squealed by. "How's work?"

"It's good," shouted J.J. "It's different. I've been overseeing two new union groups. Not exactly the same type of people I grew up with."

J.J. had spent much of his youth traveling around the world. His parents were international teachers, instructing at different American academies in Japan, Poland, and other places a notch more exotic than Indianapolis. J.J.'s peers had been the children of international business leaders, diplomats, and parents who simply had so much money that they traveled the world for fun. Many of his current workers in Indy, on the other hand, had never left the state. But J.J. was not pretentious about his breadth of travel; in fact, sometimes it seemed that he longed for the stability of staying in one place. After all, he'd intentionally spent his last five years stationed securely in Illinois and Indiana.

46

"The union wage is pretty decent, actually," J.J. said. "But I swear, some of my guys immediately dump two-thirds of it into new sound systems or louder engines for their cars." As if to voice their assent, two Jeeps roared by at the top of their mufflers, a short-lived acoustic drag race that lasted until they hit traffic again.

J.J.'s average employee was at least twenty years older than he was, had only a basic education, a modded-up car, perhaps a small house somewhere, and few ambitions for anything beyond. It struck me as an odd contrast that, in half as long a life, J.J. had traveled the world, had attained two degrees and a management position with a prestigious company, and was about to buy his first condo. His circumstances might have set him up to be the archetype of success, but he'd grown into the role. Either way, his life seemed basically perfect.

"Are your guys jealous?" I asked, as a future Supreme Court Justice screeched by, his shaved head poking out his F150's sunroof, his hand hoisting a can of Natty Light toward the moon, "about being managed by a college kid?"

"Oh, they don't want to be managers," replied J.J. "That would mean more work, more responsibility, and worst of all, less time putting jet engines into '82 Camaros."

"Jeez," I mused. "Can you imagine a life like that?"

But J.J. just gazed thoughtfully out at the Circle, as the red cable-spool truck roared by again, the driver screaming gleefully as he hung out the window.

"I wish I could," said J.J. at last. "They're some of the happiest people I've ever met."

CHAPTER 8
ILLINOIS

Choose Your Own Adventure

Eighteen hours after I left J.J.'s place in Indianapolis, I woke up in some bushes on the outskirts of a campground in southern Wisconsin, a list of strip club phone numbers scrawled on my forearm and what appeared to be a dead body lying next to me. These are the kinds of things that happen when I hang out with Johnny Green.

Johnny was my junior-year college roommate, in a room that became known as 7-Eleven, not because of its room number, but because you could stop by any time of the day or night and one of us would be awake. Also, we sold beer to underclassmen.

To this day, Johnny Green remains one of the most fascinating people I know. He was hired right out of college by a law firm to run their technology systems, which he had absolutely no idea how to do, but he taught himself in less than a week. On the other hand, Johnny Green does not know which city, specifically, he was born in. This seems like something most people keep track of, but it doesn't seem to bother Johnny.

Johnny also has a knack for getting himself into misadventures. He once went to a party near our campus in northern Illinois and woke up the next morning under a bed in a strange dorm room. When he asked someone what dorm he was in, he didn't recognize the name of the building. When he asked them what college he was at, he didn't recognize the name of the school. When he asked what state he was in, the answer was Wisconsin.

Another time, I was awakened at 2 A.M. by a wild-eyed, intoxicated Johnny leaning over my bed.

"Jury! Wake up! I need three dollars."

I groggily rolled over. "What do you need three dollars for?"

Johnny paused, then looked at me with a mischievous glint in his eye. "For adventurousness."

"You're going to go buy cigarettes, aren't you?"

Johnny stared at me with his hyperfocused gleam.

"Yes."

I woke up again three hours later to a stinky, soaking wet Johnny standing over me, offering me my $3 back. Apparently, on the way to buy cigarettes, he had come across a gaping sewer hole the city had drilled out of the street, and of course he'd opted to wiggle through the fence and investigate. He climbed eighty feet down a ladder to the bottom where three feet of water led down various sewer pathways. Johnny jumped in, picked a path, and after a series of randomly selected lefts and rights, found himself in an old mine cart that had been abandoned underneath the streets of Evanston. Unfortunately, the mine cart didn't roll very well on its tracks through three feet of water, so eventually Johnny got discouraged, found his way out of the sewer, and walked home.

I listened to this story from my bed, simultaneously shocked and not shocked at all. When it was over, I asked the only question that came to mind.

"Wow. What do you think would have happened if that mine cart had been working?"

Johnny startled, as if the realization changed everything. "Whoa!" he said. "I don't know *where* I'd be!"

There was no way I could pass through Chicago without having my Illinois adventure with my old friend Johnny Green. Though I'd promised Sarah I'd stop in and see her, that task could wait until tomorrow.

But there was a lot of pressure on Illinois. What could I do that would trump all of college? Not to mention that Johnny was involved. Everything had to be perfect. As I drove into town that evening, I started making a list. Take in a Cubs game? Recreate *Ferris Bueller's Day Off*? Do a bar crawl, of every bar we'd ever gone to in Chicago?

Johnny would have none of it. "You're aiming at this all wrong," he told me. "The best adventures can't be planned. If you make this big ol' list, you'll end up disappointed."

He cracked an Old Style from his fridge and handed it to me.

"I think we should get in your car, you pick a random direction, and then I'll pick one, and we'll drive until we see something we wanna do."

"Like a Choose Your Own Adventure?"

"Yeah! Except with more booze."

I wasn't convinced. But it was Johnny. We climbed into the Imposter and off we went.

Johnny gave me the choice between north and south, and I picked south. I gave him the choice between east and west, and he picked east. Unfortunately, in all our excited picking we got turned around and pretty much drove straight west, to Aurora. Now I had to introduce Johnny to one of *my* rules: No Going Back. He agreed it was a swell rule.

We found a riverboat casino, which apparently got around Illinois' usual no-gambling rules by floating over water. We couldn't for the life of us figure out how this made sense, unless the Fox River was somehow considered international waters, but decided the cause was worth contributing $200 to, and promptly played a dozen blackjack hands before remembering that we were both poor.

"But what now?" I moaned, as we climbed dejectedly back into the Imposter. "We were only in there for like twenty minutes! That can't be our adventure."

"Wanna go to Madison?" asked Johnny. "We're getting close to Wisconsin. Chrissy's there—we can go out to the bars with her."

"Isn't Madison like . . . a hundred miles away?"

"You're not scared of a little driving, are you?" teased Johnny. "Besides. No going back."

What could I say?

We started the Imposter and aimed toward the Madison bars, where our friend Chrissy was in grad school.

"How're things with Sarah?" Johnny asked on the long drive north.

"The long-distance thing is hard. I wonder if we would have kept dating after graduation if we knew. It's nothing like either of us expected."

"It never is," said Johnny.

As we rolled into Wisconsin, reality hit: (a) Madison was indeed 100 miles away, (b) all the bars were now closed, and (c) Chrissy had been in Europe for a month. We probably should have called first.

Upon discovering our mission to be an abject failure, I again looked to Johnny.

"Now what? It's 1 A.M.!"

"There's gotta be some kind of bar still open around here somewhere. Hey! There's a sign for an airport. They have bars that are open all the time!"

"Do they?" I asked.

"Don't they!?" replied Johnny.

We drove around in the dark near Madison, searching for airports and strip clubs.

"I'm not saying you should plunge into every relationship that comes along," Johnny continued, as I pulled phone numbers out of my cell's spotty Internet and wrote them on my arm. "I'm just saying if it seems like fun, you should go with it until it doesn't seem fun anymore."

"What if you end up in a bad situation?"

Johnny shrugged. "You're gonna make some mistakes. But at least then you get a story out of it. Remember that girl from out of state I dated? It ended up being too far, but we had some really good times for a while, and I got to learn all about Indiana. And remember that girl I dated who kept stealing things?"

I nodded. Johnny shook his head.

"That was probably a mistake. That girl was nuts."

After an hour of what I'm sure looked like sketchy prowling of the Madison area, our mission seemed grim.

"And now what? Nothing's open."

Johnny spied the emergency half bottle of Skol vodka I had smuggled up from Indianapolis. "We could go Vodkamping."

Vodkamping, if you haven't already guessed, is exactly what it sounds like: Vodka, plus camping. We began searching for a campsite, but apparently all there is to do in southern Wisconsin on a Thursday night is go camping. Every place we saw was full. I drove as Johnny started in on the Skol, despite my objections and refusal to join him.

"What if we get arrested?" I demanded.

Johnny shrugged and took a swig. "Then at least we'll get a story out of it."

We finally found a campground that seemed to have a few free spots but, to our chagrin, was charging a $10 admittance fee. We didn't have $10. Johnny handed me the Skol, I shrugged, took a shot, and drove the Imposter across a grassy field and hid it in some trees. We got out, drank some more, and discussed the smartest place to spread out our blanket away from the prying eyes of authority. Then we gave up and just tossed it into some bushes on the bank of a pond.

My old college roommate and I sat and looked out over the calm, starry water, sipping vodka straight from the bottle. Almost nothing that night had worked out. We'd gone in the wrong direction, lost money at the casino, and now were lying in a bush. But each step brought the night to another level.

"Well, except driving to Madison," Johnny pointed out. "That was pretty much a total bust."

In the morning, the dead body next to me turned out to be Johnny, thankfully still alive, though plenty groggy from drinking a third of a bottle of Skol. I pulled him out of the bushes and we headed back to Chicago, recounting our night.

"Wow," I said. "That adventure wasn't at all like I was thinking."

Johnny just smiled and looked out the window at the passing scenery. "It never is."

Once again, Johnny Green had accidentally woken up in Wisconsin.

CHAPTER 9

WISCONSIN

Sarah vs. the Brat-Eaters

I had two more things to do before I left Illinois for my family reunion and the car swap:

1. Stop to see several of my old college friends at a BBQ.
2. Try to break up with Sarah.

There comes a time in any relationship when the guy freaks out and, no matter how beautiful or awesome his girlfriend is, he thinks: "I gave up every other set of boobs in the world for this?" My freak-out had been building since the trip began. I was only 23! She was the only girl I'd ever slept with. What if there were buxomy models waiting to de-pants and devour me in every other state after this one? America is, after all, the land of opportunity.

Sarah wasn't perfect. Sometimes she was too shy, and prone to unbearable fits of irrational girl angst. She could be a little taller. Yes, these were stupid things, but if you haven't picked it up already, I was a bit of an idealist.

Most of all, I was worried about her interfering with my trip. How could I leave it all behind and find myself if every few days she was pulling me back? What if I needed to unburden myself and do this Roadtrip totally alone? Yes, she was comfortable, but maybe this trip needed to be about getting *outside* comfort.

In any case, my gut was telling me something was wrong, and at a certain point you either have to swallow your gut or do something about it. It had taken me eight states, but I had finally gathered the resolve to drop by Sarah's downtown apartment and do the deed. I would be strong and logical, and say goodbye to our two-year relationship quickly and painlessly.

Instead, she cried. Then I cried. Then I invited her to my family reunion. There's no such thing as saying goodbye to a two-year relationship quickly and painlessly.

She said she would leave me alone more. She asked me to give her one good reason why we should abandon a relationship that had nothing wrong with it. I told her I wasn't positive I wanted to spend the rest of my life with her. We thought about this, and both agreed it was a pretty crappy reason.

"But you hate this trip!" I argued. "And I don't blame you. It's pulling me away."

"Then let me come with you this weekend," she said. "I like your family. Your reunion sounds like an adventure."

I didn't know what to say. Did Sarah fit into more of my categories than I thought?

"Besides, Wisconsin is one of the Sucky States, remember?" she said, a pleading smile spreading on her tear-streaked cheeks. "You need backup, in case they've heard about you, talking your trash."

I almost loved her sometimes.

Together we carried her painting up from the Imposter and unwrapped it, unloading the burden between us. The painting was of an orange sunset, dipping down into the ocean. It was beautiful, although part of me wondered if it would have been easier simply to buy a sunset painting in Chicago.

Appleton, Wisconsin, about an hour north of Milwaukee, is home to Lawrence University, lots of people of German heritage, and an Applebee's that advertises selling apples, so that people can buy an apple at Applebee's in Appleton. Appleton is also where much of my family is from, and every two years the Jury clan descends upon Appleton like a cloud of locusts and picks the town clean of grill meat and Leinenkugels.

A few words about my family, and about why, the whole way up from Chicago, I was a little anxious about introducing all of them to my petite vegetarian girlfriend. First, although we're not entirely German (we have roots in nearly every European country), all Jurys adore bratwurst—it's one of the prerequisites for being in the family. Anyone who refuses to eat the meat is kicked out of the brood and unceremoniously catapulted into a swamp. I pictured my brother Alex, roaring like a Tyrannosaurus and dunking his head into a bucket of sausage, with Sarah standing quietly nearby, eating a bun with ketchup on it.

Second, Jurys—especially my immediate family—come from big stock, in terms of both quantity and barrel-chestedness. The boys in my family range from 6'2" to 6'5", and 220 to 290 pounds. Much of this size comes from my mother, whose dad was 6'7". But if my mother brought the height gene, my dad supplied the big-head gene. Middle brother Mark and I escaped with only somewhat larger-than-average nuggets, but Alex received the full brunt of my father's giant-dome syndrome and spent the first month of his life looking like a newborn Blowpop. We could never find hats for either of them, because as we liked to say, hat stores don't carry size "Equator." I couldn't imagine what 100-pound Sarah's and my children would look like. I pictured my girlfriend delivering something resembling a large bobblehead. Or maybe the baby would just punch its way out of her chest, like in *Alien*.

My pulse quickened as Sarah and I pulled up to the park my family had reserved, along the Fox River in Appleton. We always rented out a park for our reunions, probably because it was cheaper, but I liked to think it was because no indoor structure could contain us. Was I making a huge mistake, bringing a lamb to the lion's den? Was I was about to show up with my tiny, terrified girlfriend to some kind of primal, animal-sacrificing orgy?

It wasn't so bad. There was no bestial roar from the crowd. My mom and a couple female cousins came out to greet Sarah, and I gazed over at a gazebo filled with my relatives calmly dishing salads and desserts onto paper plates. Everything seemed a lot more ordinary than I'd pictured.

Now that I thought about it, many of my extended family members were closer to normal that I'd made out (excluding my brothers, who were still behemoths). I had one relative who was an engineer out of Stanford. I had another who drove a motorcycle. Had I trumped it all up in a projection of my worries about Sarah? Maybe we had the same kind of diversity any family has, and were linked simply by blood and a fondness for brats.

Sarah still looked a little out of place, as she talked for an hour with my taller mom, a former Chicago resident, about life in the city. Sarah didn't quite seem like part of the family, as she chatted up my lawyer great-uncle about her first year of law school while he consumed half a pot roast between sentences. Sarah required fewer Leinenkugels than the rest of us to become inebriated, and later that night she tried to learn sheepshead, an obscure card game that only ten German people and my relatives play. Sarah did not fit in. But she sure was trying.

My grandmother cornered Sarah, to try to convince her to transfer law schools to Minnesota so she'd be closer when I finally proposed, and I got a few moments alone with my brothers and dad.

"Why'd you try to break up with her?" they asked.

"I don't know, I guess I was worried she wasn't perfect."

"There's no such thing as perfect," my dad reminded, between bites of a brat log cabin on a baguette.

"I know. Maybe it's just that whole 'oldest child' thing, where everything's gotta go exactly my way."

My brothers and dad all nodded.

"She's not like us. Sometimes she gets totally upset for absolutely no logical reason!"

My dad looked at me. "You realize she's a woman, right?"

"I dunno. I guess I freaked out. I figured I had models to bang."

"Why would a model bang you?" said Alex. "You live in a car."

I rescued Sarah from my grandma and we went for a walk down by the river. I held her hand as a near flawless sunset started to sink into the horizon, marred only by a few stray clouds. My girlfriend didn't fit in, but she came a lot closer than I had expected. Maybe she wasn't perfect. But maybe basically perfect was perfect enough.

At the family reunion I learned the dismal news that the Spacemobile was still out of commission. I didn't understand what could be so wrong with a Volkswagen that it took eight days to fix, but I was pretty sure Germany was to blame. Regardless, the Imposter would have to last me a little longer.

Sarah and I left the reunion Sunday morning after doubly meaningful good lucks from my family. This wasn't the first time I'd tried to break up with her.

In college, after we'd been dating for about two months, I went away on Christmas break and came back with some of the same gut rumblings. I told Sarah I needed some space. A few days later I came to my senses and convinced her to take me back, but the damage had been done.

No wonder she wasn't a fan of my Roadtrip! Every time I went off traveling by myself for a few weeks, I'd get inside my head and come back with all these crazy ideas. No wonder she wished I would stay in Chicago. She was worried I would leave, come back, and try to break up with her again. After all, I just *had*.

Outside Sarah's apartment, she bore right through me with those blue eyes and made me promise that I'd never do this to her again. I returned my girlfriend's gaze with a new appreciation for what she must be feeling, and for what a stupid and loathsome human being I was. I promised. I would never do this to her again.

I pulled away from the curb, my beautiful, wistful, small girlfriend perfectly framed in the rearview. No matter what ended up happening, it was a picture that would stick.

CHAPTER 10

MICHIGAN

Tony the Tiger Must Die

Right before I started my freshman year at Northwestern, my first college experience involved showing up to campus a week early with 120 other new students and piling into a crowded bus for a camping trip. We were supposed to go to the Smoky Mountains in North Carolina, but of course there was an abortion clinic bomber loose somewhere in the area, so we headed to the Upper Peninsula of Michigan instead. It was an ironic change: my Detroit friends had always told me the U.P. was where all the cabin-dwelling psychopaths hung out. Anyway, they divided us campers into small groups, and we were supposed to spend a week in the woods acquiring some buffer friends before being thrown into the terrifying experience of our first year of college.

But the trip also served another purpose for me. One evening, as I trampled alone over bushes and small trees searching for a good place to hang a bear-bag, I stumbled across the rocks of a flowing creek. Looking out over the water as the setting sun's orange light ricocheted off the rippling water, I was overwhelmed with a feeling of having a blank slate. Right then, my past—my childhood, my high-school experience—was completely behind me, and only mattered now in how it had formed the person I had become. My future—what I would do in college, what I would do after—lay completely ahead. There was only the present. For the moment, I was separated from everything, standing alone in time. I felt almost like I was being reborn.

As I learned in my first semester of college, between naps in my Intro to Philosophy class, every mythology and religion has some component of rebirth. It's a way to explain the transitions in life; when something dies, something else is born to take its place. Often these transition points are marked by difficulty and fear: the angst of puberty, the midlife crisis of the shift into old age, and the tears of my mother, just one week earlier, as her oldest son boarded the bus to leave for college. Or the annoyance I was feeling now, as I struggled to resist putting my fist through the dashboard over an insane Chicago traffic jam caused by morons watching some guy get a speeding ticket.

As the Imposter and I crawled slowly toward Michigan for the first time since that meditative week, it occurred to me that on *this* trip I had so far experienced no blank slates. Just a lot of stomach rumbling. Possibly it was because I was still in Chicago, the strongest reminder so far of all the past-life connections that still entangled me. Or possibly it was because Michigan Avenue's billboard foliage and Abercrombie wildlife were the exact opposite of the Michigan wilderness I needed.

I finally escaped the Windy City and headed around the southern tip of Lake Michigan through Gary, Indiana, and its choking, smoking jungle of factories that keep Chicago running. Gary is Chicago's boiler room: industrially imperative, but well hidden out of Michigan Avenue's sight. And you sure wouldn't want to live there.

At least I finally had a strong plan for something to do in a state. Even as a rival Midwesterner, I had to admit that Michigan was a pretty solid place; I'd always fondly thought of it as being a lot like Minnesota, with fewer Norwegians. Michigan had a nice mix of lakes and big cities, a few of the nation's most important industries, and a full variety of sports teams, though not all of them won games. But I couldn't have cared less about any of these things. I was interested in cereal.

Growing up, my brothers and I were accustomed to six meals a day: Breakfast, Lunch, After-School Snack, Dinner, Dinner 2, and Before-Bed Snack. Typically, at least three of these meals consisted solely of cereal. A perfect, no-nonsense Midwestern food, cereal goes right after the jugular of the grain and dairy groups, not wasting anybody's time with silly fruits and vegetables. If they made a cereal with big chunks of pork in it, we wouldn't have eaten anything else.

We ate probably two boxes a day among the three of us. My mother would take the Spacemobile to the Wholesale Club every two weeks, fill the entire back with boxes and boxes of Wheaties, Cherrios, Chex, Rice Krispies—everything but Grape-Nuts, really—then load them all onto two huge wooden shelves in our bunker, which had been built specifically for the purpose. It looked like we were hoarding supplies for the cereal apocalypse.

I stopped briefly in Benton Harbor to try and get a look at Chicago from my new vantage point across Lake Michigan, but gray, hanging haze blocked what would've been a difficult view anyway. I passed through the verdant farms of western Michigan and the rolling, hilly homes of Kalamazoo. But I was too focused to be observant. My destination loomed: the Kellogg's headquarters and cereal factory in Battle Creek, Michigan, had been starred on my map since before there even *was* a Roadtrip.

In 1998, Kellogg's moved its factory tour, along with a museum and tourist center, into a cereal lover's Mecca near Battle Creek's single-skyscraper downtown. The attraction was aptly named Cereal City. My imagination couldn't handle this. A cereal factory tour was tantalizing enough, but a place called *Cereal City*? I pictured nothing less than a *Charlie and the Chocolate Factory* scenario, with Snap Crackle Pop Oompa-Loompas, giant swimming pools of Raisin Bran, and basketball courts where Tony the Tiger and I could challenge unsuspecting bullies to one-sided games of twenty-one. It would be like the Emerald City of Oz, the Land of Dairy Queen, and Heaven, all poured into one hearty, wholegrain bowl of goodness, served with milk, and topped with strawberries.

I fought my way through Battle Creek's midmorning traffic and finally saw it. In the distance, a giant, elevated blue sign, with a huge Tony the Tiger head perched on top of it. My head grew light. My mouth dripped.

I was about to experience the biggest disappointment of my life.

If I'd been expecting the world's largest cereal playground, what I got was the world's largest cereal gift store. Cereal City was a bloated, corporate wasteland of overpriced merchandize, dull historical video panels, and large inanimate cutouts of cartoon characters that might have been cool if I were four. And that was about it, other than a ten dollar faux-factory tour and a cereal bar that offered, instead of free Corn Pop martinis, small bowls of Corn Flakes dispensed out of two tall tanks for $3 a shot. It was pathetic. We had more cereal in our basement.

I signed up for the paid tour anyway, dimly hoping that my cereal fantasy lay just behind a red curtain somewhere. Instead, I shuffled glumly along through fake machines and conveyer belts while a monotonous guide related the intricate process by which one grain is judged to be superior to another. If there was a giant pool of Raisin Bran, I didn't see it, and I got the feeling the staff would have frowned upon my unhygienic notions of bathing in it.

I became convinced that even the original factory tour would have been lame, but the fake tour was even lamer. The rest of the tourists, mostly Michigan kids on field trips, glanced at me occasionally, wondering why there was an unshaven 23-year-old man hanging around wearing sweatpants. They reminded me of unspoiled dreams.

I finished the tour and trudged back to the Imposter, being careful to avoid eye contact with the kids' suspicious chaperone. What had I been expecting? I didn't *really* think there would be cartoon birds dropping Fruit Loop life preservers into milk lakes, did I? This was always my problem: I dreamed up these fantastic, unrealistic expectations of how life was supposed to go, and then I shut down when life couldn't live up.

I was glad to have moved on from my family reunion. Though it was refreshing to refuel my brat tank, everyone had interrogated me about my plans after the Roadtrip. "That's what the Roadtrip is *for*," I told everyone, grinning, but worried inside. Now I was ten states in, and I hadn't a single clue about the whole stupid direction thing. Would I really bolt awake one morning, smack my head on the roof of the Imposter, and go "Golly! I want to be an architect!" What if finding one's way in life was a bit bigger than one road trip? In the meantime, I kept imagining my Wisconsin relatives, smiling politely but secretly thinking, "Who's this kid think he is, too good for the Midwest?"

In all of my excitement and troubles of being out on the road, I'd forgotten what this trip was all about. So far, I'd done a pretty rotten job finding my direction. Perhaps it was time I got a little pushier about going after it.

My only consolation in Battle Creek was the discovery that, if I rearranged my cooler, I could cram in a gallon of milk to accompany the several boxes of cereal I'd picked up at the gift shop for a (very slight) discount. I was pretty pissed at Kellogg's, but not enough to pass up road cereal.

CHAPTER 11
OHIO

Mennonites in Hollywood

Kidron, Ohio, is a town so small that it's not so much a town as it is a highway between two other small towns. Even these other two, Orrville and Dalton, are places you've never heard of. They're collectively about twenty miles east of Canton, which is about fifty miles south of Cleveland. You know your town is small when you need four other towns to describe its location.

But my college friend JD, who hailed from Kidron, was quite proud of the patchwork of villages that made up his home. I was learning something about the small places of America: each of them wants to be known for something. Thus the "Home of [Insert Obscure Olympic Pole-Vaulting Bronze Medalist Here]!" signs at the borders of so many two-stoplight villages. Orrville's big claim to fame is that it's the home of Smuckers, which in my opinion is actually a pretty decent achievement, because I really like jelly. Dalton, the smaller of the two, is the home of Yost, a candy company that makes only one very specific kind of sucker. Why they don't branch out into other kinds of hard candy—or other kinds of suckers, at least—is beyond me, but the point is that Yost is not exactly a *Fortune* 500 company. But there it is on the Dalton sign: "Welcome to Dalton, Home of Yost Candy." And why not? Everybody deserves to be famous for something. Even if it's just suckers.

JD's hometown, Kidron, is right in the heart of Ohio's Amish country. Not all rural areas in Ohio are predominately Amish, but JD's area sure was. JD is not Amish. He's Mennonite, which is a lot like being Amish except that technology is okay. Which is good, since JD was a film major with me in college.

Growing up Mennonite in a largely Amish area was a unique experience for JD—his was the only family in town going to hell, but at least there was never a long line at the local Radio Shack. It also made JD the most popular kid in the county when he was growing up—all the little Amish kids could sneak over on Saturday mornings and watch his glowing box of evil.

JD's family welcomed me to their backyard campfire that night with great excitement. JD's family was one of the few families in their area code to have Internet access, and they'd been reading my nightly blog posts and had many questions, mostly about how I'd managed to drop my keys into a lake within the first three states. They offered me a seat around their fire, a bed in their house, and a beer, all while politely disregarding my used-car smell. They even complimented my budding beard. This *was* Amish country, after all.

Their enthusiasm and hospitality were a kind relief to me. Finding energy to write and reception to upload (via an agonizingly slow cell-phone modem) at the end of each long day had been hard. I didn't know whether anyone was reading my posts, or whether they cared. But JD's family cared. I was glad I was making the effort.

In the morning, JD took me to lunch at one of Kidron's only shops, a general store that resembled a large, two-story barn. In an effort to appeal to anyone and everyone who might possibly stop in tiny Kidron to spend a buck (be they Amish, small-highway traveler, or Witness Protection Program participant), the general store inter-preted "general" in the widest possible capacity, selling everything from butter churns and bonnets to sparkplugs and DVDs.

On the lower level of the store was a cafeteria-style restaurant that served a fascinating combination of traditional Amish cuisine and typical greasy road food, and there were various strange rules printed on the menu, including, "No noodles served on Tuesdays." We had no idea why this was, but it made me fear and respect the Amish tradition all the more to imagine that on their stone tablets, right up there between No Adultery and No Coveting Thy Neigh-bor's Man-Servant, was something as oddly specific as "Tuesdays = No Noodles."

"I'm moving to Los Angeles," JD announced out of nowhere over our non-noodle dishes. "I leave at the end of the month."

JD and I had been in a sitcom-writing class together at North-western, after which I'd been inspired to spend a summer in L.A. to see what the place was all about. But I had a bad feeling about the city even before I arrived, and the summer had done little to win me over. The weather and women looked great, but I had neither time nor ability to enjoy either. I spent most of my hours working inside, interning for a misanthropic film producer with whom I was warned never to make eye contact. Every year, 100,000 new graduates flood L.A. to compete for 100 good jobs, and everyone else scrounges for benefits at Starbucks. On a trolley tour of Universal Studios, the guide informed us that one actually had a better chance of being *struck by lightning* than selling a spec screenplay in Hollywood. He would know. He'd been trying to get struck for years.

So the City of Angels didn't seem like an awfully encouraging place to me. But as I congratulated JD on his decision and promised I'd drop in on him if my Roadtrip ever made it to California, I was secretly jealous. JD had no job, no connections, but he had the cour-age to jump into something as monumental as being the only person from Kidron ever to move to Hollywood.

"Why L.A.?" I finally asked, after my tide of covetous self-loathing had somewhat subsided.

JD shrugged, as if he knew what I'd been thinking. "I'd always dreamed of being creative for a living. I know it's tough to pull that off. Nobody makes it right away. Most don't make it ever. And even if it works, it's impossible to guess when or how."

"That sounds like a lot of uncertainty."

"Yeah," said JD. "But I'll never find out unless I try. And the odds are probably best in L.A. As long-shot as they are."

"Besides," he added, as he bit into a mass of locally made gelatin that the menu implied was made with genuine horse hooves. "I really need to get out of Amish country."

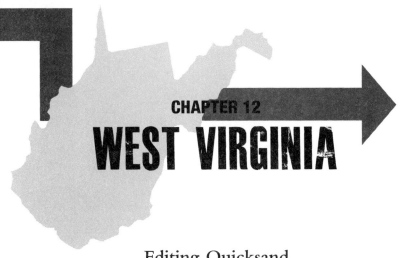

CHAPTER 12

WEST VIRGINIA

Editing Quicksand

In college, a friend of mine from Virginia liked to tell West Virginia jokes:

Q: What do a tornado and a divorce in West Virginia have in common?
A: Someone always loses a trailer.

Q: Why do birds fly upside down over West Virginia?
A: Because West Virginia isn't worth a crap.

But these were the exact same jokes we used to tell in Minnesota about Iowa, and Iowans in turn told about Nebraska. West Virginia didn't seem much different from eastern Ohio, or the whole Midwest, for that matter. In fact, the only thing I could make fun of West Virginia about while I was there was its strange shape, a meandering river outline that looks like some mutant platypus paw that a five-year-old had drawn on an Etch-a-Sketch. But at least it doesn't look like a boot stepping in dog poop, like Louisiana.

I guess every state just likes to make fun of the smallest one next to it. I wondered whether Wyoming ever made fun of anybody. Maybe they just said, "Screw it," and held a rodeo.

Teasing aside, I was having a lot of trouble finding things to do in West Virginia. Admittedly, part of my activity conundrum was due to the truncated route I was taking, across the state's northernmost platypus talon, on a miniscule highway I'm sure wasn't featured in the West Virginia tourism guide. My driving route through each state was generally determined by a combination of efficiency and any cool stuff I'd heard about in the area, and an unfortunate side effect was that not every state got four-star treatment. It also didn't help that I hadn't done a lick of research on West Virginia.

Not knowing what else to do, I called my dad.

"Dad, I can't find anything interesting in West Virginia. I feel like I should do something direction-y."

"You mean like find a fortune teller?"

"I'm not finding a fortune teller in West Virginia. You raised me better than that."

"Hey, you called me. I've got TV I could be watching."

I whizzed passed a sign for a Baptist church that had lost some of its letters and now just read "BAP URCH."

"You could find a minor-league baseball game or something."

"I can't even find a town, much less a stadium."

"Well. Maybe not every part of every state is interesting."

He said it, but I'd been coming to the same troubling conclusion. This was a problem I had foreseen: How do I do something interesting in every state when nothing interesting presents itself? Do I set my schedule even further behind and scrape under every nook and cranny for an adventure at five in the afternoon in West Virginia on a Wednesday? Or do I push on? The highways in America are meant to lure you forward, with the promises of "Gas: 30 miles! Fun: 80 miles!

Happiness: Just keep driving!" It takes a lot of discipline to resist the progress of the road.

The way my dad had said it, it also sounded like not every part of *life* was interesting. Was this some depressing allegory on the state of adulthood—that the great freedom you anticipate your whole life is mostly paved with vast stretches of nothing special?

My call-waiting beeped. Sarah. Say what you will about West Virginia; the cell reception wasn't bad.

I let my dad go and clicked over. Sarah had texted earlier that she had some good news, but any news would have been good news on this uneventful strip of road.

Sarah spoke neutrally, as if feeling me out.

"What have you been thinking about still being an editor?"

I thought about it. "I don't know." Honestly, I didn't.

I had always had the same theory about careers as I did about relationships: when it came to a job you were going to spend the rest of your life with, you should be able to find something basically perfect: nine out of ten. Editing seemed like the best marriage of the factors I was after. Creativity, and of course the steady pay that my Type-A, make-my-family-proud side insisted was important. There were full-time jobs for editors. You could collect benefits while spending your day finding the funniest combination of shots of a monkey smashing a piggy bank with nunchucks in an avant-garde yet brilliant insurance commercial. And of course, anyone's career should be something they love.

"I guess I still haven't thought of anything better," I said, finally.

"Well then. Here it is," replied Sarah, trying to conceal her excitement. "I met this guy at a law school mixer last night. He's the husband of a girl in one of my classes, and he works at a post-production company here in Chicago. He thinks he might be able to get you a job! They're looking to fill an assistant position, pretty soon after you get back."

"Oh," I said, unsure how to respond. "I wish I didn't have such a lousy track record with editing gigs in Chicago."

"Yeah, I told him about your old company," she said, her smile now glowing through the phone. "He said they're a bunch of pricks. Hopefully you'll have a better run this time."

I imaged I would. It certainly couldn't go much worse.

When I moved in with Sarah after my Minneapolis employment misadventures, I was thrilled to be hired as a runner at a prestigious downtown post house. It didn't matter that "runner" was another word for "coffee bitch": with my work ethic and smoldering charm, I'd be promoted to head of the company in no time.

Instead, I spent twelve hours a day dashing from errand to errand, no lunch breaks, scavenging scraps from the clients' cold sushi plates between runs. They hired me because I had a lot of editing experience, but I never touched an editing machine as long as I was there. I made $350 a week, running half-million-dollar checks weekly from McDonald's and Nike to the bank, while chipping in a humiliating hundred or so bucks to Sarah's downtown rent.

One afternoon, the powers that be summoned me into the VP's office.

"We're making a change in the runner position," they said, dispassionately. "Here's two weeks' severance. Pack your things."

The only "things" I had were already in my pockets. "But I've been working twelve-hour days," I said. I had been cleaning out the company's huge refrigerator, and was still holding the sponge.

"You should want to work fourteen."

I didn't want to work fourteen.

But why not? The job sucked, sure, but all creative industry jobs were like that. The sad fact was that anything a film major qualified you for involved working your way up through the bowels. Sure, these were especially stinky bowels, but it shouldn't matter as long as you truly loved the prize waiting for you at the top. I was never afraid of a little hard work.

"Look," said Sarah, pulling me back to the present. "I know you're not sure what you want to do yet. But this guy sounds really nice. And it can't hurt to have options, right?"

I hesitated.

"Right?"

I opened my mouth, but nothing came out. The phone went cold in my hand.

"Right. I mean . . . yeah!" I back-pedaled. "It has nothing to do with you, Sarah. I'm just worried about having another awful runner job."

It was too late. "That's not what it sounds like."

"I can e-mail the guy, but I don't want to commit to anything yet. Who knows where I'll end up after this trip?"

"You don't want to come back to Chicago, do you?" Sarah asked, hurt.

"No! I mean—" Nice work, Paul. "Chicago's great. But . . . what if it takes me a little longer to get back there?"

"What? Like for how long? Three months?"

"No."

"A year?"

"No!" I was up to my neck. "Listen. Sarah. I don't know for sure where I'll end up after this trip, but it might be Chicago. I don't know what I'll want to do, but it might be editing. But I *do* know that I want to be with you."

She paused. I might have found a foothold. "You said that two days ago, too. Of course I want to believe you. It's just hard when you keep doing things like this."

"I know."

"I'm only trying to help."

"I know." I really had to stop painting myself into corners. "I'm awful. I'm sorry. It's the job thing. I will come see you after the forty-eight days. I promise."

Her voice got soft, the way it always did when she was almost ready to forgive me. "Promise promise?"

"Promise promise."

We hung up. While it's true that a guy will say nearly anything to get his girlfriend to stop being angry, I meant what I'd said.

Paul Jury

I could e-mail Sarah's editing guy. Perhaps editing and I had just gotten off on the wrong foot. Hadn't I enjoyed myself back in college, splicing together sketches about Congressmen Gone Wild and the Snuggle Bear stalking people? Perhaps being rejected by the editing business twice within six months had simply soured me, temporarily, the way a guy who's been turned down for dates by two girls convinces himself that they were ugly anyway.

There could still be a future for me, in Chicago. After all, the one comfortable part of my day had been coming home to Sarah. And like she said, it couldn't hurt to have options.

The Imposter and I zipped past a "Now Entering Pennsylvania" sign. I slammed on the brakes. This was not happening again. I turned around, found a different road, and drove back into West Virginia.

I found a giant steel suspension bridge and, for lack of any other options, pulled off the highway, drove the Imposter down to the silver water, and took a nap under the bridge. *Not unlike a common troll*, I thought to myself as I drifted off. One upside of a directionless, destination-less journey was that I could stop and take naps whenever I liked. At least West Virginia had nice rivers.

That night I e-mailed my editing resume (and uploaded my reel, an experience that was hell on earth on a cell-phone modem) via an outlet in the tiny, cluttered lobby of a zero-star motel near Cameron, West Virginia. The state deserved more than an hour, no matter what Regular Virginians say about it.

The chubby, tattooed front-desk clerk gave me the eyeball as I casually strolled in, sat down on one of the lobby's folding chairs, and plugged in my computer.

"Help ya?" he asked, as if adding more syllables required too much effort.

"Oh, no thanks," I said. "I'm staying in room 102, figured I'd get a change of scenery! Remember? I checked in earlier."

The clerk peered at me. I had no idea if there really was a room 102, but it seemed like a reasonable guess, in case 101 was *his* room.

"My wife's got a migraine, and she hates it when I type in bed. Thought I'd come in here and keep ya company!"

I smiled broadly at the clerk. He watched me for another moment, then snorted and went back to watching high-school football reruns on a flickering twelve-inch TV. The ruse seemed to work. The clerk might not know who was actually staying in his motel; or more likely, he didn't care. He might only have been eyeing me because I looked like a disheveled hobo. He should talk. He was the one wearing the wife-beater.

I shut off my laptop and went outside to rearrange the Imposter for the night. My dirty laundry bag was not as airtight as I'd hoped and had begun to burden the cab with a faint odor I kept mistaking for rotting trash from passing landfills. I popped back inside the motel, paid the tattooed clerk $3 for a stack of scented-paper Christmas trees, chucked them in with my laundry, and relegated the whole bag to the trunk.

I resisted the magnetic signs pulling me toward Interstate 70 and the luxurious rest stops that waited there, and instead pulled the Imposter onto a deserted road in Cameron. I parked near a street light, for security, and under a large oak tree, for early-morning shade. I cracked all four windows a few inches for cross-ventilation.

If my path was something other than moving back to Chicago and giving editing and Sarah another shot, I had thirty-six more days to find it.

But at least I was beginning to feel like I was winning some tiny victories against the road.

CHAPTER 13
PENNSYLVANIA

Directionless

I was headed for Gettysburg. My mother, a former teacher, had made me promise I'd do at least one educational thing on my trip around America, so I picked the place where the most people shot each other. And who knew? There was a chance I'd learn that my direction was to join the army, though more likely I'd learn that compared to giving your life for your country, giving your Saturday morning to fetch Thai food for ad clients wasn't so bad.

Getting to the famous battlefield was a battle all its own. Another problem with small highways is that they're not as well marked as interstates. In some cases, they're not marked at all. The assumption must be that anyone driving this tiny road in the middle of Pennsylvania must be a local and therefore know where they're going, because why the hell else would they be here? Which is probably a fair point. But *I* was here, angrily trying to navigate a combination of Highways 16, 116, and 316 to Gettysburg. If the numbering system alone wasn't annoying enough, half the road signs were blocked by trees, or rusted so heavily I couldn't read their first digit. In Driver's Ed I'd learned that even-numbered highways are supposed to go east–west . . . unless they feel like randomly veering south through twenty miles of Pennsylvania farmland, apparently.

This was bullshit. Why didn't any of these stupid highways have mile markers? Why couldn't I figure out a totally basic question like what I wanted to do with my life? Why was this asshole road suddenly turning north for no reason at all? Why wasn't there a place where I could stop and figure all this out?

I slammed on the brakes in front of a Pennsylvania Welcome Center window and screamed at the woman inside, "What's my purpose in life!" She stared after me. I don't think anyone had ever interpreted her "Information" sign that literally.

By the time I reached the town of Gettysburg, I was so furious that I wanted to jump out of my car and start bayoneting people myself. Perhaps the Union and Confederate soldiers had also taken Highway 16 to the battle. It would explain why they wanted to fight for three days over a random chunk of land in Pennsylvania.

I finally began to calm down as I approached the battlefield. The direction signs were better maintained—probably because they had tourism money riding on them—and the realization was starting to set in that I was about to see a place where 8,000 of my ancestors had died to ensure that I even *had* forty-eight states to drive through. I pulled into the Visitors' Center parking lot, jolted the Imposter's door open with one great cathartic kick, and almost knocked over a woman in a walker. Apologizing profusely, I smothered the last of my temper.

I was too broke to pay for the guided tour, so I wandered aimlessly around the grassy battlefield, trying in vain to eavesdrop on the paid guides while pretending to look at flowers. To me, Gettysburg looked like a regular old field, though it was much bigger than I'd imagined, sprawling for miles and broken up with patches of forest, hills, occasional log fences, and even roads. I guess I'd always pictured more of a couple-acre meadow, like a game of capture the flag, except with more killing.

Two squirrels began to fight near me and captured the rest of my waning attention. So much for my gaining any profound historical insight from the field. I was about to give up and go back into the Visitors' Center to inspect the cannonballs when I heard a voice.

"Most people remember Gettysburg for Lincoln's address," the raspy, authoritative voice floated on the breeze from a nearby statue. "Ironically, Lincoln's speech was about how we *shouldn't* remember his speech, and instead direct our memories toward all the men who gave their lives here."

The speaker was a tall, lanky man who moved like a marionette as he walked with a tourist couple along the rocky wall at the edge of the battlefield. I moved closer. "Was the Civil War needed to end slavery?" the man mused to no one in particular. "Probably not; advancements in technology would have eventually killed it economically, and changes in moral opinion would have killed it spiritually. Truth is, most soldiers on both sides probably didn't care much about slavery at all. Only 5 percent of Southern soldiers had ever owned a slave, after all, and only 5 percent of Northern soldiers had ever even *seen* one. But the rabble-rousers of the time were convinced that bloody war was the only way to settle the matter."

The man stopped and gestured out to the field. I pictured mangled bodies of soldiers staining the green grass red in every direction. It seemed a huge waste. How much of it was noble patriotism, and how much of it was people tricking each other into fighting over somebody else's ideology? It seemed like people needed to do a better job of learning from the past.

"Most historians correctly view Gettysburg as a turning point of the war," our faux guide went on. "But the turning point in the *battle* was Pickett's Charge."

A few more people trickled into our group. A paid tour drifted past, and I could see their guide lasering a stink-eye at our competing lecturer.

"The South had the upper hand in the battle, but sending a massive wave of soldiers directly at the main body of the Union army was not a good way to keep it. The losses were so heavy that momentum—and morale—swung completely in a couple of hours."

Somebody asked the guide why anyone would try this courageous but idiotic charge tactic, when every World War I movie made it seem like the worst idea ever.

"They charged," he said. "Because most of the generals, especially the Southern ones, had been trained in tactics of the Napoleonic era, when charging actually worked pretty well. But by the Civil War, gun technology had evolved, and a solid defensive line could now wipe out almost an entire charge. It just took a while for human strategy to catch up."

And human stubbornness, I thought. Typical: develop the technology first, and *then* develop the responsibility to use it. But there would always be new technology. Sometimes we can't learn from the past, because the present is a totally different battle.

Our ad hoc educator wrapped up his address, and some of our group, who by now far outnumbered the paid tour, lined up to shake hands with our bearded sage. "I'll be here again tomorrow," he shouted to everyone. "Come back if you wanna hear about how the Union soldiers punished souvenir poachers by making them bury dead horses!"

I felt refreshed, like I'd finally done something adult after two weeks of slurping cheap beer in redneck bars and sleeping in my car. My mother would be pleased. I thanked our lecturer for the lessons on learning from history, and *not* learning from it.

"You really know your Civil War," I said. "Are you a professor or something?"

"Oh, no!" the man said, laughing and holding my hand a little too tight. "I work at a liquor store, in Pittsburgh."

"Oh," I nodded. "Pittsburgh? Isn't that like . . . hours from here?"

"Yup! I drive up down weekends and hang out. I love the Civil War. And if you love something, you gotta be willing to do it for free. And trust me," he said, still holding onto my hand, staring at me with a pair of big, weird eyes. "I *really* like war."

I pried my hand loose and tiptoed away.

But the guide's words echoed. Another thought had lodged itself in my brain, like a musket shot.

I wouldn't edit for free.

I turned back toward our rogue historian and waved. He'd helped me more than he knew.

And hey, a free tour's a free tour.

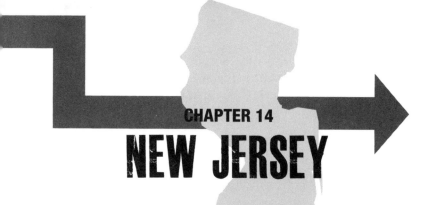

CHAPTER 14

NEW JERSEY

Drinks with a Rabbi

"Booze with a rabbi" was not something I'd pictured making it to my final Roadtrip list, but in a cheery pub in Rutgers I found myself doing precisely that. My old fraternity brother Ari, after getting all the sin out of his system in college, had begun rabbinical school and started down yet another life path that made mine seem depressing. Okay, technically Ari wasn't a rabbi yet, but "light beer with a frat-guy rabbi-in-training" doesn't have the same ring to it.

Ari had started his training by leading a Jewish outreach program at Rutgers, and after he had shown me around, we settled down to some beers at a university tavern (yes, future rabbis can still drink beer). Ari was enthralled by the idea of the Roadtrip and spent the first few pitchers interrogating me about how the trip had been so far: what I had seen, whom I had visited, and how, exactly, I had let Johnny Green convince me to sleep in campground bushes. We also speculated on new Roadtrip ideas should I survive Forty-Eight States in Forty-Eight Days and someday want to do a sequel. One brainstorm was driving to all fifty states in alphabetical order, but after realizing this trip would start in Alabama, proceed to Alaska, and then go back to Arkansas, we abandoned the idea, even before getting to the nasty Georgia-to-Hawaii leg. We also tossed around the idea of driving to every street or intersection ever mentioned in a rock or rap song, but soon realized that this trip would be spent almost exclusively on Santa Monica Boulevard in L.A. and at various unseemly intersections in Brooklyn, the Bronx, and Compton. Also, including Vanilla Ice (and why wouldn't we?) would involve a terribly out-of-the-way trip down to *A1A Beachfront Avenue.*

Within an hour, the conversation had become more serious. My growing madness (and perhaps the three pitchers of Amstel) prompted me to seek Ari's guidance on my whole Direction thing. If not editing . . . what? Actually, I temporarily skipped Direction and went right after an even bigger fish.

"Ari," I said, in a voice that was two sips away from a slur. "Do you get a lot of kids with questions about God?"

Hey, if you're on a road trip to find answers, you might as well question everything.

"Sure," said Ari, holding his pitcher and a half a lot better than I was, despite his 5'3" frame. "College is when a lot of people question stuff like that. I mean, technically I'm the social director, but if they ask me, I try to give the best answer I can."

I realized that he'd probably started this exact same conversation any number of times, with college kids who'd thought of this four years before I had. Then again, in some ways this Roadtrip *was* my college.

"It occurred to me the other day, it's impossible to prove God with logic," I reasoned. "Because if there is a God, then he invented logic. So it doesn't apply to him."

"I suppose that's true. Though I think the moment we say anything for certain about God is the moment we're wrong," countered Ari.

"All right, but let's assume. On the other hand, by the same reasoning, it's impossible to *disprove* God with logic."

"Okay," said Ari, unsure where I was headed with all this, yet patient. He was always a fantastic listener.

"But here's the thing," I went on. "Let's say there's a God, and he invented logic and gave it to us as a gift. Then he's not letting us use one of our greatest gifts to discover him? I mean ... that's just a dick thing to do. That's like giving a kid a telescope and only letting him look at things inside the house."

Ari nodded and sipped his beer.

"The alternative is either that (b) God doesn't exist, or that (c) he exists but didn't invent logic. In the latter case, that isn't any God *I* want to believe in. Can't even invent logic? C'mon God, get with the program."

Ari nodded and sipped.

"The only other thing I can think of is that (d) God invented logic, and it *is* possible to discover him through logic ... but it's so difficult that nobody's smart enough to do it yet. In which case God is teasing us. God's a big tease!"

"Are you sure you're not approaching this the wrong way?" Ari asked, finally. "It sounded before like you were saying God couldn't really be approached with logic."

"So he's just sitting up there, watching me wrack my brains with this? He's probably laughing!" I looked up at the ceiling fan. "If you're up there laughing about this, God, I swear we're gonna have words if I meet you someday! Me and you, God."

A slop of lager spilled out of my raised glass and dripped down my sleeve. Suddenly I realized I was the guy who was talking a bit too loudly at the bar. I put my glass down and was quiet for a moment.

"Sorry."

"That's okay," said Ari. "Happens all the time."

"That's actually not what I wanted to ask you about," I said.

"I think I know what you were going to ask."

"How? Did God tell you?"

"No, I've been reading your blog," answered Ari. "Your whole direction thing. You know there's not an obvious answer, right?"

"I was afraid of that. I guess I'm just wondering, I mean, how'd you find yours? You're going to be a rabbi. That's like the clearest direction anyone could ever have."

"Well, I don't know about that," Ari said modestly.

"You know what I mean. If there's a God, why doesn't he save me a lot of time and gasoline and tell me I'm supposed to be a janitor or something?"

"I don't know if God works that way," said Ari. "Coming down and casting people like a director in a play."

"Do you feel like God called you?"

Ari shook his head. "There was never a burning-bush moment when I said, 'Aha! God wants me to be a rabbi!' But you know, when I look back, everything's led me to it."

Ari set down his glass and looked pensive.

"For a long time," he said. "I didn't know what I wanted to do. Things sort of happened, and I went along with them without knowing why. Friends would always come to me for counseling, and I learned that I liked helping people. I was good at studying, so I became a chemical engineering major—"

"Kind of the exact opposite of being a rabbi," I interjected.

"Pretty much," said Ari. "But when I interned at a hospital, I realized medicine and chemicals weren't the right way for me to help people. I even had a period when I wasn't really religious."

"Fraternity rush?"

"Well, coincidentally, yes, but for a longer period than that. It was a period when I understood what nonreligious people thought, and then I made my peace with Judaism. And one day, it clicked. Everything that I was good at, everything that made me happy—and everything that didn't—pushed me to becoming a rabbi. The signs were there all along."

Ari went on, "Did God toss all these events into my life to guide me and make me become a rabbi? I don't know—again, I'm not sure I know whether God works that way. But he could have. And I do know that he made me the person I am, good at the things I'm good at, and open-minded enough to recognize the path they might be leading me on."

Ari and I paid for our beers and hiked back to his apartment. The walk was the good kind of silent. I thought about what he had said. If the people and situations in my Roadtrip had been trying to tell me something, I sure hadn't heard it yet, unless the divine message was that I was supposed to be a car-dwelling derelict. But I could start keeping my eyes open.

Ari and I fell asleep that night, both of us in his bed (since he'd just moved and didn't yet have any couches), watching the movie *Amélie*. It was categorically the most homosexual thing I've ever done in the presence of a rabbi.

CHAPTER 15
NEW YORK

The Longest Island

In the morning the Imposter and I headed up to New York City, where my brother Mark was getting a collegiate head start on his finance career with an internship on Wall Street, and brother Alex would be meeting us for a weekend of brotherly shenanigans. Unfortunately, I had to temporarily suspend the No Interstates rule to get to Manhattan, since New Jersey is basically one giant interstate. Well, technically it's a "turnpike" (New Jersey is fascist like that), but same thing.

New York City is a tutorial in individuality. Over 8 million people live in the Big Apple, each with his or her own unique story, but when all of them are out at once, pushing and jostling through the concrete grid, it seems pretty impossible that anyone could get noticed over anyone else. And yet they sure try. You'll find in New York some of the most noticeable people anywhere: screaming homeless people, flamboyant theatre folk, and three rampaging Jury brothers after a McDonald's-dollar-cheeseburger-and-malt-liquor contest. Even the buildings cry for attention: there seems to be an ordinance that the closer a structure is to Times Square, the more light bulbs it has to have. Even the Square subway sign looks like it belongs in Vegas. But with everyone and everything competing as loudly as possible to be noticed, the city simply blurs into a blinding, deafening din. No one is listening to you in New York. This can make the city seem rude and uncaring, but it also provides an atmosphere of anonymity and acceptance where everyone can do their own thing and nobody gives a damn. Anyone who grew up in a very small town might appreciate the idea.

In the hopes of experiencing a little of this New York individuality firsthand, Mark, Alex, and I decided to follow our forty-ounce evening with a Sunday morning church service in Harlem. We'd heard great things about the music and singing at some of the traditional services, and after my recent adventures, I figured I could use a little time in church. We rose early and dressed up—unusual activities for Jury boys left to their own devices—and headed to Harlem. We even made 290-pound Alex put on a pair of Mark's long pants, since he'd forgotten to bring any of his own and we didn't want him looking like a pasty-legged tourist in a Harlem church. Alex was not pleased about this: it was a humid 100 degrees in Manhattan that day, and even with the baggiest selection from Mark's wardrobe, it was like trying to cram a watermelon into a tube sock, and Alex walked around all day with a scowl, making stretching noises like he was wearing leather.

The service was expectedly enthusiastic. It was also long, clocking in at a hair under three hours, without air-conditioning. The music was full of honest, sweaty passion, reaching every ear and every corner of the cavernous, balconied old church. The whole scene reminded me a little of those exuberant TV Southern Baptist services where the audience shouts back, "Mmm-hm!" and, "Hallelujah!" after everything the pastor says. But the hallelujahs—and the most joyous singing—were limited to a few exuberant rows in the front. Everyone else was too hot and tired to yell anything. Or they were tourists.

Our refreshing but exhausting commune with Harlem zeal—coupled with having to walk back to the subway in the heat with surly, tight-pants Alex—left us yearning to simply go back and take naps in front of Mark's air-conditioner. But we had one more important stop: Ground Zero.

This was July of 2003. The rubble that had been the World Trade Center was mostly cleared, but there was still a great hole in the earth between Vesey and Liberty Streets, and a greater one in the national psyche.

I didn't know anyone killed in the attacks. My best friend Charlie's older brother Andy was supposed to be painting an office in one of the towers that day, but he'd gone to a Jamiroquai concert the night before and had slept through his morning alarm. He woke up with a headache in the middle of the newscasts as the tower he was supposed to be in was falling.

I didn't understand this karma. The Midwestern Lutheran God I had been raised to believe in rewarded hard work, not partying too much. I couldn't comprehend God's lesson here. I tried to convince myself that Andy had recently done a lot of charity work, or that God was a Jamiroquai fan. If I could still believe in God, after 9/11. It seemed unlikely that anyone's deity could have been involved in a day like that.

Two years after the attack, some of the nearby buildings still had mesh coverings, like mourning veils, to protect them from the dust of cleanup. But what stood out most was a white wooden wall that had been constructed around the site. This wall had become a several-block-long canvas for signatures and messages. People came, witnessed, and left their scrawlings, like signers of a great cast on a broken leg that would never heal. Some of the messages cried sorrow for the victims of the attack; others vented bitter hatred toward the attackers. Freedom of speech knew no limitations here. But

unfortunately, the message that stood out most was a joke—a mean-
ingless scribble on a meaningful wall. It simply read: "Hi! Aaron was
here!" It was written right above a message from a mother who had
lost two sons in the towers.

I got angry, seeing it there. If Aaron was old enough to write, he
should be old enough to know better. I couldn't decide which was
worse: if Aaron had written this to be bad and funny, or if somehow
no one in Aaron's life had ever bothered to teach him any better.

Harlem enthusiasm and Ground Zero ignorance. This was New
York individualism at its best and worst.

On Sunday evening, after a teaser of rabbi Ari's rap-song-
intersection road trip idea with brief and ill-advised stops at Flatbush
and Tillary, Church and Troy, and Franklin and Willoughby, Alex and
I said goodbye to Mark and headed for Providence, where Alex went
to college. The road was calling, and Alex had to be back on campus
at 8 the next morning for training at his summer job, something the
football team had arranged for him.

As we headed out of "The City" and into Queens, I reiterated to
Alex the Roadtrip Rules:

Rule #1: No interstates.

Rule #2: No speeding.

Rule #3: No going back.

Rule #4: Do something interesting in every state.

Alex shrugged; it all sounded fine to him. We had twelve hours to
get to Providence, and it was at most a five-hour drive, even slowing
down (Rule #2) and taking smaller roads (Rule #1). As for Rule #4,
well, we could stop and grab a Zima, or whatever people did in Connecticut, then hang out in Rhode Island the next night after Alex was
done with work.

Little did we know, it would be Rule #3 that got us in New York.

When you live in the Midwest your entire life, certain geographical facts about the rest of the country can escape you. For example, that Texas is *not*, in fact, the same size as Alaska, despite what certain disproportional maps might suggest. Or that Long Island is *not*, in fact, the same thing as Manhattan, despite the fact that Manhattan is, indeed, both long and an island. Honestly, I really did think this, before Mark rolled his eyes and straightened me out. The point is: I was relying heavily on the two-foot road atlas that evening as we headed out of NYC.

Somehow, we made a wrong turn in Queens, and before we knew it we were out on Long Island instead of up in Connecticut. As any New Yorker knows, this is a pretty sizable error, but like I said, we were from the Midwest.

Alex suggested we turn around and go back. I informed him that Rule #3 clearly stated that we could not. We had to find a new way.

"Are you sure?" asked Alex. "Seems like every single other person in the world would go back through Queens right now."

"We can't think like the herd," I persisted. "It's important that we do this Roadtrip right. Besides, if we pull this off, we'll be heroes. *Heroes.*"

"Gimme the map," said Alex.

We consulted the atlas, determined to find a route from Long Island to Connecticut without going back through Queens. I was sure there must be a way.

"Look here," I said, pointing at the blue area separating where we were from where we were supposed to be. "The water's only like two centimeters across! There's gotta be a bridge or something here somewhere."

Alex squinted at the map. Then his eyes lit up. "There," he said, pointing to a tiny dashed line that led from the tip of Long Island up across the sound to Connecticut above. "It says 'toll.'"

We were set. "Toll" obviously meant a road, like the toll roads we'd taken in our childhoods in Minnesota, when we'd visited such exotic places as Chicago. We congratulated ourselves on our cleverness and roared off eastward across Long Island, peeking excitedly around each turn for the first glimpse of our trip-saving toll road across the ocean. It had to be close—after all, according to our map, Long Island was only about fifteen centimeters long.

Two hours later, we were still driving. And beginning to worry. Alex began to suspect that there might not be a bridge at all, and I was inclined to agree; after all, he was the Ivy League engineering student. It must be a tunnel instead. We continued on, passing Hampton after Hampton.

At what point we realized we were screwed is hard to pinpoint. Perhaps it was the lack of signs for the World's Longest Bridge, Ahead. Perhaps it was when Alex noticed the scale on our map reading "1 centimeter = 8 miles." Or perhaps it was when our highway came to the end of Long Island, turned into a dirt road, and abruptly stopped, leaving us gazing out over a cliff into a vast ocean, without even a hint of light flickering from our destination.

It's hard to believe that anybody could be so stupid. The sound separating Long Island from Connecticut is at least ten miles wide; in some places, it's more. It would have taken a healthy section of my imaginary L.A.–Hawaii bridge to span it. Nevertheless, there we were, a twenty-three-year-old traveler and his nineteen-year-old brother, staring across Long Island Sound at 11 P.M., wondering where we had gone wrong.

So, we did what any twenty-three-year-old traveler and his nineteen-year-old brother would do in the face of abject failure: we went to a bar. If we didn't realize we were done for yet, the bartender quickly set us straight: the "toll road" we had seen was a seasonal ferry, and our catching it would be limited by at least three factors:

1. The ferry cost $50, which we didn't have.
2. It didn't run on Sundays.
3. It didn't run at night.

So after two or three semi-legal beers, we climbed back in the Imposter, broke Rule #3, and headed back to Queens.

Sometimes, not retracing your steps means you see more of America. Other times, it means you see every centimeter of Long Island . . . twice.

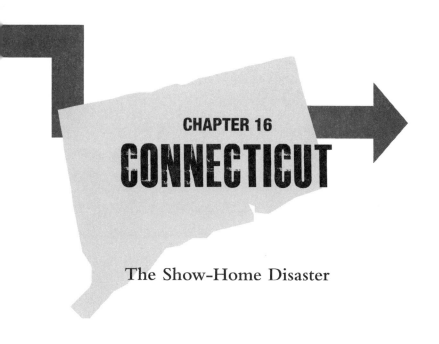

CHAPTER 16
CONNECTICUT

The Show-Home Disaster

This is the story of how my brother Alex and I almost went to jail in Connecticut. We didn't do anything really wrong, but if the misunderstanding had gone much further, we could have found ourselves with some very serious charges indeed.

When we left off, Alex and I were speeding from Queens across the Connecticut Interstate in the middle of the night in an effort to deliver Alex to his 8 A.M. first day of work in Providence. Or rather I was speeding; Alex was passed out in the passenger seat.

By this point, I was beat. I was also agitated: at the fact that our five-hour drive had turned into an eleven-hour drive; at Alex for refusing to drive during any of it; and especially at Connecticut and Long Island, for refusing to have a ten-mile-long bridge between them. I began making up haikus to express my irritation, and also to keep myself awake:

Oh, Connecticut,
You connect here to there, but
What connects to you?

Later came the slightly angrier version:

Oh, Connecticut,
Vast, multisyllabic state:
I hate you so much.

But we had to keep moving. Our rough estimates told us we could still make it to Providence in time, though we no longer exactly trusted our geography skills. Pausing for a rest could mean a trip-breaking snooze delay that might cost Alex his job. But then a Denny's appeared and we agreed we had to stop. No matter how much of a hurry you're in, there's always time for an All-American Slam.

Denny's proved to be a delicious and disastrous idea, as a catastrophic food coma engulfed us both the second I restarted the Imposter. Two miles later I could barely keep my eyes open, much less on the road, although Alex's congested buffalo snores did their best to keep me awake. I was fading fast. After being roused more than once by the shrill grinding of the shoulder warning treads, I punched Alex.

"Dude," I said, as my brother grunted out of his slumber. "I'm dying. Either you gotta drive, or else we gotta pull over and nap for a little bit."

"Then I guess we're pulling over," replied Alex, letting his head droop with a thud into the closed window.

"We're not gonna make it back in time," I said. "And seriously, I've been driving for nine hours. I think it's kind of weak that you won't drive even a little."

"Shut up, I'm full of pancakes," returned my giant brother. "It's your stupid map that got us into this mess."

"I'm gonna beat your face."

"I'm bigger than you are," said Alex.

He had a point.

And with that, he passed out again. I pulled the Imposter off the road at the next exit and rooted for a quick place to park and pass out for a little while.

As I'd learned by this point, there are good and not-so-good places to sleep in your car. Rest stops: Good. Gas stations: Depends. Government buildings and schools: Not so good. But by 5 A.M., after nine hours of driving to the end of Long Island and back, I was too tired to be picky.

I exited into what seemed to be a townhouse development. You know how, when they build a new cookie-cutter community, they always build one complete house first to use as a show home, and then build the other identical houses around it? That's what this looked like. The curbs in front of the unfinished homes were scattered with construction debris, but the show home was finished, so I pulled up across the street. Parking in front of a functioning house made me a little leery, but it seemed to be safe: there were no lights, no cars . . . not even an address, except for a dark, commercial-looking sign in the front yard. Surely something about where to call to schedule a townhouse tour, I told myself as sleep set in.

I woke up forty-five minutes later to a cop pounding on my window. One of my groggy eyes cracked open and confusion flooded in: why were we being accosted at 5:45 A.M. on a Monday morning in central Connecticut? Had we missed a No Parking sign? Did somebody want to tour a shiny new townhouse at the crack of dawn, and we were being an eyesore?

I was jolted out of my pondering by the cop, who was banging on the glass again.

"Hey!" he yelled. "Open up! What are you doing here?"

My eyes opened a little wider and I realized the cop wasn't alone. There were two cops, one fat and one skinny, standing outside our window in front of their police car. Both cops wore scowls that said we must be doing something worse than simply being an eyesore. I rubbed the fuzz out of my brain and looked forward: there was a second cop car, sitting in front of us, blocking our escape. I looked in the rearview ... there was a *third* cop car, behind us. We were boxed in!

"Hey! Answer me!" My bewilderment was shattered by the rotund cop, knocking again. "What are you doing here?"

I realized I'd better say something before people started shooting. Finding my tongue, I rolled down the window and yammered off my usual story about how I was a college graduate on a road trip across the country, and I was tired and didn't want to crash so we pulled off to sleep, and how my brother was a football player at Brown and we needed to get him back to job training in Providence. Clearly it was the same old story a Connecticut cop heard every day.

The big cop wasn't convinced. "Brown, huh? What's the name of the football coach?" Alex told him, but I don't think the cop actually knew the name of the football coach, so he tried again. "Oh yeah? Well do you know Coach Somethingorother, the lacrosse coach?"

I don't think Alex knew Coach Somethingorother, but he was smart enough to pretend that he did. The beefy cop seemed somewhat appeased.

"All right," he said. "Wait here."

He disappeared back to the rear cop car, his vehicle still blocking our view of the show home. It must have been quite a show home, I thought, to summon three squad cars. Then again, there probably wasn't a lot else happening at 5 A.M. on a Monday in Connecticut.

After a moment the fat cop returned, our license plates having apparently checked out. "Okay, I believe you," he said. "But still, what are you doing here? Why on earth would you think it was okay to sleep here?"

Maybe the townhouse developer had some big-time mob connections we should have known about. I apologized, and re-explained about being tired and needing a quick place to nap, and figuring it would be okay to park across from this show home because nobody lived there . . . .

"Wait a minute," the cop interrupted. "A show home?" He looked deep into our faces, as if trying to grasp whether we really believed that. Honestly, we did. "This isn't a show home," the fat cop said at last. "It's a day care center!"

As he said this, the thin cop was moving his squad car out of the way, and we saw it. What we thought was an abandoned model house was now crawling with mothers and their young children, ready for a long day of television and hyperactivity. And here we were, two shady, unshaven guys, wearing wife-beaters in a black Ford Taurus, parked across the street from a day care center as mothers dropped their kids off for the day. I had on a backwards black baseball cap. Alex was wearing a bandana. And I imagine we both must have been wearing big angry frowns as we slept intensely, arms crossed in our kiddy-kidnapping wagon. Truly, we could not have looked any more like pedophiles if we'd been wearing signs that read, "Free candy from strangers."

The fat cop bellowed with laughter. "You thought this was a show home? Wow, that's rich!" He headed back to the rear cop car. "Hey, guys, you gotta hear this!"

Alex and I were mortified. Mothers on the sidewalk were covering their children's eyes, as we were undoubtedly being frozen forever in the minds of several five-year-olds as Those Strangers You Don't Talk To.

Laughter echoed from the cops behind us, and the fat cop sauntered up again, wiping a blissful tear from his cheek. "That's a riot," he said. "But my partner wants to know: if your brother has to work at 8 A.M., how come you're coming from New York so late at night?" I glanced at Alex, and he nodded, defeated. I proceeded to tell the cop the whole embarrassing account about driving to the end of Long Island and back.

The cop stared at us for a moment, then died laughing. He ran back to his buddy cops. "Oh man! And listen to *this*!" More hysterics. Alex and I exchanged a humiliated glance. The fat cop came back with the skinny cop.

"Wait, wait," the cop said, trying not to lose it. "He doesn't believe me. Tell him how you thought there was a bridge!"

Giggling wafted up from the car behind us. I was glad they were having a good time, but I wanted to get the hell out of there. "Listen, are you gonna charge us with something, or can we go?"

The cop recovered, glanced around, then waved the front cop car to move. "All right, you're free to go. Just don't park in front of any more 'show homes,'" he snickered.

I put the car into gear and drove away. At this point, the adrenaline from the encounter was more than sufficient to keep me awake to Providence. But the disorientation of getting forty-five minutes of sleep followed by nearly being booked as child-molesters kept our spirits from getting too high. We drove in silence for a few minutes.

Finally, Alex looked up at me, with a faint grin.

"You have to admit," he said at last. "That was kinda funny."

"I guess," I replied. "I told you you shouldn't have put that nylon over your head before you went to sleep."

"Well, you're the one who cut all those kids' pictures out of that yearbook and spread them on the dashboard," he returned.

I punched him, he punched me back, and we roared on to Rhode Island, trying not to be blinded by the sunrise. We may have broken every other rule, but at least we kept Rule #4: Do something interesting. And Johnny Green would be pleased: we got a story out of it.

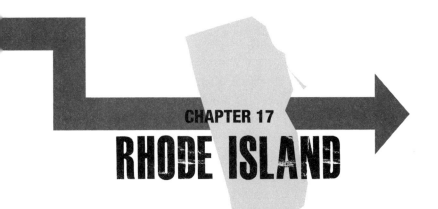

CHAPTER 17
RHODE ISLAND

Rule #3

Alex and I roared into the new day in Providence at 7:30 A.M., barely in time for his 8 A.M. work, only to find out it'd been cancelled. It was only a fluff football job, after all. Too tired to even be mad, I simply cursed Long Island and Connecticut once more and passed out next to my brother in his bed. I didn't even complain about his snoring. Hey, beds and couches four nights in a row? I was living like a king.

It was the summer between Alex's freshman and sophomore years, and he was living in an off-campus house he shared with several members of his fraternity. This house was not the fraternity itself, but when you put enough frat guys together under one roof . . . let's just say the local germs knew where the party was.

When I woke up, somewhere in the vicinity of 2 P.M., Alex had already left for the gym. I entered the kitchen to get myself a drink and promptly had one of my shoes pulled off by a sticky floor, two centimeters thick with dried beer, mud, and other liquids I was afraid to guess at. Fortunately, there was an empty beer keg nearby that I caught myself on, or I might have fallen to the ground and become stuck forever, a hapless insect on a frat-house flypaper floor.

The fact that this kind of grossed me out surprised me. I had once been in a fraternity myself, though being a frat guy at Northwestern is a little like being the bully on a chess team. But I liked being in Zeta Beta Tau. Not all fraternity stereotypes are true; sure, our house was known to throw a drunken raging beer party now and again, but we also raised nearly $50,000 a year for leukemia research, in memory of a deceased brother. Granted, our donation was followed by a drunken raging beer party . . . but I digress. One stereotype that *had* been true was that our house was disgusting. It's just really hard to put thirty college guys together and not have some diffusion of responsibility kick in. At the time, I hadn't minded the mess. But now I was squirming over my brother's repugnant kitchen. There comes a time when you outgrow college.

I climbed on top of the keg and proceeded to make myself a sandwich without touching the floor, and contemplated how things had changed since my own days of brotherhood had ended a year earlier. I had gone back to my fraternity once in the fall, to say hi, and to steal food, as was custom. "What are you doing here?" exclaimed the younger members of the house, with friendly surprise. I could tell they were glad to see me, even as I walked off with a whole crate of their cereal.

I went back to the fraternity a second time, in the winter, because a good friend still in the house had asked me if I'd come help with an event. "What are you doing here?" exclaimed the younger guys again, slightly confused at having now seen me twice, but still glad to have my help.

I went back to the fraternity a third time, reluctantly, because I'd left something there during the event. "Seriously, what are you doing here?" said one of the younger guys, wondering whether I had anywhere better to go.

That was the last time I went back. I was beginning to feel like the guy who doesn't have anything better to do than hang out at his old frat. The guide from Gettysburg was right: sometimes you need to learn from the past, but sometimes you need to forget it.

And now, as I perched atop a beer keg in my brother's nasty kitchen, one of the other members of his house wandered in. I think he recognized me as Alex's older brother. But Alex was not here. And I was squatting on a keg in boxers, clutching a loaf of bread and a knife.

"Hey . . ." he said, the strangeness of the situation dawning on him. "Um . . . what ahh you doin' heah?" he said in a sentence remarkably pronounced without any Rs. He must have been a local kid.

There was no disdain in his voice, nor any welcoming. Only bewilderment.

There comes a time when you and college . . . well, you outgrow each other.

I cleaned up the Imposter—and myself—at Alex's. I couldn't imagine that my sketchy-drifter appearance and body-odor-and-jelly smell had helped make a good impression with the Connecticut cops. I didn't shave, though: I was starting to like the mountain-man look I was rocking. But then I moved on. As much as I enjoyed my college days, and didn't think I'd matured all that much since then, those days were now behind me. And as we learned in Queens: no matter what lies ahead . . . Rule #3. There's no going back.

CHAPTER 18

NEW HAMPSHIRE

The Chairman Is Sick

Late that afternoon I plowed up into Massachusetts through Pawtucket, which quickly joined my list of favorite American city names, along with Oconomowoc, Wisconsin; Paw Paw, Michigan; and Cheesequake, New Jersey (home of the world's most delicious natural disasters). The Imposter's cooler was full of yogurt cups and knock-off Klondike bars, stolen from Alex's fraternity's kitchen. I may not be able to go back, but tradition is tradition.

My plan was to skip through Massachusetts to the Canada-hugging states on top of it, then double back to hit Boston later in the week, when Mark might be able to get off work and come hang out with me. It was an impractical route, but part of me also wanted to get far away from Connecticut for a few days.

I didn't have a strong plan for New Hampshire. Judging from the signs I encountered in the first few miles after entering the state, people from New Hampshire (New Hampshirians? New Hamsters?) are particularly proud of two things: their abundance of moose and their abundance of French people. They also have a particularly truculent state slogan, "Live Free or Die," which is printed boldly across every New Hampshire license plate. New Hampshire *was* the first colony to declare its independence from Britain, but this catchphrase seemed a tad belligerent, more like a war cry from *Braveheart* than the official motto of a state chiefly known for its production of apples and lack of sales tax.

I stopped at a little grocery store near Nashua, did a little research, and learned of a dairy shop in North Hampton called C'est Cheese that seemed pun-tastic and worth a visit, at least to satisfy the French part of "something to do in New Hampshire." I pictured giant blocks of Brie and separationist propaganda for New Hampshire to secede and become a territory of Quebec.

I picked up a fresh bread loaf at the store. I'd been learning something about bread. Since that particular PBJ ingredient went the fastest (my wholesale tubs of peanut butter and jelly were lasting like champions), I had to stop every couple of states and buy a new loaf, and I'm pretty sure I never bought the same brand twice. It seems the Bread Anti-Trust Bureau has done an excellent job of keeping any one bread company from becoming too widespread (except Wonder Bread, which has its own Nascar), and every region has its own brand. Perhaps it's a secret message about the diverse unity of our country—after all, bread is the staple of the U.S. diet. It's what rice is to China and what pasta is to Italy. It's what we feed our prisoners. Bread is patriotism. Bread is America. Sick as I was of sandwiches, I would have been a downright Commie not to eat lots of bread on my trip.

In the check-out line, I swiped my debit card. A horrifying number stared back at me. $1,500? I was already halfway through my savings for the entire trip? How? I wasn't even in Maine yet! It seemed riverboat casinos and "I'm sorry I tried to break up with you" dinners with Sarah were devouring my budget a lot faster than anticipated.

I climbed back into the Imposter, my concern dropping momentarily into panic. What was I doing? A man should be making money and taking over his father's company, not joyriding around like a hobo tourist. I was supposed to be making my family proud. I tried to squish it down and remind myself that I'd chosen this. I guessed I wouldn't buy a two-foot Gouda wheel at C'est Cheese, after all.

I pulled away into the arriving dusk and my phone beeped twice. The first signaled a text message from Sarah:

Can you call me? The Chairman is sick.

The second was a low-battery warning. Then the phone shut off.

Great. I was suddenly not sure I could afford gas for thirty more states, and now I had to drive all over New Hampshire scouring for electricity? Then I cursed myself: I had barely talked to Sarah in days, and my first reaction was to be annoyed? I should be glad anyone still wanted to talk to me.

Things were about to get a lot lonelier.

Up until this trip, I'd spent my life in Minnesota and Illinois, and almost everyone I knew lived in the Midwest or the East. For the first fifteen nights of my trip, I'd had seven people to crash with. In the next fifteen nights, I'd have only one. To top it off, I would soon be hitting the South, the part of the country I knew the least about, and I guess you could say I was a little bit nervous. What did a Minnesota boy know about the Deep South? Every state had its small-town, toothless hillbillies . . . but Southern toothless hillbillies had *accents*.

I passed a dingy old pizza joint that seemed like it might have an outlet, but I'd have to buy dinner to sit and eat their power. I had to find free power somewhere. Sarah needed me. I sighed. The Chairman was sick.

The Chairman was Sarah's cat. She had adopted the little gray wad of germs and teeth while I was living with her in Chicago, and I had convinced her to name it Chairman Meow. Sarah didn't like the name at first—she wanted to name the feline Mister, which could then be abbreviated through her baby talk to Mi'ter,—but eventually she gave in. Deep down, I think she had to admit it was a pretty fantastic thing to call a cat.

The strange thing about The Chairman's adoption was that Sarah had wanted a cute little white cat, possibly with some spots, and The Chairman was this mangy, ill-behaved, dark gray fur ball who looked like he'd just crawled down someone's chimney. But he was the only kitten at the shelter that day, and Sarah wanted a cat. Right then. Sarah always had the remarkable ability to just change her heart. And if it was a naughty gray cat instead of a docile white one that needed to be loved, well, so be it. I, always ruled by the rational, asked Sarah whether she was sure she didn't want to try another shelter, or come back another day, to find the cat she'd always dreamed of. But it was too late. She'd already fallen in love with The Chairman.

Sarah wasn't a girl who tried to find what she loved. She was a girl who loved what she found. All she wanted in return was to be loved. That was the difference between us. Sarah told that cat she loved it every day, from Day One. I could never bring myself to say it to her even once.

I drove past a library, but it had closed hours earlier. Damn you, French-hours New Hampshire.

Despite his awesome name, I soon came to hate The Chairman, whom Sarah spoiled to no end. The cat quickly learned that it could get whatever it wanted in the middle of the night simply by biting Sarah's feet. The Chairman would leap onto the bed, hungry and chomping, and Sarah would whine, get up, and trudge dutifully to the kitchen. I, on the other hand, would throw the cat across the room. I once chucked The Chairman a full twenty-five feet across the apartment, where he landed on the couch and remained in frozen shock for a minute before Sarah came to his rescue, petting him and glaring lasers at me. I spent two nights on that couch for my offense, but lessons had been learned. From then on The Chairman only bit Sarah, and I only threw The Chairman across the room when Sarah wasn't around.

And right now the little guy was probably barfing up fluff and kibbles all over Sarah's apartment. At least the sickness couldn't be blamed on me: I had only seen The Chairman briefly in Chicago the week before, and although he had been particularly bitey during my visit, I had resisted the impulse to poison him.

I pulled out my cell phone's battery and blew on it. Somehow this gave the phone another minute of power. But I wasn't getting any reception either, despite the fact that the Verizon map I'd taped to the dashboard clearly showed that this was a red zone. I would have to have words with their coloring team. The phone shut off again. My fingers tightened on the Imposter's steering wheel. The sharp needle of the speedometer edged up toward sixty.

What was bugging me? While I appreciated Sarah's letting me name her cat after a communist dictator, I couldn't shake the nagging feeling that I was pausing my trip to drive all over New Hampshire so I could comfort my girlfriend about kitty vomit.

My gut was rumbling again. I thought I had put this behind me back in Wisconsin.

Even if she hated the Roadtrip, Sarah had always supported me— couldn't I at least do the same for her? I remembered the end of senior year, when I'd shunned her and everyone else, killing myself to finish my senior writing and directing project. One evening I stopped by her house on my way to the lab for a final, marathon night of edit-ing. I was going bonkers. I had about twenty hours of cutting to do in about ten hours, and I was horrified at the possibility of letting down an auditorium full of people. But to Sarah, I wanted to apologize— for neglecting her in the past, neglecting her now, and for all the times I would someday neglect her again for some stupid project that she didn't understand. I wanted to cry. This was my biggest fear: that the things I cared about would interfere with and ruin the other things I cared about.

Sarah took my face in her hands, and asked me if there was any-thing she could do.

"There's nothing you *can* do!" I lamented. "I'm the only one who knows how to edit this thing, and it's pulling me away from you, but

I can't stop or I'll fail. But if I don't stop, I feel like I'm failing you, and—"

"Shhh," she put her finger over my lips. "I know I can't help you edit. I don't know how to work that silly machine. But what can I do to help *you*?"

I was quiet. I didn't know what else to say. "Just be with me."

"Okay." She grabbed her coat.

Sarah came with me to the editing booth that night and stayed with me for ten hours, sitting silently next to me for as long as she could stay awake, then sleeping on the floor while I edited harder than I'd ever edited in my life. We didn't exchange a word. She could do nothing to help. But to me, it was everything. I finished the show by morning.

And now, here I was, neglecting her again. The girl I cared about was miserable because I was off on yet another dumb project.

As I pictured her alone and beautiful, probably slipping her slender legs into pajamas as The Chairman finally curled up in his box to sleep, I recalled that along with everything else I was depriving myself of, I also hadn't had any carnal comforts since Chicago. Well, since way before Chicago, really; we hadn't exactly fit any lovin' in there either, because I'd been too busy trying to break up with her for no reason.

We were both making sacrifices for me to do this crazy trip. It was unfair to Sarah that I got to have 100 percent say in when those sacrifices ended.

The least I could do was find a damned outlet.

I finally located one, and with it, a powerful discovery in my ongoing quest for late-night power: ice machines. Most gas stations have ice machines outside, and ice needs to stay cold all night, right? I sat down on the curb next to a closed Citgo station, plugged in my phone, dialed, and reflected that this was a piece of knowledge I had never imagined needing.

"I'm sorry," Sarah said, "I know I promised to give you some breathing room, but—"

"I know. It's okay. How's The Chairman?"

Sarah was, perhaps, irrationally worried about her cat, as animal-obsessed girls who live alone can sometimes be. She thought The Chairman might have whooping cough. I didn't think that was something cats could get. In fact, I didn't think *anybody* got whooping cough, since at least the Oregon Trail.

"But he sounds terrible! Are you sure he isn't dying?"

"Sarah, he lived in an *alley* before they found him. If the mites and winter didn't kill him, I'm sure he's got a pretty solid immune system. Just keep an eye on him tonight, and take him to the vet tomorrow."

"Okay," she finally said, the way a five-year-old would when she eventually agreed to go to bed. "I think he's feeling better, anyway," she added. "He's biting me."

C'est Cheese was closed by the time I hung up with Sarah. I quietly headed toward Vermont to find an inoffensive place to sleep.

I hated not understanding what was pulling me away from the simple, logical choice of Chicago and my girlfriend's safe, warm bed and obnoxious cat.

But something was.

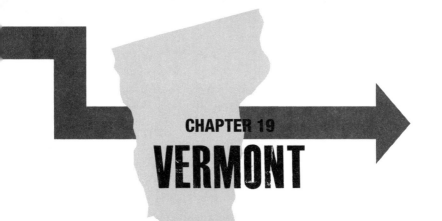

CHAPTER 19

VERMONT

Tree Blood & the One-Armed Waitress

For some reason, two of my college friends, Jeremy and Rabbi Ari, loved Vermont. As far as I knew neither one had actually been there, but they would run around the halls of our fraternity screaming, "Vermont! Vermont!" and wearing bright pink T-shirts with the state's name emblazoned across the front in huge block letters. In hindsight, I think they were just trying to annoy everyone.

Both Jeremy and Ari insisted I do something characteristically *Vermont* while I was in Vermont. Problem was, I had no idea what this meant. Stop at Ben & Jerry's? Buy some cashews, the most pretentious of all nuts, which were sold at seemingly every shop I passed? Get married to a man? I rode the Imposter up a hill and emerged above the green canopy of maple, birch, and hickory that would be blazing multicolor across New England and posing for jigsaw puzzles in the coming autumn. I pondered what I could do that would be Vermont enough to satisfy my friends, short of stopping and taking a quilting class.

In Quechee, I passed a little waterfall and my mind flashed back to the last time I'd been this far northeast. Six months after Sarah's adventure on the editing room floor, a play I'd written won second place in a small playwriting contest and was being produced at an off-off-off-Broadway theatre in New York . . . and by that I mean Buffalo. Regardless, it was the first work I'd ever had "professionally" produced, and Sarah and I drove from Chicago to see it at a tiny alleyway theatre (seriously, that was the name of the theatre: Alleyway). I made a total of $75 in royalties from the production, and at that moment I decided that writing was not really something I could make a living from.

While we were in Buffalo, I talked Sarah into venturing up to Niagara Falls. She came along to support me, of course, but law school changes a girl. The winter weather was unbearable, and we'd barely reached obstructed viewing distance when shivering Sarah had had enough.

"But don't you want to walk to the other side and see the full view?" I asked, my eyebrows frozen solid. "It would be a wacky experience, at least."

"I've got Firm interviews now," Sarah replied, through chattering teeth. "And I've got you. I don't need any more wacky experiences."

The Imposter and I zoomed past a maple syrup farm: now *there* was something characteristically Vermont. But for some reason it seemed so lame. Every time I'd tried to do something *expected* in a state—the Field of Dreams in Iowa, or the Kellogg's factory in Michigan—the result had disappointed. Besides, my eye had been lured by a restaurant's sign:

ALL THE MEAT YOU COULD EVER EAT! $7.99

In my protein-deprived state, it seemed like a mirage. What an incongruous establishment for Vermont, which I'd always pictured as having a high percentage of vegetarians. I wondered if it had been won in a trade with Texas for a dainty pancake shop somewhere in Lubbock.

It wasn't very Vermont. But this was *my* trip, wasn't it? At some point, I had to get out from under everyone else's expectations. Sure, I still had a budget, but for $8 I could cram a pretty insane amount of meat into my system. I could even stuff some into my laptop bag for the road, with the added bonus of having a pork-scented keyboard every time I blogged. Besides, I already knew how syrup was made. Tree blood.

I put the Imposter into Park, cast a last glance at the maple syrup farm, and chose the decidedly un-Vermont path.

I would not be disappointed.

Everything seemed normal about the restaurant, except for a series of blankets with moose on them that hung for decoration around the dim dining room, as if my future food was watching me. Everything seemed normal about the small barnyard of meat trays at the buffet as I took my seat, a shiver of excitement in my belly, like a kid on Christmas Eve. And everything seemed normal about the waitress who strolled over to me, except that she only had one arm.

I did a double take, as, I'm sure, did everyone else who ever entered the establishment. At my high school, one of the history teachers, Mr. Krueger, had been similarly impaired, and some of my more demented friends would sit in the back of the class and ask questions like "How do you put on deodorant?" "How do you jump rope?" "Mr. Krueger, what is the sound of one hand clapping?" Of course, they never uttered these questions loud enough for Mr. Krueger to hear; rumor had it, over years of double use, Mr. K's other arm had become so strong it could karate-chop your head so hard it would explode.

By now, I had learned a few things: that it's impossible to explode a head with a karate chop, but also that it was rude to make a waitress uncomfortable by staring slack-jawed at her pinned-up left sleeve. I retained my most unassuming face as the waitress approached.

"I'll have the All-You-Can-Eat-Meat situation, please, with a water. And a Coke. You know what, never mind, no Coke. I'll just have the water."

"Why, you don't think I can carry it?" said the waitress.

"Wh-what?" I stammered. "No. Why would I think that?"

The waitress looked at me. "Cuz I only got this one arm, duh. Don't pretend you weren't staring. I can do anything any other waitress can do, you know."

She tossed her order pad up in the air and caught it, as if to demonstrate something another, two-armed waitress would normally do.

"Go ahead. Ask."

I didn't know what she meant. "What?"

"You wanna know how I lost it. I tell that story about ten times a day, anyway," she said, peering around the restaurant. "I suppose one more won't matter."

"I don't mean to pry—"

"Playground accident," she said. "Rusty swing-set chain."

I had no idea how this made sense. "Like . . . the chain lopped your arm off?" I was beginning to feel like the meat restaurant really *was* a dream, and this was the part where it got weird.

"What? Don't be ridiculous, a swing-set chain could never slice through an arm. No, the chain cut my arm a little, but my mother didn't want to take me to the doctor, and it got infected and eventually they had to take it off. There's still a lawsuit, versus the Hydrogen Peroxide Corporation."

I was at a loss. "That's . . . a company?"

"Course it's a company. I'll be back with your water. *And* Coke."

And with that, she marched off.

I had no idea what to think. Where did they find this woman? Why had I randomly chosen the town, road, and restaurant in Vermont necessary to cross paths with her? Why was I so tempted to ask her how many pull-ups she could do? The Vermont Tourism Board people were probably rolling over in their hickory graves, knowing that this was the woman representing them. The whole scene could not have been any less Vermont. But I guarantee it was more interesting than a syrup farm.

The one-armed waitress approached another customer, who hadn't noticed anything amiss.

"Hi, could I have—"

She sighed, loudly, interrupting. "Go ahead and ask."

The waitress mostly left me alone after that. I made trip after trip to the buffet and stayed out of her way. But I'd never been so confused about how much tip to leave. She did a good job, despite the verbal abuse, but I was worried that overtipping might get me an "I don't need your charity!" lecture, while undertipping might get my head karate-chopped. I left exactly 15 percent, to the penny.

Afterward, I ducked into the maple syrup farm, just to peek. Heck, it was only across the street.

Yup, clichéd touristy lameness.

CHAPTER 20

MAINE

A Musical in Maine

In Maine, I could have gone lobstering or taken in a garden tour in the town of Rome, Maine (yes, like the lettuce). Instead, I wound up at an employment agency.

Right after I graduated and moved back to Minnesota, I started writing a musical with my musically gifted high-school friend Sean to keep the creative spirit from atrophying. In a move that would prove painfully ironic during my phase of employment blues, we chose to write a play with the theme of keeping youthful idealism alive in the harsh real world. We wanted a setting that embodied some of the vexations and obstacles associated with starting real life, so we picked an employment agency. We wanted a state that exuded a sense of naïve, noble optimism—without seeming too hick—so we picked Maine. The main character gets a job at an Augusta employment agency, realizes that life sucks, but tries to keep up his quixotic outlook ... there's singing and dancing, idealism and realism, fun with job interviews and paperwork, and lots and lots of Maine. Ah, musical theatre.

In any case, there it was on my Roadtrip To-Do List: "Maine: Visit Employment Agency." I figured doing a little research for the project—which had of course netted us exactly zero dollars so far—would give me something unique to do in the Pine Tree State. And hey, as long as I was in Maine, I might as well go research a musical at an employment agency, right? It seemed absurd enough for my vision for the Roadtrip.

I tried to explain this to Terry, the elderly but astute career counselor who had the misfortune of being assigned to meet with me. It was one of the strangest conversations probably ever to take place at the Augusta Employment Recruitment Center.

"A musical?" Terry said. Tiny but alert, she looked a bit like a mouse with glasses. Her office—and the whole employment center—was modern, well-lit, and cheery. A place where people found hope.

"Yeah, about youthful idealism in the real world and all that," I said. "You know, a coming-of-age story."

"Coming of age at an employment agency?"

"It's a good setting for the real world. The main character comes here because he thinks he can save the world."

"In Maine?"

"Yes. Maine."

There was a long pause, as Terry gave me a long, thoughtful look.

"The musical's not really why you came here today, is it?"

They really train their agents for everything up there in Maine.

"Well, it was, originally."

"But now?"

I sighed. "I was planning to come up here, just for a lark, and ask you about how I could stage a chorus number about filing. But I've been driving around the country for three weeks now and I still have no idea what to do with my life."

Terry nodded. It occurred to me that, strange as it was, this might not be the first time she'd had this conversation. Perhaps not even today.

"My friend Ari gave me some advice about just letting my path come to me, but that's not my style. I feel like I need to go after it, and I figured coming here might be a good step in the right direction. Unless," I said, eyeing her. "Our silly musical was all part of God's wacky plan to lead me to an employment agency in Augusta . . . ."

"The Lord works in mysterious ways," Terry said, eyeing me back.

"But anyway," I continued, shifting in my seat. "I'll understand if you don't want to waste Maine's tax dollars."

Terry looked me up and down, like a job-scanning robot running me through her processors. Then she picked up her yellow pad.

"There are about a million things you can do for money in this country. A *career* is a little different story, though." She jotted something down on her pad. "There are typically three factors that go into a career decision: what you've done in the past, what you're good at in the present, and what you'd love to be doing in the future. Of course, there's also an element of what's available; for instance an auto plant recently opened up in Randolph . . . ."

"The last time I tried to change my own oil, I almost set myself on fire," I said.

Terry nodded. "What jobs have you had thus far?"

I unfurled my ridiculous history of bouncing, video editing, sorting employee-satisfaction surveys for my dad, painting houses, and being a security guard. Terry was unmoved. Only five jobs in a year wasn't so impressive to someone in the unemployment industry.

"What did you like most about any of those?"

"I don't know; none of them were particularly great jobs. I guess what I liked best was all the wacky experiences they provided."

She nodded, and jotted something down on her pad. "And what are you good at now?"

"Well, I was a film major . . ."

Terry shook her head. "Undergrad majors don't mean as much these days. If there's one thing I've learned about careers, it's that they don't always progress the way you planned."

"Tell me about it."

"It only means that any place you start is equally likely to land you where you'd love to be. You just have to start somewhere," She folded her hands. "So. Where would you love to be?"

Great. This was the hard question.

"I don't know. Doing something creative."

"Like writing a musical about an employment agency in Maine?"

I squirmed a little in my seat. "I suppose. But that's not a job."

"It sounds to me like you wish you could be a writer."

I avoided her eye contact. "That's not a career."

"Sure it is. There are books, and movies, and plays . . ."

"Have you ever met anyone who made a living writing plays?"

"No . . ." she admitted.

"Neither have I."

"Maybe not in Maine. But in New York, or L.A. . . ."

"I've been to L.A. It's eight million people in coffee shops with screenplays, and every year somebody sells one but then goes back to waiting tables when they can't sell another. You can't feed a family with a dream."

Terry looked at me. "It sounds like you've thought about this."

I sighed. "I guess I realized that writing was a hobby, not a vocation."

"Well, you may need to start with a less glamorous form of writing, like copywriting, or writing textbooks or something."

"I might as well work at an auto plant." I stood up. "Thanks. I don't want to take any more of your time away from people who are actually looking for jobs in Maine."

Terry nodded. "Remember, people's first jobs usually aren't their dream jobs. Or else I wouldn't have my job. But you have to jump in somewhere."

I shook her hand and headed for the door.

"One other thing," said Terry. I turned. "What's the name of your musical?"

I blushed. "*Maine Squeeze.* Working title."

Terry winked at me. "You might want to keep working."

CHAPTER 21

MASSACHUSETTS

Car Pranks

Both of my best stories about Massachusetts have to do with cars, pranks, and the Massachusetts Institute of Technology, and nothing to do with me.

There is a room in one of MIT's fraternities known as the Carport. The story goes that once, while a member of the house was on vacation, a few of his bored brothers completely disassembled his car, carried the parts up three flights of stairs, and reassembled it in his room. The guy came home to find a fully functional Ford filling his bedroom. Whether his mechanically gifted brothers helped him correct the situation, I never heard—I only know that the guy got little use out of either his vehicle or his room for a few days.

In a similar but more famous campus story, a mysterious car appeared one morning in an unusual place: on top of the domed roof of one of the main academic buildings. The car appeared to be an operational campus patrol vehicle, with a person inside. It later turned out to be a meticulously repainted old Chevy, complete with a dummy cop and a box of donuts. Nobody knew how the car had gotten there—nobody had seen a crane or any other means of getting a full-sized car onto a roof. Nobody knew how to get the car safely down.

What is it with MIT students and elaborate, car-related pranks? Probably they just have too many brains—and too much time—on their hands. I rolled back down the coast toward Boston wondering whether, among everything else I had to worry about with the Imposter, it might somehow end up several hundred feet in the air.

I'd always meant to get out and see Boston and MIT, where my brother Mark was studying math and finance while I was trying to avoid overdraft fees on my checking account. In college, I'd been too busy, what with the pursuing of Great Things that had since failed to pan out. But now, I had time, and an excuse: Mark had decided to take the day off work in Manhattan and train up to tool around with me. It was vastly out of the way for both of us, but worth it, and there was always a chance for a cheeseburger-and-malt-liquor rematch.

Mark was running late, so I got a head start on Boston by myself. Boston's a curious town: population-wise, it's not even as big as Charlotte or Jacksonville, but the city more than makes up for it in spirit, mostly because of overzealous Red Sox fans. The town's also one-third college students, at least during the school year, which makes for a skewed commerce distribution. Growing up, we visited my grandparents every spring in Sun City, Arizona, a retirement community that, having no schools, spends all its money on hospitals and golf courses. Boston is the exact opposite: whereas Sun City has a disproportionate number of drug stores and shuffleboard courts, Boston has beer-pong bars and late-night Taco Bells.

Mark texted me as I was finishing my chalupa and returning to MIT. He was still on the train, he said—there was some kind of delay. I should go ahead and have a peek around campus without him.

Through several of MIT's main buildings, there is a massive hallway known as the Infinite Corridor. It stretches several blocks down the spine of campus, with hallways branching off like arteries into different departments, finally coming to an end (or beginning) at Mass. Avenue, in Building 7. Because, obviously, all MIT buildings are numbered.

I stood gazing down the Corridor, just as all MIT students do at some point when they begin their journey into the prosperity that awaits them. Even now in July, the Corridor was bustling with summer students who streamed off down their various paths—to Chemistry this way, to Mathematics that way. Every path seemed better than mine.

I imagined Mark there, moving with them, leaving me behind.

Like Craig in St. Louis and J.J. in Indy, Mark was the epitome of What You Were Expected to Do. But it was worse because he was my brother.

Mark is two years younger than I, and growing up, our sibling rivalry raged like an inferno that engulfed our house's furniture, our parents' patience, and occasionally Alex, when he got too close to one of our brawls. As the oldest, I absolutely could not bear losing to Mark in anything, so my odd chess and Monopoly losses to him were generally punctuated by game boards thrown across rooms and bishops lodged into wall plaster. I was bigger than Mark through most of high school, so I maintained an edge in the face-smashing category (the only category that matters in a house full of boys), and got to feel like my alpha position was intact.

Then Mark got taller than me. Then he got into MIT. And then, after his junior year, he started a summer Wall Street internship, where he made more money in two months than I'd made my entire year since graduating. My college internship, if you'll recall, was working in L.A., copying scripts and having coffee mugs thrown at me, being paid only in whatever candy I could steal. The film industry had its own angle on success, but the odds were long. Too long. And I couldn't bear losing.

I gazed through a window into a computer lab filled with tomorrow's leaders, clacking their keyboards, practically accumulating interest just sitting there. The ultimate embarrassment for any oldest child is having your younger siblings be more successful than you. Especially while they're still in college.

My phone rang. Mark.

"You're going to hate me," my brother said. "I'm not coming."

"I thought you said you were on the train."

"No. I was on the train here. I asked my boss if I could have the day off. He laughed at me and said, 'You're on Wall Street now.' I never got out of Manhattan."

"Well, you're not missing much. Yesterday I went to an employment agency in Maine. This morning when I woke up there was a tree branch that had fallen ten feet from my car. I don't have health insurance. Later I got so bored I actually dozed off in a park for a few minutes." I looked down the hallway. "I don't know how or where I got turned around, but it's a strange road I've ended up on."

"I know," said Mark. "I sure am jealous of you, man."

What?

"I wish I could be there. It would be a hell of lot better than sitting in this stupid office."

I gazed back into the computer lab of tomorrow's successes. For the first time I noticed that they weren't smiling.

"I don't get it," I said. "If you knew you couldn't come this morning, why did you say you were on your way?"

"You said you wanted to see Boston and MIT. I figured you might not do it otherwise. I know how you are about driving way out of the way for nothing." Mark said. "Sorry I tricked you. But that's what we do at MIT: pranks involving cars."

A couple of grinning students ran out of a lab and back down the hallway, skipping out on class, carrying what looked like a potato gun.

"Hey," said my brother. "Have an adventure for me."

I hung up. The potato gun students busted out the in-door, laughing, into the summer sun.

I turned. And took my first step down the Corridor.

CHAPTER 22

DELAWARE

Late-Night Outlets

The monster drive back through Massachusetts and eastern New York and down into Delaware gave me plenty of time to think, and plenty of time to become excruciatingly bored. Cell reception is pretty good in the colossal suburb that is southern New England, and to combat my burgeoning loneliness, I called every friend and relative in my phone book. Sadly, most of the conversations went something like this:

"Hey, it's Paul! I'm driving through Delaware!"

"Oh. Um, that's cool . . . ."

"What are you doing?"

"Nothing. Uh, kinda busy at work right now, can I call you back later?"

Few of them did.

I also got a hold of my parents.

"We got Grandma set up on our old Dell," my mom said. "So she can read your blog. She's really enjoying following along! She wishes you wouldn't use so many curse words, though."

For some reason, I didn't feel like calling Sarah.

The South was looming, but my mind was stuck on New England and the Midwest. The frowns on the faces of the MIT kids. The maniacal mirth of the union folks in their souped-up cars in Indy, shrieking around the traffic circle like it was a merry-go-round. The faces should have been reversed. But they weren't.

Perhaps it was a good thing that I was about to be alone for a while. I'd been focusing so much on what other people were doing; it was time I went off on my own for a bit. It would be my own personal vision quest, like when a young tribal boy goes off into the wilderness to become a man and hallucinates about talking buffalo and such. Didn't Jesus go off and have a vision quest in the desert for forty days before he decided he was ready to be the son of God? Or was that Moses? Was it blasphemous to talk about Jesus having a Native American vision quest? I wished I had paid better attention in Sunday School instead of making doodles of the apostles shooting lasers at each other.

I threw my phone into the backseat and crossed over into Delaware. If I was about to enter a dozen states of solitude, I might as well use it to forget everyone else and find myself. I didn't need people. I was Rugged Adventure Man, wrestling grizzly bears and tripping about buffalo.

There's not much to say about Delaware. It's the first state, which I guess means the guy from colonial Delaware got to the courthouse five seconds before everybody else on State Registration Day. It's also home to the headquarters of a shockingly high percentage of U.S. corporations, since some slippery Delaware laws make it extremely affordable to incorporate there. This really means nothing to anyone passing through the state, except that when you're stopping for gas and bread, you're slightly more likely to have a well-dressed VP come out and ask you how your gas and bread-buying experiences could be improved.

I got some strange reactions at the gas station, and sizing myself up in the restroom mirror, I understood why. I was a fright. Three weeks without conditioner had rendered my hair completely unmanageable. I tried in vain to straighten things out by dunking my head into the sink, my unsanctified crown bumping against the porcelain bowl. It would be easier to just switch to a full-time baseball cap. My clothing's wrinkled state had transcended the level of "I don't know how to iron" and reached "homeless person." I began to seriously doubt that my dozen sets of clothing were going to cut it. But money was still too tight to waste any doing laundry—given the choice between looking presentable and eating, I'll take the latter. Still, the dirty clothes bag had become potent enough to make me a little woozy when I opened the trunk. I plucked out a few of the most offensive pieces, shut them into all the Imposter's windows, and roared off into the distance, rotten clothes flapping in all directions like a redneck parade float.

I peeled my eyes for a place to charge my now-exhausted phone. On my growing list of strange things I'd learned on the Roadtrip, the following places are decent spots to find a functioning outlet in the middle of the night:

- **Lobbies of seedy motels.** Or good hotels, but you don't tend to find as many of those on the side roads. As I learned in West Virginia, most hotels' third-shift front-desk employees don't know who's actually staying in their hotel and who's drifting through and stealing electricity.
- **Car-repair shops.** These are no guarantee, but I'd noticed that auto shops are more likely than other stores to have external outlets, I guess in case the mechanics need to wheel out one of the huge diagnostic machines to tell somebody their car needs a new everything. Just watch out for guard dogs.

- **Near big sports fields.** Sometimes there's an outlet near where the lights turn on, or by the control panel for the sprinkler system. This can be inconsistent, however, and you always risk getting soaked by the sprinklers.
- **Denny's.**

That night in Delaware, my ice machine discovery in New Hampshire led to an even bigger jackpot for late-night outlets: Coke machines. I don't know why I hadn't thought of this before. Look for them outside convenience stores. Or supermarkets. Or wherever, really; you'd be amazed at the places where you can find a Coke machine these days, thanks to the Coca-Cola Corporation's stranglehold on the American economy. In Vermont I saw one next to a phone booth.

The particular machine I found outside a closed real-estate office was pretty close to the wall, and I had to muscle it out a bit before I could access the sweet electrical nectar behind. In the middle of this operation, a man walking a dog strolled by to see a shaggy guy in a backwards cap and a filthy button-down sumo-wrestling a Coke machine.

He stopped. Gave me a glance. Then continued on his way. I guess transient-looking vision questers shoving around Coke machines in the middle of the night is a common occurrence in rural Delaware.

CHAPTER 23
MARYLAND/D.C.

Capital of the Universe

Before the Roadtrip, the biggest solo travel I'd ever done was a two-week trip to France before my junior year of high school. My host family did a commendable job of taking me to every famous landmark in France, but after a while they all started to look the same. I felt like I was on an extended tour of a huge museum, not visiting a country. All I wanted to do was go to the local pool hall and do whatever real French people did—chain-smoking while talking about how great Paris is, or surrendering or something.

When you see the Eiffel Tower, you're not seeing France. You're seeing the Eiffel Tower, along with the 20,000 other tourists who think that the Eiffel Tower has something to do with living in France.

I felt like this while I was jogging through Washington, D.C., past the epic American landmarks featured on every piece of currency I didn't have in my wallet. D.C. seemed like it was all grassy malls, rich people on important calls, and tremendous old stone buildings with ordinances about the minimum number of pillars they must have. There had to be another side to the city, but I wasn't seeing it. You can't go to the Washington Monument and think that's what all of D.C. is like, any more than you can go to D.C. and think that's what all of America is like.

I was suddenly glad I'd made the "No Interstates" rule. As much as it had been a pain in the butt (both literally and figuratively), it was helping me see the *real* United States. America is not the White House. America is a surly, one-armed waitress yelling at you in a meat restaurant in Vermont.

Disappointingly, the most memorable thing about my jog was that I again lost my car keys, which fell out of the same red shorts I'd been wearing at Lake Wappapello. So I retraced my strides past the monuments, this time with eyes focused on a two-foot swath of grass in front of me, until after an hour I found the keys near the foot of the Washington Monument. It felt like some obnoxious allegory about American tunnel vision and dependence on technology, or a message that the universe wanted my trip to continue, despite my repeated idiocy. Or perhaps the lesson was simply that I should have thrown away those shorts in Missouri.

After my running-shoe tour, I drove up to Bethesda to make one more visit before I started my solo vision quest. My college friend Samantha was working at a news company there, and I picked her up after work for tapas and sangria (Spanish for "Get drunk for lunch") at a colorful Spanish restaurant with chili peppers painted on everything. It was the kind of place first-daters take each other to show they have culture. I dug into the various plates of unpronounceable entrees despite my feeling that I was getting sick. After all, forty-eight states meant forty-eight states' worth of germ exposure.

"My five-year high-school reunion was last weekend," said Samantha.

In college, Samantha had been renowned for her low alcohol tolerance and was endowed with the appropriate sobriquet Two-Can

Sam. But after four glasses of sangria (perhaps more for me, as I was eating all the wine-soaked fruit in a desperate attempt to get some vitamin C), Samantha was still articulate. Apparently, she'd been practicing.

"How was it?"

"I didn't go. But I heard it was pretty sloppy."

My own five-year was looming in Minneapolis in a few months.

"I would have gone," said Samantha. "But I had a work event, and then it hit me that I'll probably never see most of those people again. Well, maybe at other reunions, but everyone will be wasted again and it won't count."

"What about the people you actually *liked* in high school?" I asked.

Samantha shrugged. "I keep in touch with them anyway. And I've got other people I like now. It took me a whole year, but I finally figured out the five percent of people at my work who aren't utterly lame to hang out with."

"Does that mean you're going to replace me, too?"

"Well, I don't think I can, now," said Samantha. "You drove all the way out to D.C. to drink sangria with me."

Sam smiled and flagged the waitress for another pitcher.

"You think that'll happen for our college friends, too?"

She shrugged. "Probably. I think that's the way it always happens. One phase ends, you say goodbye to most of those people, and you make new friends."

"I don't have any new friends," I said.

Sam looked at me. "Well, at least you're doing a hell of a job cementing things with the old ones."

The new pitcher arrived. Samantha seized it.

"Anyway," she said. "I say it's good that I'm the last familiar face you'll see for a while. Force you to get out there. It'll be like New Student Week all over again. Except without the passing out in gutters."

I peered at the tremendous glass she was pouring me.

"Well. Let's not get ahead of ourselves."

Two-Can Sam had come a long way, and even after plenty of San-gria, she was still coherent enough to realize that neither of us had a chance in hell of driving my car home. Thankfully, Sam had also been practicing her ability to boss her younger brother Jamie around, and he swung by to pick us up.

Jamie was interning on Capitol Hill and spent most evenings at the Hill bars, D.C. schmoozing, which is like Hollywood or Wall Street schmoozing, except everyone dresses more preppy, name-drops political connections and pedigrees, and talks about how great D.C. is. That's the unique connection between these three very different cities, New York, L.A., and D.C.; each represents a different corner on the elusive Money-Fame-Power triangle, but each is completely convinced that its corner is the best. Maybe D.C., with Power, is the closest to being right . . . but then again, Money can buy power, and Fame can make you rich.

"You're only in town until tomorrow?" Jamie said, as Saman-tha and I delicately deposited our engorged bellies into his car. "We should take you through the city!"

"I already kind of saw it," I said.

"No, not the postcard stuff," said Jamie, shifting into gear. "I'm gonna show you everything you need to see to appreciate the *real* D.C."

Jamie zipped back onto the freeway as Sammy and I tried desper-ately to resist succumbing to the postprandial lassitude that accompa-nies a 6 P.M. tapas binge. Jamie was headed for The Hill but swerved off at an unexpected exit.

"A lot of people think D.C. is only pretentious snobs and presi-dential wannabes," he said. "Don't get me wrong, there are a lot of those, but the city's got its tough side, too."

To punctuate, he turned down a street that could have guest-starred on a *Cops* episode.

"A lot of the city used to be quite the war zone, back in the crack days in the eighties. It's gotten a lot better, though we were still number two for murders last year," he said, almost proudly. "I think the Beltway Snipers helped bump us up ahead of Detroit. Still can't seem to sneak ahead of New Orleans, though."

I looked out the window. The grass of downtown had given way to cement. Broken glass and street dwellers littered the sidewalk.

"*This* is the real D.C.?" I watched a bum relieve himself behind a dumpster.

Jamie looked at me in the rearview. "No. But this is one part of who lives here." Abruptly, he turned back onto a main road. "All right, you get the idea. There's not that much to see here, and it's actually kind of dangerous."

Jamie swung us on a wide, circuitous route toward downtown, through sprawling middle- and upper-middle-class neighborhoods that I realized probably made up the majority of the city. Finally we pulled up to a somewhat dingy-looking restaurant labeled "Chili Bowl."

"What's this place?" I asked. "A D.C. restaurant staple?"

"Sort of," said Jamie. "But mostly I'm just hungry. You guys are already drunk and full of meat."

Jamie ate his chili dog and drove with his knees as he pulled up to one last stop. The Lincoln Memorial.

"I thought you said the *real* D.C." I said.

"This is the *real* D.C. Another part of it, " Jamie replied. "Every day I drive through these monuments on my way to work and smile. Sometimes I come have my lunch out here."

"And look," he smacked my shoulder and pointed. "Check out Abe's hands."

I looked. Nothing seemed amiss. Giant stone Abe's left hand was clenched in a fist, while his right was a little more open, with the index finger sticking out a little.

"Abe's left hand is making the sign-language letter A, and his right is making the sign-language letter L. His initials! Honest Abe is throwin' up signs!"

Jamie laughed and went over to point this out to another tourist.

I softened my stance a little. Maybe D.C. isn't exactly America. But maybe it represents it. And isn't that all we ever asked of it?

Jamie came back. "Yup. Greatest town in the universe!"

He drove us back to Samantha's, pleased as can be. I couldn't help but imagine that somewhere in Paris, some local was driving an out-of-town friend around the Eiffel Tower, with the exact same grin on his face.

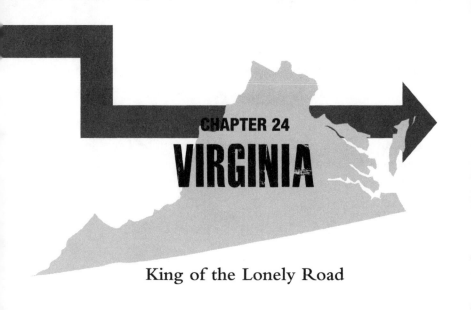

CHAPTER 24

VIRGINIA

King of the Lonely Road

Having nearly lost my car keys twice because of the same defective pocket, I decided to throw my red running shorts away. I couldn't risk a third key drop—maybe this time over a pit of lava. I chucked the insolent pants into the garbage outside Samantha's and headed for Virginia.

Samantha, bless her heart, had sent me off with a care package of food from her parents' pantry, including a half-pound bag of M&M's. With my sparse diet, it was like giving a whole bottle of tequila to a wino. On my way through Arlington, I spotted a Costco and got the brilliant idea to make trail mix—to add some variety to my road diet, and to keep me from inhaling the entire bag of M&M's before I even got past the Beltway. Heck, it might even be nutritious; when one eats absolutely no vegetables for seven weeks, it's important that one gets plenty of sugar and raisins. I didn't have a Costco card, so I had to talk a Korean man into buying me the peanut and raisin jugs—I certainly wasn't going to pay regular grocery store prices—while I waited outside like an underage kid outside a liquor store. I imagine it looked quite suspicious to anyone watching two guys exchange a ten-dollar bill for two snack tubs outside Costco.

I was becoming pretty satisfied with my ridiculous diet. Between cereal, sandwiches, and trail mix, I had grain, dairy, some protein, and even some fruit covered. That just left ... well, vegetables, and fruit other than processed jam berries and month-old raisins, but so what? I'd been on the road for four weeks and hadn't yet gotten scurvy.

Finally free of the giant ring of suburbs around the nation's capital, I picked up the Blue Ridge Parkway and headed south along the eastern edge of the Appalachian Mountains. The purple layered hills that rose over the ageless colonial towns and old-timey gas stations inspired thoughts of patriotic song lyrics, but somehow I had pictured something bigger. More mountainy, even. Compared to the towering Rockies I would be driving through in another few weeks, the Appalachians seemed like speed bumps.

Near Roanoke, I came across a murky lake and figured I would take another shot at my growing obsession with swimming in a mountain stream. The lake was mostly surrounded by houses, but after some searching I found an ambiguous alley that rode the border between two properties. I emerged onto the bank with my suit and towel to find a weedy bank sloping a few feet down into the reedy water, and a man fishing.

He stood among the sparse plants in the rutted dirt bank and cast his line. His bobber popped into the water, which, as I drew closer to it, looked like it had been the recent beneficiary of an oil spill. The man was a gaunt black fellow with skin even darker than the tar-colored water. He slowly reeled in his line, speaking to me without glancing up.

"This is private property, you know."

"Oh, sorry. I was gonna catch a swim. Is this your property?"

"Nope, just fishin' here. But you oughta watch out. You're trespassin'."

I considered pointing out that my trespassing was probably better than his trespassing *and* poaching, but decided against it.

"My name's Terrance," he offered. "Lived here all my life."

"My name's Paul," I said. "Never been here before."

"You're lucky. I've seen a big downfall around these parts. Mostly this lake."

I was going to ask how a lake could have a downfall, but the gasoline on the surface sufficed to explain. I breathed in the pungent smell of progress.

"It's the urban sprawl," he lamented. "From the city. Now e'ry square foot near water gets taken up by some yahoo. It's polluting the lake, and depleting the fish."

I considered pointing out that fishing was another way of depleting fish, but decided against it.

"I used to come fishin' here with my dad," Terrance went on. "This very spot. Used to pull out bass until we couldn't cook 'em all! But not anymore." He cast his line out again and hit something that resembled a diaper. "Where'd you say you were from again?"

"Minnesota. I'm trying to drive to every state."

"I took a road trip once," said Terrance. "All over the South, and over into Texas. Thought I might leave Roanoke, after my brother was killed. But I ended up right back here at this lake. At least I still had my dad, though."

"Where's your dad now?"

"Heart attack, after the plant laid him off. It's only me, now. Roanoke's doin' fine, but it's us little folks that suffers." Terrance finally looked up at me. "You're not gonna swim, are you?"

"No," I said. "I suppose not."

"Good idea," he advised, casting his line out again. "This lake is chock full of disease."

I eyed Terrance's fishing pole and considered pointing out that . . . well, never mind.

I said good day to Terrance and continued south, suddenly terribly glum. Would I end up like him? Also, my sickness was getting worse; my sinuses were beginning to bulge, and my throat was starting to swell. I had even lost my trail-mix appetite, which was always a bad sign. It was probably a good thing I didn't go in the lake.

An evening gloom crept over the lavender hills as I stopped near a little village called Horse Pasture to find a bathroom. I looked for a restaurant and was disappointed not to see any fast-food options. Drive-through chains, I had been finding, were the easiest places to snatch a quick restroom if you couldn't find a library or big grocery store. Usually you could walk right in, thanks to the restaurants' general policy of hiring people who don't give a damn. But even if you encountered a stickler manager as you tried to tiptoe past him to defile his bathroom, you could always stop, browse the menu for a minute and go, "Jeez, what to eat, so many options! You know, I think I'll use the bathroom before I make up my mind." Then you'd do your sinister business and ninja-roll out the side door before anyone realized you weren't coming back.

Instead I had to be seated by the waitress at a sickly, ten-stool café near Horse Pasture until I could sneak past the "For Paying Customers Only" sign, into the bathroom, and then out the back when the waitress wasn't watching. I left a dollar tip for the water she'd brought me. I felt bad. I'd been using restaurants far less for buying food than for leaving food behind.

That night, I slept outside St. Peter's Episcopal Church near the southern border of Virginia, my excuse ready: if anyone asked why I was camped outside a church at 5 A.M., I'd tell them I just wanted to be closer to God. I cracked the Imposter's windows enough to solve the temperature problem and parked the front tires uphill a bit, to make the reclined seat a little more horizontal. As for the being-on-display part, well, I'd sort of gotten used to it.

What a bizarre new set of skills I had acquired on my Roadtrip. Though a lot of lessons were still slow in coming, I realized, with a depressing sense of accomplishment, I'd become something of an expert at living in a car.

CHAPTER 25

NORTH CAROLINA

Trolley Fight

Okay, a Roadtrip progress report. So far:

- Twenty-four states down.
- Twenty-five days in. Almost on pace.
- 4,500 miles driven, the distance from the Panama Canal to Alaska. With all the big states left, 12,000 miles may have been a gross underestimate.
- Seventy-one PBJs eaten, according to the tally sheet on my dash. The sandwich and I had by this point grown to a place of mutual hatred, but I was too poor to stop eating them.
- $950 in my checking account. This was not good.

As for my route:

My college friend Jeff had once shown me an algorithm he'd worked out for an engineering class of the shortest distance to drive to every state capital. (Guess which one of us was offered a job after graduation?) At this point, my trip looked less like an algorithm and more like more like Moses' Roadtrip through the desert.

I found myself in Asheville needing something to do in North Carolina when I rolled past a small building with a sign reading "Trolley Tours—$12!" I stopped. Behind the counter of the bright shop was a pudgy bald man with a pale head and a bright orange nose, like a snowman's.

"Hi there," I said. "What's on your Trolley Tour?"

"Oh, you know!" he said. "Everything you ever wanted to see in North Carolina! Colonial history, tourist attractions, how the town was founded . . . . You interested in Asheville history?"

I slapped my money down on the wooden counter. "I am now."

The man smiled. "Trolley leaves from here in ten minutes. Don't be late, or we'll leave ya behind!"

The trolley pulled up as I walked outside. Downtown Asheville was a curious collision of old and new—a neon Internet café sat next to a decrepit old church. I suddenly wanted to know the town's story. Twelve dollars was a lot of money, but it would be nice to let someone else drive for a while. Besides, what better way to see colonial Carolina than in a tacky gray trolley?

As I climbed on to the open-air trolley and sat down on a padded middle seat, my phone rang. It was Sarah. She hadn't called me since New Hampshire.

Could it be she was starting to get used to the Roadtrip?

"Hey. There's something I need to talk to you about."

Maybe not.

"My parents were wondering. How would you feel about giving the Bahamas another shot?"

Uh-oh.

A couple months before the Roadtrip, Sarah's parents paid for the two of us to take a vacation in the Bahamas. It was a generous gesture, but the trip was problematic. And not just because I felt like a gigantic sponge mooching off Sarah's folks.

Something changed in me on that trip. A year into my potluck of jobs, the one thing I had culled from them was an appreciation for the crazy experiences they offered. Who knows—driving around from job to job may have inspired the idea of the Roadtrip. Sarah, on the other hand, was a third of the way through law school and had grown accustomed to the stability it provided. She was also exhausted. I wanted to run around and experience the island. She wanted to relax.

My nagging eventually won out, and one afternoon we wound up on a cliff overlooking the swirling cerulean sea. It was not a large cliff, mind you—we were typical tourists, not adrenaline junkies—but it was big enough to make you think. I jumped in. Sarah opted out. I came up from my Caribbean baptism stung by the impassioned tail of adventure. Sarah came back from the trip bitten by the ambivalent jaws of being ready to go back to law school and start a normal life. Whatever "it" was, it was out of her system. But "it" had just gotten into mine. And "it" had been causing trouble for us ever since.

"My mom can get the same timeshare deal as last time." said Sarah. "We only have to pay for the flights. We don't have to go right away; I've got exams until winter break anyway. But she has to reserve the rooms soon if we want to go."

I squirmed in my contoured seat, and tried to choose my next words carefully. Alas, it didn't really matter which words I chose. I was about to have the biggest fight I would ever have on an Asheville Trolley.

How do you explain to someone that you don't want to commit to a trip with her because, although you're still excited about a possible future together, you don't want to lock yourself into anything? And that a trip with her just wouldn't be as fun as the trip you just took *without* her? And that you can't talk about it right now because the trolley's about to leave and you paid twelve bucks to go see a bunch of old houses and plantations?

"Sarah," I pleaded, as things quickly started heading downhill. "It's not that I don't want to go on a trip with you; I just feel weird planning it right now when everything's up in the air."

"I haven't called you in six days," she said. "And you can't even give me anything? You think this last week has been easy for me?"

Ah, so that's what had been going on, on the other end of my silent phone. A volcano brewing.

"I feel like you're leaving me behind," she said.

"Would you even want to come on this trip?" I asked.

"I don't mean your Roadtrip. But no," Sarah said. "Sleeping in weird, scary places isn't my idea of a good time."

"What's wrong with a little danger?"

"What's wrong with a little security?"

I glanced around. Camera-wearing Carolina tourists in bright T-shirts were staring at me. I stepped off the trolley, and the midday Asheville traffic rushed around me.

"Well, maybe I'm feeling left behind, too," I said.

"You?"

"Yeah. What about you, and all my friends? You all know where you're headed, and I'm left in the dust. Forgive me if I need some space to figure it out."

"Space?"

"Yeah. Space."

"Oh, come on!" Sarah said. "Don't talk to me about space. I'm not the girl who sifts through your e-mail and wants to know where you are every single second. I don't even know what state you're in!"

"North Carolina."

"Great, North Carolina. We haven't talked in a week, and you're talking about space? You shouldn't want this much space. You should want to be near your girlfriend!"

"I do! I just need to be alone right now. I need this trip."

"And what about what I need?"

I sighed. Being wrong is never so bad that a little guilt can't make it worse.

"I know, I know. I'm sorry, I apologize a million times, okay? Listen, why is this such a big deal? Forty-eight days isn't that long!"

I felt a tap on my shoulder. "What!" I snapped, whirling on the pudgy bald guy who was trying to tell me that the trolley was about to leave. His pale face went even paler, and he crept away.

"It's not the forty-eight days," my girlfriend said. "It's the fact that I don't know if that's the end. You said you'd come back to Chicago, but you sound like you don't even want to."

"Maybe I don't know if I do."

I stopped. But now the words were out there.

"I'm sorry," I said. "But I can't lie to you."

Sarah took a deep breath. I couldn't tell whether she was about to cry or breathe fire through the phone.

"I should just stop caring," she said. "I should never have taken you back the first time, and gotten all invested again. Look at all the misery I've been through."

"I never meant to make you miserable," I said, feeling horrible.

"It doesn't matter what you meant to do. I love that I'm in love with a creative, ambitious guy who wants perfection. But at the same time it's killing me."

"I'm not doing this trip to hurt you."

"Well, it is. And as long as you keep doing it, it's going to keep hurting, because I'll know that I'm not your number one priority."

"You are!" I said, not knowing whether I meant it, or whether it was just the thing I was supposed to say.

"Bullshit, Paul. I'll believe it when I see it. And until you show me, maybe I need to start thinking about how to stop loving you."

For the first time ever, my girlfriend hung up on me. I turned around, and the trolley was gone, leaving me behind in a heavy cloud of stifling, blinding exhaust, and silence. Abruptly, the black road under my feet felt a whole lot lonelier.

It was everything I had always worried about. The things I cared about were interfering with the things I cared about.

I slammed my phone into the Imposter, grabbed a pair of stinky shorts, and did the only thing I knew how to do. I took off running.

CHAPTER 26

SOUTH CAROLINA

Alone & Sick in the Imposter

I don't know how far I jogged through Asheville, but I probably saw everything the trolley did, only without the friendly guide's charming narration: "And over heeeeere, we have the annual Asheville debutante pageant, to see which overbearing mother gets to relive her glory days through her stifled daughter. . . ." It didn't matter. I wouldn't have paid attention to any of it.

I ran right through the sunset and climbed back into the Imposter in the muggy dark. I didn't know how to deal with Sarah, so I simply did what by this point felt natural: I kept driving. My head and throat were burning, but I was close to the South Carolina border. I might as well pick up another state while I was here.

I needed time to think. The road at night was good for that: a black cocoon of solitude, yellow hash lines metering out my thoughts. The only distractions were the moths splattering on the windshield.

I drove on again into the darkness, around blind curve after blind curve, waiting for a cliff or a lightless semi to appear in my path. I was through half the states and had as much uncertainty as ever. Maybe more. The road ahead was just as scary as it had always been.

My reverie was broken as I sped across the state line and ran over a rabbit. At least, I was 90 percent sure it was a rabbit, and not someone's midget obese cat. There was no way to avoid it—I was going 70 and this small mass of fur ran right under my tire. I saw a flash of eyes and the silhouette of ears, and had half a second to decide whether to swerve madly, flip the Imposter, and probably hit the thing anyway . . . or go straight. I went straight. There was a sickening thud, and the Imposter's right side lifted an inch off the ground for a moment.

My eyes shot to my rearview. I saw, with a chill, that the creature was still moving. I pulled over. Backed up. I got out. The invincible Imposter was fine. But the rabbit was not. It was still alive but its back was broken. It lay twitching on the concrete.

My dad's stories from his farm days told me what was needed. I went into the brush, found a large enough rock, and returned to the animal. I hesitated. But it had to be done. Something was suffering because of me. I apologized to the rabbit, and acted swiftly.

With another rock I pushed the carcass over to the ditch, and then climbed back into the Imposter. Something had died for the sake of my pointless progress.

I drove past a sign for Interstate 26, the fast track back through Asheville and north. But I forced myself instead onto a foggy frontage road and found a secluded stretch of shoulder to try to sleep it off. To sleep it all off. I gave up quickly on consciousness and nodded off.

I pried my eyes open twenty minutes later to the sound of a car crunching gravel as it drove slowly by me. A cop car. I guess I didn't have everything figured out about living in a vehicle, after all.

The muscular black cop and his short white female partner sauntered up to either side of my car and shined their flashlights on me. They weren't out of line. But I wasn't in a place to pretend to be overjoyed to see them.

"Where ya comin' from?" asked the black male cop.

"Originally, Minnesota," I muttered. My eyes and head hurt. "Most recently, North Carolina."

The officers looked at each other.

"Where ya goin'?" asked the white female cop.

"Eventually, Minnesota. Right now . . . I don't know."

The cops exchanged another glance. I wasn't doing myself any favors in the suspiciousness category. I didn't care.

"Got a better explanation than all that?" asked the male cop.

"I'm on a road trip. I graduated college a year ago, and . . . I'm trying to drive to all the contiguous states."

The black cop shined his flashlight around the interior of the Imposter, then into my face.

"Why?"

I sighed. "I don't know."

"Well, we got a call about a suspicious black car with out-of-state plates parking near some residences," the female cop said, gesturing over a hill where I guess I must have missed some houses. "You know we gotta check it out."

It was hard to argue with her.

"You can't stop here. You can drive around as much as you like, but what you're doing right here isn't normal, and is likely to make people uneasy. All right?"

I nodded.

"Go find someplace safer."

The cops shut off their flashlights and left me in the glare of their high beams. They waited until I pulled away, followed me back onto the county highway, then let me go.

I kept driving to Interstate 26. Crossed the overpass, turned left, and drove north onto the interstate. So much for Rule #1.

It only took me a few minutes of eighty-mile-an-hour driving to find what I was after: a rest stop. Safe, comfortable, and society approved.

I checked my phone: no reception. I thought I wanted to do this Roadtrip solo, and now I wasn't so sure. But that's what happens when you do your own thing: by definition, you do it alone. The world doesn't need people making their own rules. The world doesn't cheer when you're running your own race. Who was I to think I was special? Particularly not when I was hurting somebody else. Was that all independence was, a euphemism for selfishly seeing to your own needs over everyone else's?

My throat ached. I could be working somewhere, building a life for myself. I recalled the smiling Indy Lifers and the frowning MIT students: perhaps those expressions would be different when payday came. I was tired of being poor. And tired of driving. And tired of doing without beds and clean clothes and sex . . . and for what? So I could learn something about my "direction"? I hadn't learned shit so far, except that I was sick of being alone. Oh, and I had now hit the South. The chords from *Deliverance* twanged in my head.

It was 650 miles to Chicago. On the interstates, I could be there by the next evening. That was the smart move. That's what would save Sarah. Beyond that, it was another half-day's drive back to my dad's business and my mother's chicken-noodle soup. Maybe that's what could save me.

But not tonight, in the darkness, sickness, and fog.

CHAPTER 27
GEORGIA

Beers in High School

I was awakened early the next morning by a call from my mom.

"Paul? You okay?"

"Yeah," I managed, pulling my head out of the gap between the Imposter's passenger headrest and the door, where it was wedged. "Why?"

"I read your blog from last night. You sounded down. You described the night as, hold on . . . 'blacker than a panther at midnight in a cave. In a black hole.' Your metaphors always get really lame when you're in a funk."

"Yeah, I'm okay." The sunrise streamed through the windshield and burned my tired eyes. The sun was pushing itself up for another day, whether I liked it or not.

"I had a fight with Sarah, and I'm kind of sick." I climbed over into the driver's seat. "It's nothing. I'll be fine."

"Well," said my mom. "You know you're always welcome to take a break and stop in with us for a few days if you need some company."

Wonderful. A temptation I didn't need. "Yeah, I'm afraid there's not much company down here."

"What about Luke?" my mom said.

Luke. I hadn't thought of him.

Luke had been a high-school baseball teammate who, after getting his journalism degree, had taken an internship at CNN Sports in Atlanta. We'd fallen out of touch, but my mom still kept up with Luke's mother.

"He might still be in Atlanta," she said. "You could at least e-mail him. Here, I think I've got his contact info . . ."

Sometimes having a friendly Minnesota mother was very helpful.

Last I'd heard, Luke hadn't liked his internship much, so it was a long shot. But the possibility of a familiar face was worth it. I fired off a quick e-mail.

I drove on, and cut back onto the small highways that snaked their way through the Carolina hills at the base of the Great Smoky Mountains. Something was pushing me on to Georgia. It was only fifty miles west, and I'd have to swing through there anyway, even if I still opted to hook north afterward.

Luke and I had been teammates on, among other places, an unfortunate Fall Ball team that was probably the worst either of us had ever played on. We were the two primary pitchers, and until that point had been mowing down batters in spring and summer leagues, inflating our hopes of someday being paid millions to toss a small leather sphere through the air a few times a week. But Fall League was something else. It was where all the serious suburban players came to forget about soccer and football and focus on milking division-one schools out of scholarship money. Our ragtag bunch of city kids was ill-equipped to handle the challenge. The first pitch I threw that season was crushed into a line drive that knocked a dent in the metal 380 sign on the centerfield wall.

Our team lost nearly every game that season, and Luke and I took turns being hammered on by high-school juniors with twenty-inch biceps and names like Brock Van Chisel. Mellow Luke adapted to the tone of the season, but it was a tough lesson for a pusher like me: no matter how hard you try, sometimes your team—or your own arm—lets you down. My dreams of being the first seventeen-year-old to win the Cy Young were being shelled off the mound in the early innings.

Luke came into the locker room one afternoon to find me having a heavyweight title match with a locker door, after a double-header double-loss where I'd given up a couple of home runs that may still be traveling now. Luke's shelling in the first game had not been much better, but he seemed to understand something I didn't.

"Take it easy," he said. "Somebody else will need to punch those lockers again after the night game."

"It's over," I moaned histrionically.

"Nothing's over. You think you're never going to pitch well again? Well, maybe, if you break your hand doing that," said Luke, eyeing my knuckles. "Your chances are still the same as they were before. Better, probably, because now you know not to throw 0-2 inside fastballs to Brock."

Luke slapped me in the chest with his glove and headed off to ice his arm.

"You just have to not be afraid to lose a bunch of times before you win."

Luke and I hadn't kept up much after our baseball paths diverged. Maybe I subconsciously wanted to distance myself. Or perhaps, as D.C. Samantha had said, you simply can't keep in good touch with all eighty of your high-school acquaintances.

Well, I was reconnecting now. Leave it to a forty-eight-state Roadtrip to toss social protocol out the window.

I pulled over again and checked my mail. Luke had already responded.

Yeah, still in Atlanta. Come by the CNN building when you get downtown, give a buzz.

Late that afternoon, I pulled up outside Luke's building. He climbed into the Imposter and shook my hand, as if not a day had passed since we last saw each other five years earlier.

"C'mon," said Luke. "We'll grab some cheap takeout. I have a case of brew back at my apartment."

"I should take you out for some drinks," I insisted. "It's the least I can do for you letting me crash on zero notice."

"Trust me," Luke smiled. "We should drink at my apartment."

I was about to find out what he meant.

Luke's apartment building was a school. Literally. Someone had taken a retired 1970s high school and carved a ninety-unit apartment building out of it. And not all that much carving had been done.

Imagine walking down the hallway of your old high school, past the lockers and drinking fountains, and then you turn left and open the door to your apartment. Small classrooms and teachers' lounges had been converted into studios, and bigger rooms had been sectioned off into multibedrooms. Bathrooms and kitchens had been added, but the high ceilings, giant windows, and even the occasional bell remained. Trophy cases had been cleared and repacked with building information for new tenants.

The renovation wasn't limited to classrooms. The ingenious builders had found ways to divvy up the cafeteria, the gymnasium, even the auditorium. Luke's apartment was part of the auditorium's backstage, and could only be accessed by walking to the front of the remaining part of the theatre that was being used as a corridor and going up three steps to his door. Luke pointed out that he had the unique experience of being able to walk out of his apartment onto a stage every morning.

I couldn't get over this. I didn't even realize this was something that was done, architecturally, and for the first thirty minutes of our chow mein banquet in Luke's apartment, I could not stop my eggroll-stuffed mouth from asking questions. In the chemistry rooms, did they incorporate those safety chemical rinses as their showers? Did anyone live in the lunch room, and did they get to use the giant pizza-oven? Could the people living in the ends of the gymnasium request that the basketball hoops be left up in their living rooms? I know *I* would have wanted one.

We lugged a case of Natty Light out into the hallway leading up to Luke's stage door. The old auditorium seats had been replaced by walled-off apartments, but the sloping center aisle still provided a corridor past all the doors. At the back end of the hallway, a couple of back-row seats had been allowed to remain against a wall beside a door that lead out to the main lobby, and we set up shop with our beers for a little baseball trivia.

"Winningest knuckleballer of all time?" quizzed Luke.

"I don't know. Joe Niekro? I think he used to scuff balls when he played for the Twins."

Luke shook his head. "Phil Niekro. Sucks to get beaten out by your own brother."

I took a drink.

"Winningest left-handed pitcher of all time?" said Luke.

"I know this one. Warren Spahn. I'm a lefty, remember?"

Luke took a drink.

"You thought I would say Sandy Koufax, didn't you?"

Luke nodded. "Best Jewish pitcher of all time."

We both took a drink.

"So what does your family think of your whole Roadtrip?" asked Luke.

"I guess they're fine with it. Though my grandma of course wants me to come back home and marry my girlfriend."

"Your grandma sounds like a hater."

"Nah. She's just not used to an age where kids think they can take a year off and drive a car all over creation."

"Sounds familiar." Luke nodded. For a moment, silence filled the hall. "Wanna hear something weird?"

"Sure."

"On my sixteenth birthday, my dad sat me down in our living room. You know what he said to me? He said, 'You can be president.'"

"That's not weird," I said. "My dad said the same thing."

"But then I was talking to him the other day, and he started talking about *his* dad. You know what his dad said to him on his sixteenth birthday?"

"'You can be president'?"

"No. He said 'You're a piece of shit. Don't ever think you're better than anyone else.' In a loving way, of course."

"Of course."

"It's like, his generation, people were just trying to get by. No big expectations. These days, everything's so awesome, people expect the world. Look at this."

He clicked a button on his phone and showed me a browser window with the Tivo logo on it.

"I can be sitting on the toilet at work, and tell my computer at home to record *Law & Order*. Then I get home, click another button and a little wireless adapter sends the stupid show to my computer, so I can make a DVD out of it. *Through thin air.* And I'm supposed to be president."

"That's a lot of pressure."

"Yeah. Now I know how all those Chinese only-children must feel."

"I don't think they can be president. Don't they still have a dictatorship over there?"

"You know what I mean."

I thought for a moment. "I wonder if this recession is going to usher in another 'You're a piece of shit' era."

"I think we'll recover. But who can say?"

"You know," I started, "I think I'm more prepared to tell my kid he's a piece of shit than I am to tell him he can't have a cell phone until he's sixteen."

Luke nodded and gazed at his phone. "I hear you."

Luke cracked another beer for me, and the sound echoed around the school walls. It was like a high-school fantasy was finally coming true.

"So," I said. "What's happened to you in the last five years?"

Luke shrugged. "Not much to tell. Got my journalism degree, which meant I spent most of last summer job-hunting and hating myself."

"Sounds familiar."

"I would have loved to follow the Twins or something, but the only thing that presented itself was this internship down here in Atlanta. So I moved in September."

"How was it?"

"Sucked," Luke said. "I didn't know anyone in Atlanta. Barely had enough to cover a ratty room in a rough neighborhood."

"But you came."

Luke nodded. "It was like I'd always dreamed of pitching in the Majors, then one day a coach comes up and says, 'Hey kid! You can't pitch, but you can shag balls in the outfield during practice.' What could I do? I had to take it. I couldn't stay in Minnesota doing nothing. And at least it was a job in writing and in sports."

"So how was it once you got here?"

"Sucked. Long hours. Hardly any pay. A lot of getting coffee for people who thought I was after their jobs. Well, I suppose I was, but not like I was trying to screw anybody. I thought they'd promote me because I was qualified. I mean, I don't wanna sound like an a-hole, but I did have *some* credentials."

'Some credentials,' was putting it modestly. Luke had gone to Mizzou, probably the best journalism school in the country, and graduated near the top of his class. And he was fetching coffee.

"But heck, everybody at CNN went to a good journalism school. It was hard the day I realized I wasn't the best anymore."

"The internship ended at Christmas," he continued. "They said I could come back and do another one in the new year."

Luke set his now empty beer can down sideways on the decline of the auditorium aisle, and we watched it gain speed and finally clang against the bottom of the stage under his door.

"I tell ya, I sure didn't want to come back to Atlanta. I got real nice and comfy in Minnesota, those few weeks. And then one morning, I got up, forced myself to get back in my car, and drove back to Georgia."

"Why?"

Luke shrugged and cracked open a new can. "I figured, you're gonna get hammered a few times. You can either punch a locker or keep throwing. But it was tough, man." He gestured to the arching walls around us. "You have to let this be the closest you ever get to going back. Trust me. Think about most of our other friends. If you go back to Minnesota again, you'll never leave."

"What's wrong with Minnesota?" I asked.

"Nothing, except I don't think you belong there. Minnesota's great," Luke said. "But it can still be great in memory."

I nodded and gazed down the corridor.

"So you did another internship?"

Luke took a drink. "One day, I was like 'You know what? I'm still good at this. I don't need to be Cy Young to have a fine career. Maybe the ninety-eighth percentile is still pretty good.'"

"Yeah," I said. "But wouldn't it be better if you were Cy Young?"

Luke shrugged. "Couldn't you still be happy if you weren't?"

I had no response. "So what happened?"

Luke shrugged. "Beats me. It wasn't like I started working any harder, but one day, it just clicked. They let me do a couple sample articles for CNN.com's sports page. One day the boss called me in and offered me a job. All of a sudden I have a weekly column on the Braves' farm system."

"Dude, that's great."

"Thanks. I don't get it. But it doesn't suck."

"So, you're like on salary now."

"It's a writing gig, so I sure ain't rich," he looked up. "But I live in a place with thirty-foot ceilings."

"And benefits?"

Luke shrugged. "I don't have to get into work until ten-thirty. That's a benefit."

Suddenly, a door opened and an old woman poked her frumpy head out.

"Can you two please not talk in the hall? People are trying to sleep."

I checked my phone. It was 9:30. This hadn't been part of the fantasy.

We stood and packed up our beers—we could finish killing our livers in Luke's apartment.

Luke tossed a crumpled can into the box and looked at me.

"Dude, I was reading your blog today at work, after you called. A day care center? Pretty entertaining."

I shrugged. I guess our idiocy did make for some decent stories.

"And all those plays and stuff? You ought to be writing, too."

I didn't know how to respond. "Maybe," I said. "It's fun. I guess I just don't think there are any jobs in writing."

"Sure there are," said Luke, the sportswriter. "You just have to not be afraid to lose a bunch of times before you win."

We hauled the rest of the Natty Light back toward Luke's room, leaving a couple empties on the old lady's doorstep. It seemed like the high-school thing to do.

Outside his door, Luke paused.

"One more," said Luke. "Pitcher with the most *losses* in major-league history."

"Beats me" I said. "They keep that stat?"

Luke nodded. "Cy Young. Look it up."

He smiled and stepped back into his apartment.

CHAPTER 28

FLORIDA

The Jellyfish Cop

Every time I visit Florida, I lose my shoes.

I don't know why, but it happens every time. On my first trip to the Seminole State—the Cheez-Its-smuggling mission with Charlie, Jeff, and Elizabeth—I left a pair of tennis shoes under a bed in a hotel room. On my second stint—a brief layover before my brothers and I left for a cruise—I fell asleep in the airport and awoke to find my shoes had been stolen, although my laptop, wallet, and video camera were untouched.

This Florida shoe-losing tendency is uncharacteristic—anyone who knows me will agree that I'm at least a reasonably organized guy. Yet I seem to have attained a mad-scientist level of absent-mindedness about footwear in Florida. It might have something to do with partying too much every time I visit.

As I headed down toward Gator Country for a third time, I was determined not to lose anything. Twenty-eight states in, I was having a hard enough time not losing my mind.

I had left Luke's Amazing High-School Fantasy Apartment after breakfast and continued south, revitalized by hot oatmeal and sunshine. I still didn't know what to do about Sarah, but even if I wanted to drive back to her and patch things up, I should swing south first and pick up the rest of the southern states on my way.

I turned my phone back on and there it was. A voicemail from her.

I dialed quickly and listened, not knowing what to expect.

"Hey. It's me. I wanted to apologize."

I certainly didn't expect *that*. She sounded defeated, hollow.

"I'm sorry I blew up. I shouldn't have cornered you into the whole Bahamas thing. If you don't want to go, it's fine."

"It's hard for me," she went on, "to compete with this trip of yours. But I guess it's just something I'll have to get used to with you."

The message paused, as if she was trying to figure out what else to say.

"I'll leave you alone," said Sarah, finally. "I promised you this Roadtrip, and I won't go back on my word. Anyway, you need to be the one to decide what you want to do."

I saved the voicemail message and texted her back.

I will. I promise. I'm sorry.

There was no reply.

I crossed over the border near Tallahassee and used the event as an excuse to call all my Florida friends. None of them were living there anymore, but it had helped having Luke to talk to in Georgia. A voice on a cell phone was better than nothing.

Finally I reached my college pal Kris, a South Florida native who was now living in Chicago.

"Kris," I said. "I'm in your state."

"Are you hitting Miami?" Kris said. "I can tell you some good restaurants that'll give you free food if you say you're homeless."

"I don't think I can," I said. "Miami's like ten hours from here. I'm sort of behind schedule from the Long Island and reunion detours."

It was true. Sickness and trolley fights had taken a lot out of me, and making the leviathan drive down the entire spine of Florida and back again no longer seemed like a fun or feasible step toward my forty-eight in forty-eight goal. Anyway, I recalled, I'd already done that drive—twice, actually, as I'd first helped my friends smuggle a brick of marijuana to Miami, and then helped them smuggle it back again. The prophesied Miami-to-Seattle leg could wait for another Roadtrip. Besides, I rationalized, there was nothing wrong with changing my mind, right?

"What are you going to do?" asked Kris.

"I dunno," I said. "I thought I'd try Pensacola."

"Pensacola's not in Florida," Kris said. "It's in the South."

Ah yes. The North Florida/South Florida gap.

"Pensacola is like the poor man's Miami Beach," Kris said.

"Is that their motto?"

"Pensacola's terrible."

"They filmed *Contact* there," I pointed out.

"They filmed *Contact* in a studio. Also, I question your manhood if you liked *Contact*. All I'm saying is you can't go to Florida and only visit the Panhandle."

And so it goes in the bipolar state that is Florida, where the bottom half doesn't want to be associated with the top half, and nobody wants to be associated with the Panhandle. The two halves really could not be more different. Southern Florida is essentially an extension of Latin America, and is probably one of the most ethnically diverse places in the world. Northern Florida is . . . white. Southern Florida is a weird mix of old people, young people, old people trying to be young by wearing horrifying neon Speedos, and everything in between. Northern Florida is . . . white. It's said that Florida is a place where the more north you go, the more South it gets. Kris, who is of Cuban descent, said that whenever he went north of Palm Beach, he tried to make sure he didn't speak with any accent.

I'd always thought that, if we weren't so attached to our nice round number of exactly fifty states, Florida should be the first one to get split, have the halves renamed South Georgia and North Cuba, and let them duke it out over Disneyworld. Okay, maybe California too, where the north half could be renamed Computer Hippie Land and the south half El Hollywood. But no. Instead, we have two Carolinas, two Virginias, and two Dakotas. Go figure.

I said goodbye to Kris and turned east at Tallahassee anyway. I felt bad letting him down, but I didn't have a choice. And Pensacola didn't seem terrible to me. Heck, it was a beach on an ocean. For a Minnesotan, that was three-quarters to paradise.

I rolled into the sleepy seaside town after dusk. Finding no one around, I decided I would redeem myself for missing Miami by sleeping right there on the beach. It seemed like the Roadtrip thing to do.

I was jolted awake at 5 A.M. by a four-wheeler racing down the sand and missing my head by about three feet. I had assumed many potential risks when I chose to sleep on a beach, but I hadn't anticipated this one.

Up and adrenalized, I went for a jog—this time slower than my flight in Asheville. Racing wouldn't fix anything any faster, and the budding dawn over the Pensacola sand demanded a slower pace. To my right, as my feet pounded the bike path, was the purest white beach I'd ever seen. It was like running through an Arctic sunrise, except warmer.

Much warmer. After about an hour, the smiling sunrise soured into a scowling midmorning sun, and I remembered that I was in Florida in the middle of the summer. Sweat stung my eyes as I returned to the spot where two four-wheeler tracks swerved out of the way of a panicked sand angel.

Up to this point, I had still been goose-egged in my quest to swim in a mountain stream. My dips in Missouri and North Carolina were in flat places, and Vermont and Virginia had taken me through mountains, but I'd never found my way to any accessible water. That Pensacola beach was no refreshing mountain stream either, but it was water, so into the ocean I plunged. Fearful of venturing out past the break into the unfamiliar deep waters, I stayed shallow, wearing boxers and a smile, trying to make the best of what I had.

I was promptly stung by a jellyfish.

At least I think it was a jellyfish—being stung by random crap in the ocean is not something a Minnesota boy has a lot of experience with. Whatever it was, it hurt like hell, and by the time I scrambled out of the water and raced across the sand, a nice four-inch blotch had already appeared on the front of my pasty white thigh. My leg began to swell, as did my alarm. *Could I die from this? Was I supposed to counteract the poison with urine?* For some reason the idea of lying sideways on the Pensacola sand peeing on myself seemed oddly inappropriate, even for someone who'd just slept on a beach.

I jumped into the Imposter, sopping wet and swelling, and peeled out to find the nearest hospital.

I was promptly pulled over by a cop.

The officer took forever to saunter up to my window as I sat there, shirtless, wet, and panicked. I should have been worried the cop would approach with his gun drawn, thinking he'd pulled over a half-drowned, naked meth addict.

"Kind of in a hurry there, aren't ya?" drawled a gum-chewing cop from under a bushy brown moustache. He was a tall fellow—probably mid-six feet, and he had to lean way down to rest his elbows casually on my open window.

Despite the fact that my quad was beginning to inflate like a pink balloon, I felt inclined to argue that I hadn't been speeding. I might be dying, but there was still the matter of having four tickets on my records.

"Sorry, I thought the sign said thirty, and I thought I was under. I have this rule about speeding," I said. "Also, I've been stung by a jellyfish."

The cop did not seem to be nearly so concerned. "It's a school zone, this time of the morning. Limit drops to twenty. You didn't see the sign?"

"I'm sorry, I must have missed it," I said. My leg was throbbing, as if a small techno rave was forming inside it. "Listen, is there a hospital somewhere around—"

"Also, fine's doubled in a school zone," the cop continued. "Lots of kids around." He glared at me, accusingly, as if I'd been trying to run them down on purpose.

"I'm sorry, I didn't see any kids. But seriously, is—"

"*Lots* of kids," the cop persisted, staring at me. "You always drive like that, when there's kids around?"

I stared at him, not sure what answer he was after. I wondered if he could smell the combination of fish and fear wafting up from the Taurus. "But I've been stung by a jellyfish! And isn't it summer?"

"Summer school. Ain't as many kids as usual," he admitted. "But they're there, awright. Lemme look at your leg."

Confounded, I showed him my leg, hesitant to mention that 6:30 A.M. seemed a bit early for summer school. The cop frowned, regarding my puffy limb for a moment. He popped his gum.

"It's not too bad. I'll be back."

Without another word, the cop went back to his car, and I was left in the Taurus, leg burning, salt beginning to soak into my now-dry skin. Another eternity went by as I waited for the officer to return, presumably with a vial of jellyfish antidote that every Pensacola cop carries in their car. Instead, he came back with a paper.

"I'm giving you a warning," he said. "But if I catch you speeding through another school zone, I'm gonna drop the hammer on you." He handed me the paper. "The hammer. Children are our future."

I didn't know what to say. "Um . . . thanks?" I managed. "But honestly, do I need to go to a hospital, or something? Can I die of a jellyfish sting?"

"I told you, it's not bad," said the cop, standing to his full height. "You may not even have been stung by a jellyfish."

He strolled away. I was waiting for him to come back and hand me a pair of $3 children's goggles. But he was gone.

I started the Taurus and headed for Alabama. I called Craig, my cancer-curing doctor friend in St. Louis, and he assured me that no, I was not going to die of a jellyfish sting. If it even was a jellyfish sting. After an hour or so my leg stopped throbbing, and the swelling went down.

Once again, things on the Roadtrip had worked themselves out. Maybe I needed to be patient and let some other things work themselves out, too. I left Florida, the morning adrenaline injection putting the finishing touches on my waning sickness. I smiled, thinking that I might just have discovered the best way yet to get out of speeding ticket.

And that's when I realized I'd left my shoes on the beach, back in Pensacola.

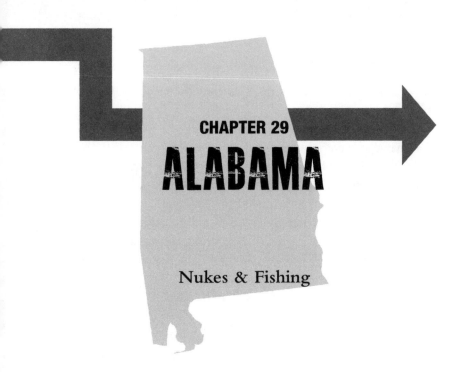

CHAPTER 29
ALABAMA

Nukes & Fishing

In Alabama I bought peaches. You'd think this would be something I'd do in Georgia, but how could I resist? They were ten bucks, for a whole basket of them. My new game for the next few days would be to see how many peaches I could eat before they went rotten or I died of explosive peach-diarrhea. It also couldn't hurt to have some fruit in my diet—maybe my illness had been a low-grade case of scurvy, after all.

I followed the county highways that parallel Interstate 10 and drove west across the southern Alabama coast toward Mobile. I'd never thought of Mobile as a port city—I'd always pictured it as being full of mobile homes. I suppose I'm guilty of some stereotyping here, but you have to admit the name is misleading. But it turns out that a nice little chunk of Alabama is coastal, and the massive Battleship Parkway bridge, which stretches several miles across Mobile Bay, gave me hope that my giant bridge to Hawaii wasn't such an impossible dream after all.

I'd run out of friends to call. I'd listened to every CD in my collection at least a dozen times and switched to local radio stations, partly to hear somebody else's voice, but also to listen for country songs with snappy titles like "I'm 'a Punch Your Lights Out for Jesus." I needed a breather after the madness of my Florida jellyfish morning. I also needed some company, and when I saw three men fishing off a wharf near the Mobile city limit, I pulled over and simply walked up to them and introduced myself. An unsurprising side effect of a solitary seven-week Roadtrip seems to be the willingness to approach just about anyone and talk about just about anything. Now I knew how the elderly must feel.

The fishermen accepted me easily into their group, as if letting a random stranger into your conversation was part of the fisherman code. They seized the opportunity to get some new insight into their important topic.

"What do you think?" said Bob, the apparent leader of the group, a robust fellow with a shock of reddish blond hair poking out of a mesh cap that read "Today is Bob Day." "Huge war breaks out tomorrow. Every country for itself. Who wins?"

"I dunno," I said. Bob's two companions—Clarence, a slightly chubby black guy in an old, torn jean jacket; and Jorge, a short, quiet Hispanic man in a Yankees hat—rounded out the diverse trio. Bob looked a little Irish. I didn't want to offend anyone's roots. "Are weapons allowed?"

"See?" said Clarence, to Bob. "He said the same thing. We're not number one for literacy or life expectancy anymore, either."

"Who gives a rat's ass?" said Bob. "America's number one because we can kick everyone else's ass. Plain and simple!"

"China and India have like a billion people each," Clarence informed us. "What if they ganged up on us?"

"They can't gang up on us!" shot back Bob. "What part of 'every country for itself' don't you understand? Otherwise, Israel would have to be on our team, because we have all their cab drivers."

Clarence and Jorge shook their heads. Bob turned to me. "Of course weapons are allowed. Future wars are gonna be fought by stealth bombers and robots, anyway, so population doesn't matter. Besides," he added, to his friends. "What are most of those billion people in India doing? You could air-drop in a hamburger and they'd all kill each other fighting over it."

"That's very racist, Bob," said Clarence. "Most Indians are Hindus, and don't eat cows."

Bob pulled up a fish, unceremoniously whacked its head against the side of the dock, and tossed it into a bucket. "Whatever. Air-drop in a 7-Eleven, then," he looked at me. "So what brings you to Mobile?"

I told them about my Roadtrip. They all nodded, approvingly.

"You should sleep outside Wal-Marts," said Clarence, when I told them of my sleeping spot debacles. "They actually *like* people to sleep outside their stores."

"What?" I asked. "Why?"

"I dunno," said Clarence. "But they do. I guess so you'll wake up and go buy something."

"That's capitalism for ya," chipped in Bob.

Mentally, I added Wal-Mart to my list.

"Well, you've found yourself about the best fishing spot on the Gulf Coast," Bob boasted. "We've been coming here for years. Last summer, Jorge there caught over a thousand fish from this wharf. Best fisherman since *The Old Man and the Sea*."

Bob got excited and turned to Jorge. "Aw, tell him that one story though, the truck story?" Jorge just shook his head. Bob hesitated about a tenth of a second before charging on with the tale himself. "Damndest tragedy I ever heard. So Jorge's kid needs braces, right? Well the orthodontist needs a thousand bucks for a down payment, and Jorge doesn't have it, so he goes fishing for it. He's at it every day for a week, from before dawn until nine at night. And dang it if by Friday he ain't got the money."

"You can make a thousand bucks in a week selling these fish?" I asked, peering into their paltry bucket, astounded.

Bob paused briefly. "What? Nah, dummy, Jorge crews sometimes on a charter boat. Helps rich tourists catch fish."

He resumed his story, booming to the whole dock.

"Anyway, he's walking out of the charter office Friday evening, all set to take the money home to his family. And wouldn't you know it, some jackass has run his car into Jorge's truck. Hit-and-run type deal. No way to trace 'em. Thousand dollars to get the thing moving again. Money was gone again, just like that."

Bob turned to me, like he was bestowing priceless advice upon his world-bound son.

"Don't ever do anything just for money, kid. Because money can be gone," he snapped his fingers. "Bam. Just like that. And then what was all that time worth?"

"Good thing Jorge likes fishing so much," Clarence piped in.

Jorge smiled, subtly. I don't think Bob saw it, as he turned back to me.

"So America wins, right, if we can use weapons?"

"Sure, I guess so. We have the most nukes, right?"

"Actually, Russia has the most nuclear weapons," Jorge said, finally speaking up. "I read they have around twelve hundred, and we only have a thousand."

"C'mon, Jorge! We're the richest!" said Bob. "And like anyone really knows exactly how many nukes a country has?"

"China has more active soldiers than we do," volunteered Clarence.

"Clarence," said Bob. "I'm starting to suspect that you're some kind of socialist."

"And technically, Luxembourg's the richest, if you go by average income," said Jorge quietly. Bob ignored him and surged on.

"America will always be the best! We're the land of opportunity!"

"I'm just saying a lot of that opportunity's going to start moving overseas in the next fifty years," replied Clarence.

Bob stared, disbelieving, at his friend. "Seriously, what are you, a China-lover?"

Clarence shrugged. "They have good wontons."

"Don't we spend way more money on military than anyone else?" I asked, hoping to redirect the subject. "What are we spending all that money on, if not nukes?"

"Tanks," said Bob. "AK-forty-sevens."

"A lot goes to the Pentagon, for undisclosed purposes," said Jorge.

"Lasers that can shoot your ass from space," said Bob.

"Iraq," said Jorge.

"Don't get me started on Iraq." Bob warned.

"Mercenaries?" I ventured.

"Agh! Mercenaries!" Bob exclaimed, like I had stabbed him. "Now that's the worst thing you can be. Worse than a prostitute. Your life is the most valuable thing you got. Die for your own freedom, that's great, but kill and die for a buck?" He looked at me again, shooting more wisdom out of his violently pointing finger. "Never do anything just for money."

"Jorge, do you know?" asked Clarence. "We spend way more money on military than anyone else, right?"

"Yes. More than the next twenty-five countries combined," said Jorge. "All of Europe, Russia, China, Japan . . . add all those together, and we still spend more."

This was a pretty impressive statistic, and it took its effect on all of us, even Bob.

"Wow," said Bob, finally. "Maybe we should buy more nukes."

"How do you know all this stuff, Jorge?" I asked, after a moment.

"I had to do a lot of research," Jorge said, modestly. "For my citizenship test."

He pulled up a fish, and set it in the bucket. Clarence began to reel in another one.

"So you guys all work down here on the charters?" I asked.

"Nah, just Jorge," said Clarence. "Bob owns a fishing equipment company. Rich son of a bitch." Bob grinned widely as Clarence went on. "I just come out to get away from the missus."

I turned to Bob. "I thought you said you shouldn't do anything just for money."

"No," he replied. "I said you shouldn't do anything *you hate* just for money. Nothing wrong with having dough, if that's what's important to you. How do you think Jorge's kid got her braces? Not from his poor ass, that's for sure!"

He punched Jorge in the arm. Jorge just smiled that tiny smile, and fished. I looked closer at Clarence's and Jorge's fishing poles. High-end stuff, especially for a wharf in Mobile. Expensive. To match Bob's. Presents, I realized, for two longtime, loyal fishing pals.

"Call me a greedy son of a bitch," said Bob, grinning toothily. "But makin' money makes me happy. 'Specially if I can do it fishing."

I wished them all good luck, got back into the Imposter, and headed west.

On the outskirts of Mobile, I drove by another southern mansion, even grander than the one in Kentucky. This time I stopped. One side effect of a solitary seven-week Roadtrip is loneliness. But another is freedom.

The mansion turned out to be nothing—locked doors and closed gates.

But I was glad I'd checked.

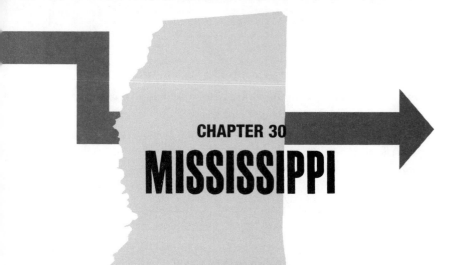

CHAPTER 30
MISSISSIPPI

The Waffle Heir

A comedian (whose name I can't recall, so I'm reduced to stealing his joke) once quipped that the Mason-Dixon line should be replaced by the IHOP–Waffle House line. It's hard to disagree: these days, nobody knows who Mason and Dixon were, but everyone south of Dixon's line knows about Waffle House.

Indeed, it seems that a city's proximity to the Gulf of Mexico is directly proportional to the number of Waffle Houses it has. I passed a food/gas/lodging sign in Mississippi that had arrows pointing to *three* different Waffle Houses (and one Chick-fil-A) off the same exit. I began to theorize that all Waffle Houses were owned by the same evil, bent-on-world-domination megacorporation that also owns all the near–Waffle House knock-offs: Waffle Shop, Waffle Iron, and the mysteriously named Huddle House. (Which is admittedly a pretty good restaurant, though whatever a *huddle* is, I'm not eating it.)

Not being one to oppose the new world order, I took my Mississippi stop at a Waffle House on the outskirts of Biloxi, hoping to mollify my hunger for both breakfast and human interaction. I wanted to see what all the fuss was about. I also wanted to find out what grits were. It turns out they're not made from gravel, as my friends in Minnesota had tried to tell me.

I entered the busy restaurant and made a beeline for a seat alone at the counter, which is the international restaurant signal for "Yes, I'm here alone and it's okay to talk to me." A late-thirties blonde woman seemed to be running the shop, assisted by an older blonde woman who carried plates of shallow-squared batter discs in and out of the kitchen.

"You guys are busy for two P.M." I announced as the younger woman—Janet, according to her name tag—strode by and smiled.

"Well. People want their waffles."

Janet had a kind, maternal look, like the Waffle House was her beloved, if sometimes unruly, child.

She also had a medium-sized southern accent. I'd been noticing this, since hitting the South: the smaller the city, the more severe the drawl. In the tiny, muggy towns, words ran together, as if it were too hot to pronounce each syllable. But nobody I'd met in Atlanta had much of an accent at all. They probably roll their eyes every time a movie actor bumpkinizes their dialect to play a southern character, the way Minnesotans roll their eyes every time the movie *Fargo* comes on (Fargo is actually in North Dakota, for the record). Nobody in the Twin Cities talks that way, except for the occasional "Oh sure" my mom will let slip during a post-service chat in the community room of our Lutheran church.

Biloxi was sort of halfway in between. Nobody sounded like they had a tire-less pickup truck in their front yard, but I'd heard a couple "Y'alls" on the way in.

Janet brought me a menu. "I'm surprised it's so crowded," I said. "Especially with that other Waffle House literally five blocks up the street."

The older woman walked past again, disapprovingly clucking her tongue. Janet pushed a glass of water in front of me and shook her head.

"Don't mind her. She just doesn't care for that other Waffle House."

"Oh?" I wondered how different two Waffle Houses could be. "Why not?"

"Aw, there's nothing wrong with it," Janet said. "We've had a bit of trouble with them in the past, that's all."

Trouble? "Like what?" I asked. This sounded almost juicy.

"Nothing," Janet said. "Just a bit of a feud, that's all."

What? I sat up. This was too good to be true. Was I about to be a hapless bystander in a Mississippi Waffle House Feud? I pictured shotguns, and the stealing of whisks.

"It's not really anything anymore," Janet said, seeing my interest. "But it used to a bit of an issue, back when Momma ran the store."

She gestured to the older blonde woman, who made her way past us carrying several dirty plates. She was still clucking at me, like I was some kind of spy.

"What do you mean, a feud?" I asked. "Like . . . Hatfield/McCoy–style, people shooting each other?"

"No, of course not," she eyed me strangely. "It's only a restaurant. Just some Waffle Houses sometimes have issues with each other, over customers, and the way menu items are made, and such."

"That Betsy's a damn crook, I tell ya," cursed Janet's mom. "Stealin' my recipes."

"I got it, Ma."

Janet's mother snorted and went off into the back. Janet pointed out an old man wearing a VFW cap and a flannel shirt. His loose, wrinkled jowls jiggled as he ate, as if someone had pulled his face partway off.

"Like, see Old Hank over there? Regular customer. Comes in almost every day. But he used to go to the other store. The owner accused us of stealing him."

Old Hank took a toothless bite of his grits and gummed away at them, like a cow chewing cud.

"Then one day, the special syrup that Momma perfected mysteriously showed up at their store," she shook her head, as if bemoaning a dark day she would never forget. So much for my waffle world domination theory.

"Isn't there like . . . a corporate office that regulates stuff like that?"

"Oh, sure," Janet said. "Especially recently. But Waffle House tends to give a lot of leeway to franchise owners. There's a lot of stuff happens in stores that they don't know about." Her eyes followed a suspicious-looking man who was leaving the store. "You'd be surprised."

I didn't know what to say. All of a sudden there seemed to be a whole new level to this bustling Biloxi store, more than just a place that ironed a mean waffle. Janet shook it off.

"But anyway, like I said, things have been fine for a few years now, between us and that other store. Ever since that Chick-fil-A moved in right between us," she smiled. "Nothing unites folks like a common enemy!"

"So you own the store?" I said, trying to keep her from wandering off. "And your mom before you?"

"Feels like there's always been a Waffle House in our family," said Janet, filling a few other customers' coffee cups.

"I've got a family business I could take over," I said. "Not as cool as waffle feuds, though."

"Oh, I'm sure it's fine. You gonna do it?"

"I don't know. I'm not very good at it. My dad's been really cool about not pressuring me to get involved, but I feel like secretly, any dad would want his son to follow in his footsteps. I'd hate to disappoint him."

"Well, do you *wanna* do it?" asked Janet. "That's what matters, ain't it? You only got one career in life." She paused. "Nah, that ain't true, most people got like twelve. But you should *aim* like you only got one. Try to get it as close to perfect as you can."

I got excited. "Like it should have nine out of ten traits?"

She glanced at me quizzically. "Well, I don't know if there's that many traits to a job, but sure. What are you, a survey person or something?"

"My dad is."

"Hey mister," said a tiny voice to my left. I looked down. A little blonde girl stood there behind the counter, a plate stacked with waffles held firmly in each hand. She put mine down on the counter in front of me. "You want some coffee with your waffles?"

I smiled and shook my head. Janet patted her daughter's blonde curls.

"She knows she's got a restaurant waiting for her someday if she wants it. Guess she's eager to get started."

"It must be nice to work around the people you love."

"Yeah, but you gotta do what you love, too," Janet said. "I'm just lucky I got both. But I won't be mad if she changes her mind." Janet covered her daughter's ears and whispered. "Long as she doesn't become a stripper or something."

I ate my waffles, said goodbye, and left a nice tip. I'd never met a Waffle Heiress before.

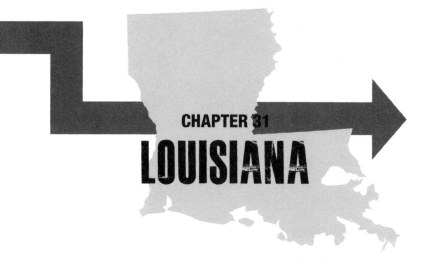

CHAPTER 31

LOUISIANA

The Food 'n Bait 'n Pet 'n Explosives Store

The only other time I'd been to Louisiana, it was Mardi Gras. Well, technically it was New Year's Eve, but I get the impression Mardi Gras season in New Orleans lasts from Advent to Easter, plus weekends, holidays, and every night after midnight. So official Mardi Gras might have been a long ways off, but people were already drunk and whipping out their body parts.

Thirteen of us had road-tripped down from Chicago for a college football bowl game and found ourselves on a packed Bourbon Street. We were new to the scene, but the jubilant New Orleans residents were eager to fill in the details. A bellhop at our hotel directed us to our first stop at a Mardi Gras "Spirit Store," where the sales clerk enthusiastically informed us that "Necklaces of beads are the only currency in the economy of getting girls to show their taddies." Out in the streets, a security guard hastened us toward a crowd where a fire truck with sirens blaring was honking for people to make room. We assumed this meant the party was being broken up, until two

firefighters jumped onto the back and hoisted a couple of girls onto the truck, where they revealed themselves in a monsoon of beads, lit by the spotlight of a nearby cop car.

I vaguely remember lobbing beads toward some girls perched on balconies, because that's what everybody else was doing, and wondering why nothing was happening. I felt a tap on my shoulder and turned to see a wise old black man standing there, cool and comfortable amid the chaos.

"I see your frustration," said the bearded sage. "It's because of inflation. Girls on balconies these days often require three or four necklaces of beads before they will show their jubblies. But they will, eventually. That's what they're up there for."

I'd never felt so enlightened by something so base.

My solitary trek across Louisiana this time was another story. I didn't see a soul on the long drive across the toe of the boot, diagonally up toward Shreveport on the ankle. Flying across the empty Pelican State byways, alone except for the humid country breeze and the static twang of Creole jazz on the radio, I experienced a very different Louisiana from the one through which I had slowly crawled, two years earlier, squashed among a thousand people screaming and peeing on mailboxes.

I stopped at an old cotton plantation near Natchitoches, but there wasn't a tour, not even a Gettysburg-style bootleg one. There wasn't anyone there at all, in fact, because I was speeding through, in stubborn refusal to let anyone else govern my schedule.

I wandered past the magnificent plantation house and past the somewhat less posh slave quarters. It wasn't the same without anyone to give me the background. Hadn't I already learned this lesson, about imposing my will on places? But I still had a deadline looming. And Sarah. And technically I still had an editing interview set up. What would be my excuse for postponing? "Oh, sorry, Boss Guy, I was driving loops around the country and didn't feel like coming back."

I took a few pictures of the plantation and moved on, trying to ignore the feeling that I was again sprinting through the scenery.

It had been a monstrous long day of driving, and my fixtures were calling for a bathroom stop. I had started to look for an inviting patch of bushes when I passed a building, sitting alone at the intersection of two deserted highways.

Store! The sign read. *Food 'N Bait 'N Pet 'N Explosives 'N More!*

I slammed on the brakes. They had me at "Pet 'N Explosives."

I entered the store. The place was like a Rambo version of the Amish General Store in Kidron, Ohio. It was the size of a basketball court, with dingy gray walls supporting a low ceiling laden with fluorescent lights. There were dozens of shelves lined with things you'd expect to see in a typical convenience store—spatulas, windshield-wiper fluid, nondairy creamer—and dozens more lined with things you wouldn't—camo outfits, carpet samples, and a somewhat disturbing aisle of life-size baby dolls. Along one wall was a row of capacious plastic tubs three feet deep with water and packed to the brim with various thrashing creatures: a tub full of minnows, a tub full of leeches, and several tubs full of increasingly larger fish, each apparently used to catch the fish in the next tank. The fish in the final tub were shockingly large, and I wondered what they could possibly be bait for. Alligators, I hoped.

Immediately next to and above the bait tubs were several rows of shotguns and rifles, a couple of which seemed to be pointing into the bait tanks. The phrase "shooting fish in a barrel" popped into mind, and I was struck with the vision of taking down one of the shotguns and blasting it right into a tub of minnows. It was a terribly cruel and disturbing idea, but I had to give credit to whoever had coined the phrase: it sure would be effective.

I used the bathroom (where bright red targets had been painted on the inside of both urinals) and passed the cashier, the other sole occupant of the store, save for a large, balding cocker spaniel that rested at his feet. I wasn't ready to leave yet.

"Food, pets, and explosives?" I asked.

The cashier looked up from his magazine, surprised but not inhospitable.

"Yup! There ain't that many stores round this area. You never know what people are gonna need."

The man was Asian, I guessed Chinese, and he could have been minding a shop somewhere in Beijing. But here he was in northwestern Louisiana, and when he opened his mouth, a perfectly Americanized southern accent rolled out. It was a little disconcerting.

"What kind of explosives? Like fireworks?"

The cashier gestured over to a couple of shelves, near the guns.

"A few. But got some heavier stuff. M-eighties, and such. Some of it's near weapons grade."

I glanced over the shelf, which held some fairly intimidating packages, not all of which looked legal.

"Do you need to have, like, permits for this stuff?"

He shrugged. "Beats me. I only work here second shift. Rob, the guy who owns the store, is a big hunting enthusiast."

I bet. Though I couldn't imagine what part of hunting involved weapons-grade explosives. Blasting out prairie-dog towns, I fantasized.

The cocker spaniel had gotten up and was sniffing at my crotch.

"Gǔnkāi!" the cashier yelled at the dog, in Mandarin. I startled, the old animal backed off, and the shop clerk resumed his southern accent.

"Anything particular yer looking for?"

I shook my head. "Not really. I'll be honest with you. I just think your store is kinda awesome."

The cashier smiled and set down his magazine. "C'mon. I'll show you around."

He hopped up and led me down a Christmas ornament aisle, past a lawn chair made out of deer antlers.

"I take it you ain't local."

"Yeah, passing through," I said. "I was just down at the plantation by Natchitoches."

"Nice place. They tell you the hogshead story?"

"No," I said. "There wasn't anyone around."

"Story goes," said the cashier, without pausing. "The master of the plantation heard about one of the slaves organizing an escape. So he gave the slave a choice between two punishments. One, he could spend twelve hours a day, six days a week working in a different cotton field than the rest of the slaves, and sleep in different quarters. Or two, he could climb into a hogshead barrel, which the master had nailed a bunch of nails into, so the points barely stuck through the inside of the barrel. Then they'd close up the barrel and roll it down the longest, steepest hill on the plantation."

He paused. I waited for the conclusion of the story. "The slave chose the hogshead barrel," the cashier said at last. "I guess he figured a couple days of pain was better than a lifetime of loneliness. *GŬNKĀI!*"

He gestured angrily at the cocker spaniel, which had climbed up onto a chair and was trying to get at the fish in the end tub. The dog jumped down and ran shamefully back behind the counter. The cashier shook his head.

"Silly dog."

"What happened?" I asked. "At the plantation?"

"The Civil War happened," said the cashier. "The master joined the Confederate army and was shot and killed in the first battle."

He pushed open a door to the back of the store. "That's probably the best story, anyway. Other than that, it's mostly just a regular old plantation. You ain't missin' much."

I wasn't, now.

"I suppose you're wondering about the 'pet' part of the sign," said the cashier, leading me outside. I hadn't been, actually—I'd assumed the bait fish and dog served double purposes. But he pointed to several large hutches, in which a few dozen rabbits hopped around. "We used to have some lizards and guinea pigs too, but it was getting expensive to clean all the cages. The rabbits also—" he stopped himself and turned to me. "You ain't like a crazy animal lover, are you?"

"No. I do not particularly love animals." It felt like an odd statement to say.

"You can also eat the rabbits," he said, confidentially. "If, you know, you wanna. Same price."

I nodded, in a way that suggested that I understood but that I almost certainly would not be eating any rabbits. We went silently back inside the store.

That was the end of the tour. I picked up a $2 bag of ice for the Imposter cooler. I felt bad that was all I was buying. But the cashier didn't seem to mind.

"Do you work all night?" I asked.

"Only until eleven," he said, as he rung me up.

"It must be pretty quiet. I mean, it's quiet now, and it's not even dark yet."

"I don't mind. There's a lot of magazines."

"Do you like it?" I asked. "Working here?"

"You know what?" said the cashier, thinking. "I do. I know everybody wants to get rich for doing nothing, but everything ain't just about me. People need places to buy stuff, too."

"And my house is just up the road. I can kiss my sleeping daughter every night, and my wife every morning. I guess that's what's most important to me."

"Do you ever get lonely?"

He shrugged. "Sometimes. They drop in to visit once in a while. And sometimes, strangers passing through wanna talk. Not all of them," he smiled at me. "But some. You're never alone, as long as you're not afraid to use your mouth." He furrowed his brow. "That came out weird. But you know what I mean."

"Yeah," I said. "I do."

I picked up my ice and headed for the door.

"Hey," the cashier said. I turned. "You wanna take a rabbit? For the road? As a pet, I mean."

I paused. "No thanks. I'd probably just kill it by accident. Appreciate it."

He waved. I smiled and said goodbye to the latest of my new friends.

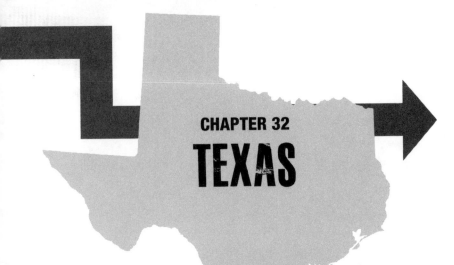

CHAPTER 32

TEXAS

Ryadum, Sheadumbaum Heeah!

I crossed into Texas south of Shreveport late that afternoon with a daunting question on my mind: How was I going to handle Texas?

"Everything's big in Texas," the saying goes. But it's not simply an audacious motto. Texas *is* big. It's number two in state size, behind only Alaska. It's number two in population, behind only California. It has *three* of the nation's top ten biggest cities. The year before the Cheez-Its debacle, Charlie and Jeff had made South Padre Island their smuggling destination. They left from Minnesota late one night. Ten hours later, they were already in Texas, and overjoyed with their progress. Ten hours after that, they were still in Texas, and going insane. Texas isn't big. It's ginormous.

I couldn't pick one part of Texas and call it representative. Not that I could do this for any state, but especially not for Texas, where every major city is its own little world. My dad had traveled through the state extensively for his business, helping Texas people feel better about their jobs, and helping them figure out their paths when their jobs went away. He gave me his two-second summaries. "Houston is two million people and no zoning ordinances," he said. "Dallas is the biggest city in the world not located on a major waterway. And San Antonio ... well, San Antonio is what would happen if Mexico mated with Venice, Italy." He was referring to the canals, but I pictured a guy in a sombrero eating pizza, which there are also lots of in San Antonio, especially after the bars close. "And then," he said. "There's the ninety-nine percent of Texas that's not any of those places."

These places didn't even necessarily get along, either. My college friend Jim, a Dallas native and die-hard Cowboys fan, only took one season to declare his loathing for the new Houston expansion team.

"I hate the goddamn Texans," he told me out of nowhere one night at dinner in our dorm's dining hall.

"You're a Texan," I responded.

"No, not people from Texas. The Houston Texans. The football team. I hate them so much I want to vomit in anger."

"Weren't they like four and twelve this year?"

"It doesn't matter," said Jim. "They're the stupidest team ever, and they all need to die."

I chewed my reheated lasagna thoughtfully for a moment.

"I challenge you to give me one logical reason why you should hate the Texans."

But Jim just stared at me. "I hated the Oilers. Why wouldn't I hate the Texans?"

Sure, these kinds of rivalries happen in every state. They're just bigger in Texas.

And so, as the saying goes, how was I going to mess with Texas?

I wasn't.

Texas was simply too huge, too overwhelming to try and conquer it all. I didn't have the time or the oomph to hit every one of Texas's 254 counties. For now I would stick to eastern Texas, make my way up past Dallas/Forth Worth to Paris and see what happened. Someday

I could return and give the Lone Star State its due with its own Roadtrip. Texas in Forty-Eight Days.

In Linden I ate too many peaches and decided to sleep outside the town post office.

You'd really think I would have learned by now.

I don't even know what I was thinking: maybe I planned to wake up and leave before anyone found me. Maybe I hoped any onlookers would just think I was anxious to mail something. Possibly I was simply so bored I was willing to do anything to have someone to talk to. If this was the reason, I would get my wish. Sort of.

In the middle of the night I woke up to yet another police flashlight tapping on my car window.

I should have found a Wal-Mart.

I lurched into semi-consciousness. It was not a good wake-up. It was one of those where you sort of open your eyes but you're only 17 percent awake and have no clue what's happening. All I knew was that there was light and sound and that I seemed to be in some sort of automobile. I *was* able to discern, however, the exact words of the uniformed officer who now stood outside my window.

"Radum, sheadumbaum heeah?"

I won't overgeneralize and say that all Texas police officers speak in incomprehensible twang, but this one sure did. Not that I would have been able to understand what was going on even if he'd handed me a telegram—I was, after all, at about the coherency level of a stoned toddler.

Mumbling nonsensically for a minute (in my muddled state, I wasn't exactly a champion orator, either), I fumbled to roll down the window. Finally I succeeded, and the cop spoke again.

"Radum sheadumbaum heeah?"

"Muhshoisabuh?" I replied. It was like a radish trying to communicate with a porpoise.

The cop turned to his buddy cop with a skeptical look, as if he had understood what I said but didn't like it. He scratched his chin then slowly turned back to me.

"Radum sheadumbaum heeah!" he said again. He must have just woken up too.

This went on for a few more minutes, until finally somebody above had mercy and removed the Tower of Babel that was clogging our communication. I was able to make out that, obviously, the cops wanted to know what I was doing, camped in a post-office parking lot. And I responded that, just as obviously, I was on a road trip, groggy from partially fermented peaches, and in need of a place to sleep. The cops glanced at each other, and then said something that made even less sense.

"Aright, ya can go back to sleep."

The cops moved off, and I sat there, stunned. They didn't mind that I was sleeping outside their post office. They just wanted to make sure I . . . to make sure I was nice and disoriented, I guess. It seems Texas cops are as lenient with their laws as they are with their pronunciation.

I scratched my head for a minute. I'd never been allowed to go back to sleep in one of these situations before, so I took advantage. After all, I was still only about 32 percent awake.

I woke up at 7 A.M., bought a few stamps from the dispenser outside the post office as a thank you, threw out the rotting remains of my Alabama peaches, and headed northwest.

Strange as it sounds, I was beginning to *like* these occasional run-ins with the police. They were always a surprise, always a little scary, but always led to good stories. It also helped that I hadn't been arrested. So far.

Now that I thought about it, *all* my favorite stories so far—from Missouri's snake-filled lake to Connecticut's show-home debacle to Florida's jellyfish cop—had just sort of happened, without any planning from me at all. Could it be that, in all these years as a planner, I'd been missing something?

I pulled over in Paris, Texas (home of the Eiffel Tower of pulled pork sandwiches), to clean out the Imposter a bit, and added a "No

Driving at Night" rule to my list. Aside from the clouds of bugs dying on my windshield and increased chances of liquefying a deer, I tended to make bad decisions about what to eat and where to park. And I just didn't see as much.

No sooner had I finished plucking stale M&M's out of the Imposter's seat cushions than my mom called with some fantastic news: the Spacemobile was operational! I had honestly forgotten about it by now; it seemed to me the definition of "totaled" should include a car that can't be repaired in less than four weeks. But apparently the Volkswagen dealership had brought the van back from the dead, and the Teal Demon rode once more. Finally, the Roadtrip I had always dreamed of could become a reality.

I made arrangements with my mother to rendezvous in a few days in western Minnesota to make the car swap, the now-seasoned Imposter heading to the bench and the Spacemobile getting the call to take charge of The Roadtrip—Part II.

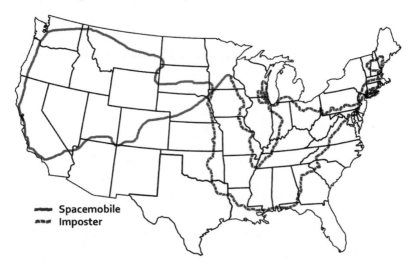

— Spacemobile
— Imposter

Once again, I was changing my route. And why not? My map already looked like it had been navigated by a blind, drunken orangutan.

CHAPTER 33

OKLAHOMA

Little Beauty

Hitting Texas meant that the East—and two-thirds of America's contiguous states—was now behind me. But the West—and two-thirds of America's landmass—was still ahead. I had a new route, and my next four states, besides swinging into Minnesota to get the Spacemobile, would be Oklahoma, Kansas, Nebraska, and South Dakota. The heart of the heartland. The middle of Middle America. The corniest of the states that grow corn . . . and wheat, and hay, and soybeans too, I knew . . . but I was from the city part of Minnesota. Corn was the only one I could identify from a passing car.

I could practically smell the Spacemobile, practically feel my butt cushioned high in its captain's chair as I was regarded with looks of perplexed awe from everyone I passed. I was so looking forward to our grand reunion in Minnesota, four states away. But as I studied my map and the big, boxy states between that moment and me, there didn't seem to be much else to look forward to.

My dad knew this part of the country well. As the son of a traveling pastor, he'd grown up on farms around the Midwest and lived in Omaha in two of the eleven houses he'd occupied by the time he was ten. In his work, he'd traveled extensively from Texas up through the Dakotas, and he always spoke about the plains with a certain reverence.

"You can see forever," he'd intone to us kids during car trips through farm country. "Standing in the middle of fields after harvest, it's like looking at the world through a giant wide-angle lens. You'll see a grain elevator on the flat horizon, only a half-inch tall, and realize it's still forty miles away."

I understood the *importance* of this part of the country—heck, it probably fed more people than anywhere else in the world. But I didn't see the beauty.

"It's just fields!" I'd complain. Granted, I was at the age when I could have driven through a field of dinosaurs and still found a way to be bored.

"Look at the colors," my dad marveled. "The clouds. It's not a big beauty like the Grand Canyon. But it's a little beauty. Sometimes you don't even notice it until it's gone."

I'd peer out the window for a second, then go back to my Game Boy. "Whatever. Looks like a bunch of nothing to me."

"Be patient," my dad would advise.

I was never very good at patience.

Whatever my dad had meant, I saw very "little beauty" through my first 100 miles of Oklahoma, as I drove up from the Texas border on a speck of highway pressed between the drought brown Oklahoma land and drab gray Oklahoma sky. For over an hour, I didn't see a town. I didn't even see a *sign* for a town. But I was excited to try out my new strategy.

Louisiana had been the last straw: every time I tried to force an experience—Kellogg's, D.C., the plantation—the result had disappointed. In Oklahoma I wouldn't force anything. I would simply go with the flow, let fate take the wheel, and see what happened.

I might have picked a bad state in which to try this.

All states have their nowhere areas—areas where towns rarely top a thousand people and gas stations are named things like "Diesel-Does-It" and the more minimalist "Gas Station." America's the third-largest country in the world—both in population and landmass—but 95 percent of its people live in a few hundred metropolitan areas. In the West, the states grow but the populations don't, so the nowhere areas get bigger. There are long stretches in the West where you won't see anything manmade besides the road you're on and perhaps a cow fence on the side of the highway. So far, Oklahoma had been a giant one of these stretches.

Eventually, I came across a drive-up tourist information booth. I won't call it a "Welcome Center," because it wasn't: the place was more like a tollbooth or an agricultural inspection stop, except that inside the booth was a fifty-something woman in a park-ranger outfit, sitting with a bunch of tourism pamphlets as she scribbled randomly in what looked like a coloring book.

"Hi there," I greeted her as I pulled up and rolled down my window, letting in some of the choking prairie dust. "I'm passing through on a road trip, and I was wondering if you could tell me what's interesting to do in Oklahoma?"

The woman looked befuddled for a moment, as if she'd never been asked this in her forty years of working in Oklahoma tourism. I think she usually just handed out pamphlets and gave directions. Or else nobody ever stopped. At last, her face brightened.

"Well, there's Route Sixty-Six!"

"Okay," I said. "What's there?"

"It's a highway!" the woman answered proudly.

"I know that," I said patiently. "I mean, what's interesting about it?"

"It's famous," the woman replied.

"For what?"

"There's a song about it," said the woman. Clearly, this was all the explanation anyone could ever need.

"Okay, maybe. What else?"

"There was a musical about Oklahoma. It's called *Oklahoma!*"

"I've heard of it. Did they write it here?"

"I don't think so," said the woman. "But they perform it here sometimes."

"Um . . . anything else?"

The woman thought for a long moment. "Will Rogers was born here. And this famous Indian dancer, I forget the name."

I remembered something. "Hey, wasn't there a big land rush here in the eighteen-hundreds?"

"Oh yeah! I think there was!"

"Like, a bunch of people lined up at the border and waited for somebody to fire a gun so they could run in and settle land?"

"They lined up?" she asked, genuinely curious.

"Or something like that. Something about 'Sooners'?"

"That's the name of the football team!" the woman announced.

"Right," I said. "Anyway, that sounds cool. You know where I can go to find out more about it?"

"Sounds like you already know quite a bit!"

"No, I mean like a historical area or something."

"Not that I know of."

"A museum? A plaque?"

"You know, I'm not really sure. You could try at the next information booth. It's a hundred miles up on Route Sixty-Six!"

I gave up and drove away, puzzled. You'd think a tourist booth would be a great place to learn about a state, but I'd learned more from three guys fishing. Clearly the woman was a crazy person who had murdered a park ranger and was squatting in her information booth.

But she had mentioned Route 66, I thought. Where it had all begun, that spring day back in Chicago.

My dad had told me about the college road trips his buddies had taken along the famed road. But 66's history went back further than that—it was one of the main roads the Dustbowlers had taken west during the Depression. It was the quintessential road-trip road, the Main Street of America, the king of small highways before there were interstates. And mine was a trip *about* small highways, I thought. *Fate was testing me.* Maybe my grand lesson was still lurking here, waiting to be discovered.

My highway merged right into 66 near the town of Bristow. But Route 66 looked like a regular old road to me, except with more rib restaurants. I must be missing something. I stopped at a small grocery store.

"Hey," I asked the forty-year-old, buzz-cut clerk. "What's the deal with Route Sixty-Six?"

"Construction," he said, as he bagged someone's soup cans and pot roast. "They're fillin' in some of the potholes."

"No, I mean what's interesting about it? I'm visiting."

"Oh!" said the clerk, his mood lightening. Anything to help a stranger. "Well, it's about the most famous road in all of America. There's a song about it!"

Of course there was. I was beginning to think it was Oklahoma's state anthem.

"It goes all the way from Chicago to Los Angeles," the clerk said.

"A lot of roads do that."

"Yeah, but it used to be the *only* road," he said, epically.

"All right," I said, losing patience. "But what's special about it *now*?"

The clerk thought for a moment. "There's a lot of potholes."

I sighed. "Fine. Can I just buy some raisins?"

This was not going well. I continued up Route 66, into Bristow and out the other side. I stopped at a café with a giant Route 66 mural on the outside wall. I sat in a corner booth, ordered a blueberry muffin, and plugged in my computer to look up "Route 66" on the Internet. Indeed, it had once been the Oregon Trail for cars, but nobody took it anymore because it had been replaced by six more efficient routes.

"Find anything?" asked the slender nineteen-year-old waitress, whom I'd told about my quandary.

I shook my head. "Not a thing. Interstate Forty-Four literally goes right over the top of it, all the way from Tulsa to Oklahoma City."

"My grandpa says it used to be a big deal. The way to California. Everybody took it," she explained. "A lot of little towns grew up around it. Like this one."

"And now?"

She shrugged. "It's just a road."

"You can learn about the American march west," an older woman chipped in from behind the counter, likely the owner. "And all the Dustbowlers."

"Okay. Where can I learn about these things?"

She had no answer.

I shook my head, exasperated. "Gettysburg, you can learn something about. The Lincoln Memorial is cool to look at. Route Sixty-Six . . . there's nothing here!"

Heads around the restaurant popped up. I backpedaled. "Besides your lovely town, I mean."

The diners went back to eating. I took a dejected bite of my muffin and sighed. "What grand lesson am I supposed to learn here?"

The owner cocked her head.

"It's a highway, not a wishing well."

She went back to filling up another customer's Pepsi. I sat for a moment, then looked up "Oklahoma land rush" on my computer. The first and biggest rush had happened at high noon on a March day in 1889. The Sooners were the people who cheated and snuck in early. I looked up "Oklahoma the musical." It wasn't playing in the state. Then I looked up "Interesting Things to Do in Oklahoma." The top entry was "National Wrestling Hall of Fame." I'm not kidding.

"What do *you* do around here?" I asked the returning waitress.

"Not much. Friday nights, everybody goes to watch the local high-school football game."

"And the other days?"

She shrugged, and poured me another glass of water.

"I watch a lot of TV."

I'm sure there are fascinating, enriching things to do in Oklahoma. Someone should tell the Oklahomans about them.

I took my muffin to go and drove up Route 66 a bit further. Nothing changed. And nothing would. I kept following 66, all the way until I had to turn north on Highway 75 in Tulsa, hoping it would lead me somewhere. The whole way, Route 66 kept looking just like every other highway I'd ever driven.

Maybe it really is just a road.

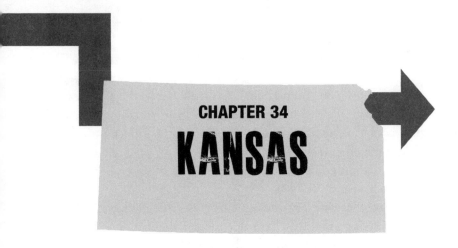

CHAPTER 34

KANSAS

Children of the Corn Maze

I entered Kansas, still confused. I'd let fate drive in Oklahoma, and . . . nothing. What was the lesson here? That highways die, cheaters get football teams named after them, and going with the flow doesn't work? Perhaps my dad was right—not every part of every state was interesting. In forty-eight states, you're bound to hit a few duds.

I moved OK to the bottom of my Favorite States List and hit Kansas, more determined than ever to find something to do, get to the Spacemobile, and get my trip back on the fast track.

I stuck to the country, avoiding Kansas City, Topeka, Wichita, and Kansas's other wonderful big cities (actually I think that's all of them). I was sure there were things to see there, but I felt compelled to stick to the country, to see if I could glimpse some of that "little beauty" my dad had been talking about. I had the growing feeling that whatever I ended up doing, it wouldn't be taking over his business. I felt bad. I wanted to see if, in some other small way at least, I could still follow in his footsteps.

I also avoided the bigger cities because I'd just been through New York, D.C., and Atlanta, and I was concerned Kansas City wouldn't have the giant stone presidents or apartments carved out of high schools to keep up. But after two hours of driving through identical, gridded farm towns, I was beginning to fear I might have made a mistake in not heading to Kauffman Stadium and watching the Royals lose 57–0 to the Yankees.

Then I saw it.

"Crawford County Corn Maze!" the sign proclaimed. "Also, last gas for 40 miles."

I was excited. First, I needed gas, but second, I'd always wanted to visit a corn maze. Every Minnesotan has this on their bucket list. What wasn't to like? I liked corn. I liked mazes. And what better way to see the beauty of the corn than to plunge right into it? It'd be like *Children of the Corn*, except without all the murder.

Unfortunately, it was very late afternoon by the time I reached my destination—getting to the maze was a bit of a maze itself. It was closed when I drove up.

I felt a pang of indignation. How dare this farmer—on whose land the corn labyrinth was built—not think to keep his maze open for me? I scouted the tall wooden fence around the perimeter of the maze, looking for a way in, being careful to avoid the farm house on the corner. I'd thought fate was making it up to me. But maybe sometimes fate needs a little help. After all, you don't need a chaperone to navigate a corn maze. All you need is determination, ingenuity, and the willingness to park your car in a hidden grove of trees and climb a fence.

I tumbled down from the top of the fence and landed in the dirt on the seat of my jeans, pushed my way through a few rotten stalks, and was instantly lost in the largest maize maze (I've always wanted to say that) I'd ever imagined.

To compare this corn maze to the dinky hedge mazes one finds at their local botanical garden would be an insult. This corn maze was huge. I imagine it occupied almost the entirety of the farmer's several-acre plot, with scores of three-foot-wide corn corridors twisting and sprawling in every direction. I say "imagine" because I was never able to gauge precisely how big the maze was, given the ten-foot-high, foreboding brown corn walls that thwarted any attempt to get a fuller view. All I knew was that this maze was mammoth. I was a kid at corn Disneyland

I found my way to the center of the labyrinth, where a post held up a drawing of the maze from above. It was shaped like a giant bird, with wings outstretched. You were supposed to enter through the beak and exit near the hindquarters, as if you were a worm finding your way down a digestive tract. I think I broke in through a kneecap.

The maze was also tough. It was unbelievably intricate, with hundreds of different paths leading this way and that, and cheating was not an option. One thing I didn't know about corn mazes is that corn makes excellent walls. Unlike the widely spaced corn in regular fields, the stalks in this maze were planted one after another, with barely an inch of space between them, like soldiers in a musket line. And corn stalks are thick. You can't bend them out of the way and jump paths; your only option is to really kick at the stalks and break them down. I felt bad enough about breaking into the corn maze—I didn't want to break out of it.

Two hours later, however, I was beginning to change my mind. Having easily fulfilled my wish of finding my way into a corn maze, I was becoming more and more fond of the idea of finding my way out. I couldn't see further than a few rows away—so much for the beauty of the corn. I could barely see the sky, the way the stalks stretched up tall and seemed to lean in over me, like the skinny evil trees of some enchanted forest. I was beginning to feel claustrophobic in Kansas, the widest open place in the world.

This wasn't fun anymore. I'd tried every possible path but I kept ending up back at the same maze map, with a bold red "You Are Here" arrow pointing tauntingly at the creature's jowl region. I ran my finger over the drawing. It reminded me of my Roadtrip map. This was exactly what I hated about not having direction: the uncertainty of how or when the solution would come. I didn't like not having control. I didn't like feeling helpless.

I tried to solve the maze on the sign, then memorize the moves required to exit—left, left, right, left, straight, left, right, straight—but I kept forgetting the steps or not recognizing what was a path and what was a place where a gopher had eaten a couple of stalks. My childhood of playing video games was at long last finding real-world application, and I was choking. I could see the editors of *Nintendo Power* standing over the corn maze watching me, like giant ghosts in the clouds, sadly shaking their heads.

The sun began to set and my pulse began to rise. The only thing worse than being lost in a corn maze is being lost in a corn maze at night. In my increasingly paranoid imagination, I saw my bones decaying in front of the den of the dreaded, mythical Corn Beast, who patrolled his maze after dark. I tried jumping, to see if I could spot the exit, but the corn was too tall. I tried running, but I only wound up back at the jowls faster. I considered yelling for help, then remembered I'd snuck in. The only thing worse than being lost in a corn maze at night is being lost in a corn maze at night with an angry, shotgun-toting farmer chasing you.

What do you do when you're lost? You ask for help. But there was no one who could help me, because stubbornness had forced me to break in and isolated me in here. Once again, I was going at it alone.

I sat down and watched the last bead of the sun disappear through the tiny gaps in the waving, grasping stalks. The maze suddenly became more ominous. Would someone find me if I stayed here until morning? Did I have enough warm clothes to spend the night? Was I really contemplating sleeping in a corn maze?

That's when I heard a snap, behind me.

I'm sure it was just a gopher, but I lost it. I started kicking. I kicked down four corn walls before I finally found the edge of the bird, then flew into the final wall like a linebacker trying to breach the offensive line. I pulled two stalks apart near the outer wall, climbed back over the wooden fence, and once again landed on my butt in the dirt, panicked and panting. I tumbled back into the Imposter, covered in corn-husk shards, a long retaliatory scratch running up my arm.

I peeled away, adding corn-maze-vandalism and trespassing to my growing list of Roadtrip crimes. I was shaking a little, and was disgusted with myself. Something had felt really right about letting fate and determination combine to get me into adventure. But something felt really wrong about breaking the rules and breaking out. Once again, fear and impatience had gotten the best of me. I hoped this wouldn't come back to haunt me.

Crawford corn maze, if you're reading this, I'm sorry I ever challenged you. I'm even sorrier I kicked down some of your corn. I had to. I was freaking out. I hope it grew back.

And honestly, you should know that I did think about returning and leaving $20 in the maze as an apology offering. But no one would ever have found it. And the Children would have gotten me. Night is when they feed.

CHAPTER 35

NEBRASKA

Tornado Girl

Not long after I escaped corn prison and resumed my voyage north, it began to storm. Hard. In the last shades of twilight, I watched thick, ominous clouds roll in over the few budding stars, and then everything was black. Thunder rumbled low through the heavy Kansas air. A startling crack of lightning turned the night to day for an instant, and the deluge began.

I pulled under the awning of a closed gas station to seek refuge from the downpour. Straight-line winds arose and whipped the gas pump hoses around like jump ropes. I was awfully glad I had opted not to sleep in the corn maze.

The rain didn't stop all night. I sat alone in the Imposter, trying to sleep but being awoken every few minutes by thunder. I began to worry. About how little money I had left. About the radio silence I'd had from Sarah since Florida. About what would happen if lightning struck a gas pump.

I felt trapped in my car in a storm in a strange place, afraid I would get blown away, bumper over bumper, into the Kansas wind. My usual instinct rumbled, to break out. To run. But there was nowhere to go.

Things were not conforming to the Roadtrip plan. I wanted to get the Spacemobile back. No storm could carry that thing away.

In a little over twenty-four hours, I was supposed to meet my mom in western Minnesota for the car swap, and I was suddenly nervous about seeing her. Would I have the tenacity to keep going? It would be so easy to follow her back to Minneapolis, crawl into my old bed, and accept the perfectly good life that awaited me in the Midwest.

By morning the rain had stopped, but the brooding sky retained an eerie shade of greenish gray that hung over me as I crossed into Nebraska. Ominous black clouds swirled over dark grass, separated by a purple horizon that made every building and tree pop unnaturally, like the surreal colors of an early film. I was headed to visit my college friend Trent in Bellevue, but when I called him to figure out exactly where he lived, I got a strained response from my normally relaxed friend.

"Uh, hey, man," said Trent. "So, I know you're heading to see me, but there's actually a huge tornado headed this way. Like, right exactly where you're going."

"What, like through your town?"

"Uh, yeah. And they're predicting others, all around. You might want to go a different way . . . it's cool if we don't meet up this time. Um, okay, good luck, I'm going to the basement now!"

Trent hung up. In college this guy played Tetris through fire drills, even once when we accidentally set a bowl of Everclear on fire in the room above his. I suspected this was serious. They didn't call this Tornado Alley for nothing. I wondered if Crawford corn karma was coming back around on me already.

I was not new to tornadoes. In Minnesota we had a brief season of them every year, right between Minnesota's other two seasons, winter and road construction. Growing up, I'd been through three tornadoes. The first was harmless enough, keeping a quarter mile distance, out in the water, at our cabin in northern Minnesota, and merely sending in a small tidal wave that nearly drowned Mark. The second and third tornadoes were closer. The second broke water-slides and pulled the roof off the building we were hiding in during my family's trip to the aptly named Noah's Ark Water Park in the Wisconsin Dells. The third hit a convenience store near my elementary school during our fifth-grade Fire Prevention graduation. As a result, our disaster-prevention ceremony had to be postponed because of disaster, proving that Midwest weather was not without a sense of irony.

So while I knew that tornadoes were nothing to trifle with, I wasn't nearly at Trent's alert level as I pulled into a gas station near Omaha to get enough fuel to move through the area.

Not everyone shared my unconcern. As I strolled into the station to pay for my gas, the nose-pierced teenage girl behind the counter was hanging up from an apparently traumatic phone call. She looked as if she'd been crying.

"How's it going?" I asked.

"Oh, just great," the girl said, her voice cracking with sarcasm and alarm. "There's a tornado coming, and my boss won't let me go home."

"Oh," I said, not really sure how to respond to this. "Well, at least you're indoors, right?"

"She's such a bitch," the girl continued. "She's just getting back at me for that sick day I took last week. She thought I wanted to go to the Moonshiners concert, but I really was sick! And now she wants me to be here when the building collapses."

"Hopefully the tornado won't come through here," I said, hoping to assuage her. "You know, often they don't even touch down."

"Oh, it'll come through here, all right," continued the poor girl. "And then she'll be sorry. She was only mad about the sick day because she wanted to go cheat with her ex-boyfriend, but she had to work. We all know she's been screwing around since March."

I awkwardly fingered a bag of beef jerky I was thinking about buying.

"That's probably where she is right now," the girl said, to no one in particular. "Down in her ex-boyfriend's storm cellar, making out, while I'm here, about to get sucked up by a tornado! I hate this job. I never shoulda quit working at Diesel-Does-It."

I felt bad. I wanted to stay and console her, but I also kind of wanted to get the heck out of there. "Um," I said at last. "Can I pay for my gas? The credit card thing on the pump is broken."

"It doesn't matter if you pay or not," replied the girl, frowning up at me with a stony look. "We're all going to die, anyway."

She continued to stare at me, and I uncomfortably fished into my pocket, put enough cash on the counter to cover the gas, and backed slowly out of the store.

It was an easy move to flee the area, and leave Tornadoville, Nebraska, to its own problems. At the door, though, something stopped me. Everything wasn't just about me. I turned. The girl had already gone back to angstily texting.

"Hey," I said. She looked up. "Will you remember that I said something?" She eyed me like I was crazy, then nodded.

"Do you really hate your job?" I asked.

She stared at me through streaked mascara, probably wondering what the heck this had to do with anything. Then slowly, she nodded.

"Everything will be fine," I said, sincerely. "I promise. You're not going to die. And sometime later this afternoon, you're going to *realize* that everything will be fine. And when you do, will you promise that you'll really think about what you'd love your next job to be?"

The girl just stood there, then nodded vaguely. I couldn't tell whether it had registered or not. Finally she spoke.

"How do *you* know everything's going to be fine?"

"I'm a Minnesotan," I smiled. "I've been through more tornadoes than you know."

With that, I headed back to the Imposter. The girl watched me all the way to the car, and watched some more as I pulled away.

Within an hour, the rain and wind had lessened. It was still cloudy, but somehow the grayness felt lighter. Less frightening. Almost . . . cheerful.

I turned on the radio and heard that no tornadoes had touched down.

CHAPTER 36

SOUTH DAKOTA

The Spacemobile Lives

From Nebraska, I swung northeast back through the corner of Iowa and slept outside a library near Sioux City. In the morning, for the first time in five weeks, I crossed back into Minnesota.

My mother had driven the finally cooperative Spacemobile from Minneapolis all the way to the tiny town of Pipestone, lodged in the southwestern corner of Minnesota. The town was named, not shockingly, for yielding a type of stone that Native Americans had once made pipes out of. Everyone wants to be known for something.

I had been living for—and yet dreading—this moment. I pulled into the parking lot of the Pipestone Tourist Center and there was my mom, leaning against the side of the weathered van, which could be described as blue, teal, or turquoise . . . it really all depended on how the light was hitting it that day. In the drizzly weather, it looked a sad aqua. I knew it would be tough to leave again.

And it was. But surprisingly, not because of her.

As we poked around the center and took the obligatory tour of how genuine Pipestone Stone Pipes were made, my mom asked me about Sarah. She asked me what I'd been eating. She didn't ask me what I was waiting for her to ask.

As we got back to the cars, I couldn't stand it anymore.

"Mom, do you want me to come back with you?

My mom looked at me like I'd asked her to help me rob a bank.

"What?" she said. "Of course not. You're almost done with your Roadtrip. Aren't you excited?"

"Yeah, of course I am. It's just . . . I don't know where I'll end up, after all this. I don't wanna let you guys down."

My mom nodded. She got what I was feeling.

"Of course I miss you," she said. "But part of being a mother is letting your kids go at some point. I know you'll always be only a phone call away." She paused. "Well, maybe not when you're traipsing around in Montana and Wyoming, but you know what I mean."

She held out the Spacemobile keys.

"Besides," she added. "I didn't drive all the way out to Pipestone for you to wimp out and come back home with me."

In that moment I knew that part of me had almost been hoping my mom would force me to stop this madness and come home. But she wasn't. Her boy was starting his journey into the world, and it was time for him to be a man about it.

"Good luck," she said, hugging me. "Go make us proud."

My shoulders quivered a bit. But my mom stood stolid. Having said goodbye to the last of her three boys when Alex headed off to Brown almost exactly a year ago, she was an old veteran at this.

Under the silver Minnesota sky, my mom held me close. Even though I smelled like death.

No, the rendezvous was tough to leave because I realized I had something else to say goodbye to. The Imposter.

As excited as I was to be getting the Spacemobile back, the trade-out came with mixed feelings. Other than its propensity for getting me into trouble with the police, that little black Ford Taurus with BIGJURY license plates had served me nobly for thirty-five states and 12,000+ miles during five of the most memorable weeks of my life. The sleeping hadn't been so bad (despite certain elements of bad luck), and I had certainly saved a lot in gas money, compared to what I would have done in the gasaholic Spacemobile. The Imposter had handled like a champ through the Midwest, East, and South, and all the ridiculous loops therein, and never once complained. And suddenly, I would miss it.

An Imposter no longer, the Taurus had established itself as the Real Thing.

But now was no time for nostalgia. I had the West to conquer. On this Roadtrip, there was no going back. Only moving ahead.

I missed the Taurus even more as I departed Pipestone and the Spacemobile immediately began to play some of its old tricks. As much as I'd trumped it up, the Spacemobile was in many ways a horrible car. Granted, compared to sleeping in the exposed Taurus, the Mobile was a four-star hotel room, but perhaps I'd built too much of a perfect picture of this car as the paragon Roadtrip vehicle. Because Lord knows it had its share of problems:

- First of all, Volkswagen had modeled the Eurovan after a 1980s German delivery truck. This came in handy when we would assign it to haul entire dorm rooms' worth of furniture across the country, but it also meant the car was geared absurdly low. First gear went from about 0 to 5 mph; second gear went from 5 to 10, and getting the car to 75 practically caused a hull breach.
- Despite this, the Mobile's speedometer went up to 140 mph. Why a German delivery truck would ever need to clock at that velocity was

beyond me—the one time I'd gotten the van to 80 made it shake like a space shuttle re-entering orbit, and even going 70 created a thwopping wind vortex in any open windows, loud enough to mute airplanes and cover the screams of passengers as their eardrums burst.

- There was an engine warning light next to the tachometer that was always illuminated. It had never gone off as long as we'd owned the car. The day it *did* go off was the day we'd worry.

- While the rest of the van was made of titanium mined from Venus, the Spacemobile's bumper was made of Styrofoam and would fly off whenever it bumped anything or when a bird landed on it. As a result, we generally drove around with no bumper at all, giving the back of the car kind of a missing-feature look, like a face with no nose.

- And finally—and this quirk would prove to be by far the most aggravating on the Roadtrip—the Spacemobile had recently developed the habit of simply shutting off whenever the tachometer dropped below 2.5 revs—in other words, whenever I let up on the gas for more than a few seconds. Something with the idle motor, I would later learn. So any time I wanted to coast, or changed gears too slowly, the engine would simply die, and I had to stomp the clutch, crank the key again, and restart the van mid-drive to get my power steering back. This was bearable on the unswerving, cruise-control highways of the Midwest, but soon I would be in the mountains.

There were other issues, like that the emergency brake didn't work and that the car carried the faint but constant odor of baked rubber, but these were the main ones. Amazingly, though the van had just spent most of a month at the dealership, none of these issues had been resolved. What *had* they fixed? There really weren't a lot of remaining options.

But dammit, it was good for sleeping in. The most brilliant feature of the Spacemobile's unorthodox design was that the middle two seats faced backwards, allowing the back row to pull forward and fold down into a queen-sized bed, where three people could easily sleep, or four if they lay on their sides tight-pack slave-ship style. Unlike in the display-case Imposter, in the Spacemobile I could simply crawl into its cavernous back, pin some curtains over the windows, and burrow into my nest of pillows, blankets, and bags. It was like sleeping in a mobile, upholstered igloo.

I glanced back into my new cozy bedroom as the Spacemobile shut off again. It was frustrating to look forward to something for so long, only to have it stall out on you at every turn. But I could still appreciate that one little thing.

I moved into fifth gear, restarted the van at 40 miles per hour, and crossed into South Dakota.

"Juxtaposition" is when two opposite things are placed next to each other, especially for a contrasting effect. I only knew the term because our tenth-grade French teacher, Madame Johnson, had forced us to memorize it when we were studying Impressionist art, as in the muted tones of a classic Monet, juxtaposed with the bright pink piece of bubblegum someone had stuck to it during first period. But the word for some reason echoed in my head as I drove across the giant cornfield that is eastern South Dakota. It could have been the state's quiet, gentle tan landscape juxtaposed with the roaring, audaciously blue van that now thundered purposefully down its highways. Or the way my nostalgic euphoria over saying good-bye to my mom and the Taurus juxtaposed with my annoyance that I had to turn the Spacemobile off and on again every time I hit an intersection.

I was headed for another juxtaposition: eastern South Dakota vs. western South Dakota.

I'd come this way before, on a train ride to a church trip in Idaho, where our bubbly camp counselor constantly reminded us about God's love appearing to her in the rivers and trees and flowers, which generally made us all want to punch her, except that she was so goddamn nice. On the day-long train ride, though, all we teenage campers could talk about was how God must have forgotten about eastern South Dakota, because he hadn't put any people there. Except for Sioux Falls—where a fortuitous combination of lax usury laws and educated, accent-free citizens brought a massive wave of insurance and credit-card companies opening call centers. The city's population had doubled in thirty years. The geographical center of the contiguous U.S. might be in Kansas, but apparently the Standard English center was in eastern South Dakota.

Most of eastern South Dakota looked like a flat, featureless desert, where the sand had been replaced by corn and the occasional Wall Drug sign. Highways went straight for hundreds of miles. And thus we were shocked when we reached western South Dakota and discovered it to be full of tree-covered mountains, scenic rivers, and the fascinating Badlands. We couldn't believe the two halves could be part of the same state. We all agreed that the western half was better, and should clearly secede, except that two is more than enough Dakotas already. Also, nobody wanted to see a horrendous compound-state-name like Southeastern Dakota.

I was headed to Pierre, South Dakota's 14,000-person state capital, to visit my high-school friend Laura. And though it's located squarely in the center of South Dakota—as capital cities are meant to be—Pierre is, unfortunately, a patently eastern South Dakota city.

The most unique thing about Pierre (pronounced "Peer" so as to dissuade any association with the French) is that it's oddly perched precisely on the time-zone divider between Central and Mountain Time, and the region has the strange policy of letting each neighboring city pick which time zone it wants to be in. Laura had her clock set to 4 P.M. because she worked west of the city, but her neighbor, who worked downtown, had his clock set to 5 P.M.

Despite getting to celebrate the New Year twice every year, Laura wasn't too high on Pierre. She'd lived in town for a year and a half after taking the only job she could find with her environmental biology degree. Six months after graduation, she'd left everything and moved from downtown Minneapolis to the middle of South Dakota to start life from scratch. Laura had been simultaneously terrified and excited.

"I told my parents it sounded like an adventure," she told me, as she showed me around town in her car.

"Was it?"

"I guess you could say that. I'm adventuring the heck out of here to grad school in twelve days."

Laura's job—for two more weeks at least—was as an environmental consultant for the government. Most everyone in Pierre did one of these two things, she said: environmental stuff, or work for the government. Except for the not-tiny minority that oversaw the waste dumps between prison sentences. "The dating scene is a little spotty," Laura reported as she drove.

I looked out the window at the little Midwestern capital, trying its best to smile under the dismal sky and sporadic rain. Trimmed, grassy courtyards gave way to a modest capital building with a serene lake beside it. I shrugged. "It seems quaint."

"'Quaint,'" Laura corrected, "is just another word for 'dull.'"

As if for evidence, she pointed to the town welcome sign, which proudly proclaimed the best slogan the town's marketers could come up with: "Pierre! The Capital City!" I swear it really says this.

For dinner and drinks, Laura took me to Longbranch, Pierre's most happening hot spot, where she was afraid to go except when she had friends visiting. We sat at the dimly lit bar working on large hamburgers as a few over-forty patrons milled about.

"It's not really Pierre's fault," Laura admitted. "There just aren't any young people. Every kid leaves the second he or she turns eighteen. The town's all old people and families . . . whose kids leave the second they turn eighteen, because there aren't any young people. It's a vicious cycle. Not quite the place for a single city girl in her twenties."

The bartender came back and refilled my beer mug—for free, apparently, as two-for-one happy hour operated on both Mountain and Central Time.

"I'm sorry it turned out to be such a bust," I said. "At least it motivated you to jump on your grad school applications."

"Yeah," said Laura. "And you know, I guess it was a good experience for an extroverted girl to totally uproot herself. It really taught me some self-sufficiency. Showed me what else is out there."

"Besides," she added. "Can't hurt a mediocre-looking girl's confidence to suddenly get asked out on dates all over town."

Laura was underselling herself—she was actually pretty hot by Minneapolis public school standards. "C'mon," I said. "You're at least a six-and-a-half."

Laura smacked me. I went back to my beer.

"Yeah, but all that stuff's about you," I pointed out. "How *you* changed. Doesn't speak much for Pierre. Sounds like about the worst place in the world to live."

"Well, no, the people are really nice," Laura said. "My work takes me to visit all these random folks, in Pierre, and in the little farm towns all around it. They always invite me into their homes. They're always so open, so genuine, so willing to share their stories. Sure, I meet the occasional toothless hillbilly in a shack somewhere, but they're usually the most fascinating of all."

"Their towns are dying," Laura continued. "And they're trying to preserve their history however they can—even by telling it to a random government employee like me. I guess it's not such a bad job."

"If you don't mind living in the middle of absolute nowhere."

"It's no party town," Laura agreed. "But, I guess I do kind of like the openness. You can see for miles. And the air smells so good. I can't even describe it. It's . . . fresh. Crisp. I didn't notice it at first, when I'd go to work every day, but after a while I started slowing down, and driving with the windows open."

She looked out the bar window, where an oak tree's dark branches scraped the glass. "It's weird," Laura went on. "There aren't many trees, but you start to really appreciate the ones there are. How their leaves glitter in the breeze. And then there are the Technicolor storms .... It's not waterfalls and grand mountain scenery. But it's small beauties. You know what I mean?"

Laura trailed off, not expecting an answer. A shimmer of wistfulness appeared in her eyes as she realized:

"Dammit. I'm gonna miss this stupid place."

I spent the night on Laura's couch, and at dawn, I left Pierre. As the town faded in my rearview, the clouds that had plagued me all through the corn states finally began to break, splitting the sky in two, one half deep gray, the other half burgeoning blue with morning sunshine. A faint rainbow extended halfway across the sky and stopped where the clouds did. I looked around. The low angle of the rising sun painted a vivid world, different than any I'd seen before. The hues of the sepia wheat, the jade grass, and the gold fields all popped in the new light.

On the flat horizon ahead, a grain elevator stood only half an inch tall. I would be there eventually.

Until then, I slowed down, and drove with the windows open.

All at once, the flat fertile farmland of the Midwest gave way to the arid hills of the Badlands as I crossed into western South Dakota. The contrast was as I had imagined. You don't really think of "scenic splendor" when you think of South Dakota, but the western half really does have it all: lakes, mountains, the Black Hills, Mount Rushmore . . . and, on the day I was there, half a million bikers there for the annual Sturgis Harley-Davidson rally.

Here was one more juxtaposition to savor in South Dakota: the last thing I expected to find here was a giant Harley party. Every year,

500,000 Harley-Davidson enthusiasts—in numbers rivaling the population of the entire state—flock to Sturgis for a weekend of trade shows, races, parties, and, well, whatever else bikers do. Every street in Sturgis was lined up and down with motorcycles. The town felt like the set of a post-apocalyptic Robert Rodriquez film, called, I hoped, *Chopper Land.*

I stopped at a crowded saloon for lunch and found myself on the only free stool in the joint, next to a group of fifty-year-old bikers. One of them wore a purple Vikings bandana. My in. Nothing breaks ice better than football kinship.

"What do you do in Minnesota?" I asked.

"I work at a marketing firm downtown," the biker said, tugging at his short graying beard. "I just grew this out the past couple weeks for the occasion. My boss was starting to give me some weird looks, but I'll shave it again for Monday."

The rest of his crew, I learned, consisted of a bartender, a tax attorney, and a hairdresser who had dropped her kids off at school on her hog the day before on her way to Sturgis. They lived all over the country. Most of them rode rarely, some only once a year.

"No, we're no gang," the hairdresser laughed when I asked about it. "We used to party together, in the seventies."

I studied again the sea of leather-clad patrons filling the bar. The room now seemed less like an imminent brawl and almost like a class reunion. Albeit, at a very intimidating high school.

I told the bikers about my Roadtrip. Two of them, a retired couple from Arizona who'd taken Route 66 over from Tucson before cutting north in Amarillo, asked me about my experience on the old road.

"You know," I said. "It was kind of a bust."

"What were you expecting?" the wife asked.

"I don't know. But it felt like just another road. Kind of a shoddy road, at that."

"It *is* just another road," said the husband. "But once it was one of the most beautiful roads out there. We've taken it every summer since seventy-three."

"And now?"

He shrugged. "Once in a while, time's gotta leave stuff behind. It can still be beautiful in memory."

The Minnesota biker brought over another pitcher and poured glasses of beer for everybody, even me. "We have the best highway system in the world, now, thanks in part to that road. It doesn't matter that it's not part of it anymore."

They all held up their glasses.

"It doesn't matter that it's been replaced?" I asked.

The Minnesota biker put down his glass and grabbed the tab before I could offer to pay for my beer.

"A road's a lot like your past. It's only important for where it's led you."

Many of the bikers I saw still cursed, still had beards, and still smelled bad (it's hard not to, when you're in 100-degree heat and wearing leather). And every single bar in Sturgis was *packed*. I guess stereotypes have to come from somewhere. But there was a lot about bikers I didn't know. I suppose my mother would say this was a good thing.

I stopped at a gas station and saw a bunch of cyclists gathered in a circle, holding hands. Not holding hands as they circled tauntingly around a mugging victim. Holding hands in prayer. The backs of all their leather jackets read "Jesus Riders." Granted, they were standing right in the middle of the pumps so that no one else could get gas, but nobody seemed to want to ask them to move.

I passed a sign on the edge of town that read, "Welcome, Bikers— you are a symbol of American independence!" There was something to it, though I'm not sure what the message had to do with the mortgage brokerage the sign was decorating. These people had driven from every corner of the country, on every one of America's roads, to find themselves, or re-find themselves, in a random town in South Dakota. Just like I had. I thought back to my friends on the wharf in Mobile. Maybe America was number one simply because it provided us—all of us—the freedom to do a trip like this. America is a college kid in a van hoping to learn his direction. America is a sweaty biker in a Jesus jacket, gazing up at Mount Rushmore. America is juxtaposition.

I didn't stay and try to talk my way into a biker party. I had to get up to see the four giant stone presidents nearby, and get on with my trip. But the trek to Mount Rushmore provided the most vivid juxtaposition of them all. Motorcycles may be noisy and unsafe, but they're also sleek and reliable, and there could be no greater contrast than the tableau of a thousand roaring Harleys, streaming around the struggling, stalling Spacemobile on the hills of Rushmore, like black ants rushing around a giant dying blue beetle.

CHAPTER 37
NORTH DAKOTA

Gemstones & Dinosaur Bones

The Spacemobile was getting worse. I couldn't even apply the brakes now without the engine shutting off. Also, a short in the horn had incited a minor case of Car Tourette's in which the van intermittently honked whenever the temperature got higher than eighty degrees, much to my embarrassment and the annoyance of every driver around me. I'd stop in traffic and all of a sudden "HOOOOONK! HONKHONK HOOONK!" I'd pull up to a drive-in window, they'd ask for my order, and "Sure, I'd like-HOOOONK! HOOONK! HOOOOOOOONK!" This was a new one, even for the Spacemobile. Fortunately, it didn't start until after I'd put some miles between me and the half million bikers of Sturgis. But I pulled up behind a pickup truck with a gun rack in Bowman, North Dakota, and had to feign rocking out to a Nirvana song on the radio until our stoplight turned green.

I also discovered that I would still have to find motels and Coke machines to charge my phone and laptop; the Spacemobile's cigarette lighter, like the Imposter's, didn't work. Why would it? Nothing in the electrical system was allowed to work.

It was going to be a long next 5,000 miles.

Why had I even wanted the Mobile back in the first place? I guess it was just always the plan. Fine, if the Spacemobile wanted to shut off every time I stopped, then I wouldn't stop. I'd push on to my goal, whether the Spacemobile liked it or not.

The Sprint Mentality was rumbling. But at least the Spacemobile was driving.

For now.

I cut the corner in North Dakota, driving across only the southwest tip, just enough to cross it off my map. It was a cop-out, but as a Minnesotan, I'd already visited North Dakota three times, which might be a world record. And let's face it: North Dakota isn't exactly brimming with notable features, except maybe a shockingly high number of nuclear missiles rumored to be hidden in fake grain silos throughout the state. I read somewhere that if North Dakota were its own country, it would be the world's third leading nuclear power.

Despite my shortcut, the forty miles I drove across the southwestern corner of North Dakota took hours. Construction had reduced the only North Dakota–Montana highway in the area to one lane, and there were lines of cars in both directions waiting to use it. Why so many people wanted to go back and forth between North Dakota and Montana, I couldn't figure, but they were queued up for the opportunity.

After a lot of stopping and starting (which was unbearable in the narcoleptic, honking Spacemobile), I found myself in the unique position of being the first car in line while we waited twenty minutes for it to become our direction's turn to use the road.

Controlling our end of traffic was a wild-eyed man with skin that resembled an old baseball mitt. He didn't have much of a uniform, save a stop sign and an orange safety vest that hung over a sun-faded, sweat-drenched flannel shirt. He also wore a cowboy hat, which I supposed was standard-issue attire for North Dakota transit department workers in the summer. I rolled down my window.

"Hot day for a job like this, huh?" I said.

"Try doing it for thirty days in a row!" yelled the man loudly, though he was only about five feet from the Spacemobile. "It was a hundred degrees most of last week! My name's Sam."

"Hi, Sam," I said. "I'm Paul."

"HOOOONK!" said the Spacemobile.

"Sorry," I said. But Sam didn't seem to mind. "You've been here for thirty days in a row?" I asked. "Don't you get any weekends?"

"Weekend guy's been on vacation," Sam answered. "But I don't mind! Lots of overtime!"

I considered this. "He's been on vacation for a month?"

Sam didn't seem to be listening. "I need the money, these days! Not really gettin' any, from my other job, 'cuz of the scientists."

This seemed too good a conversation not to pursue. "Scientists?" I asked.

"Scientists," he confirmed. "Ever been to a museum?"

"Sure," I said.

"Ever seen those big dinosaur skeletons?"

"Sure."

"Chances are, I discovered some of the bones you saw! That's what I do, dig up dinosaur bones. Found a lot of 'em! I don't know anybody at the museums, so I give the bones to some famous scientist guys, who can get 'em in. But the scientists put their own names on them, and I don't get any credit."

"Where did you find all the bones?"

"Here and there," Sam said. "Mostly in North Dakota. Couple in Montana. They're not real hard to find."

I could think of about a million follow-up questions to this. But I didn't want to break up Sam's momentum.

"HOOONK! HOOOOOONK!" shouted the Spacemobile.

"Sorry," I said. "It just kind of does that."

"That's all right!" said Sam. "I had a car once that oozed soap bubbles out of the vent when I turned the windshield wipers on!"

Somehow I wasn't surprised.

"So you give the fossils away for free?" I asked. "Nothing in exchange?"

"Oh, I get something in exchange," said Sam, his eyes gleaming. "Precious gemstones. The scientists give me precious gemstones in return for the dinosaur bones. That's why I'm okay with the whole situation. Life's pretty darn good. Just that it should be my name on those bones, not theirs."

"Oh," I said. Oddly, it all kind of made sense. "So do you still have the gemstones?"

"Most of them," Sam said. "Sold a couple to the morning-shift guy. He collects 'em. That's where he is right now, off in South America hunting for more!"

"So he's on vacation too?"

"Yup, like three weeks now!" said Sam. "Even more overtime for me! Even in the heat, I don't mind. Gotta make money, if I don't want to have to sell any more of my gemstones!"

"Wait a minute," I said, doing the math. "How long have you been out here?"

Sam looked at me with wide, excited eyes. "Without a break?" he said, "Oh, about fifteen hours!"

Sam grinned at me with his huge jack-o'-lantern smile, sweat dripping down his face, as the pilot car pulled up to lead our line of cars through the construction. Terry in Maine was right: there really are about a million things you can do for money—or gemstones—in this country.

I gave Sam a bottle of water from my cooler, and headed west.

CHAPTER 38

MONTANA

The Spacemobile Dies

Bad Idea #1: Not stopping for breakfast.
Bad Idea #2: Not stopping to charge my cell phone.
Bad Idea #3: Thinking the Spacemobile would last for more than two states.

About ten miles from the Montana–Wyoming border, the van started acting funny. And I mean funnier than the stalling-all-the-time, broken-cigarette-lighter, no-bumper-having act it usually puts on. Things had been going fine as I headed southwest through barren Montana toward Yellowstone, but then, without warning, the transmission started stinking and the engine began topping out at 40 mph, which was slow even for the Spacemobile. And then, at the top of a huge hill on a tiny highway in southern Montana, the Blue Beast came to a halt. I tried to coax it over the crest of the hill, to coast down the other side to the nearest town, but the van just quit. The Little Engine That Could . . . couldn't.

I was incensed. The Imposter had made it through thirty-five states without so much as a peep, and all I did was belittle it. The ability to always keep driving uninhibited—the basic requirement of the whole trip—was the one thing I'd always had control over. And then the Spacemobile couldn't even make it 1,000 miles before dying on me? I mean, clearly it was a bad car, but only being able to make it through two lousy states? The Spacemobile was quickly moving from jalopy to caricaturish mega-jalopy.

I needed a plan. I couldn't call a tow truck; my sleep on the side of the road near Little Bighorn the previous night had afforded no chance to charge my now dead cell phone. I needed to find a city. Or at least a sleazy gas station with a Coke machine. I consulted my two-foot atlas and saw that there was a town called Aberdeen off the exit I'd just passed, at the bottom of the hill I'd just made it 90 percent of the way up. I decided to try to reach it. I should have known better: this was the same map that had suggested there was a tunnel connecting Long Island to Connecticut.

The Spacemobile was facing uphill, on the shoulder of a four-lane highway with a thirty-foot grassy dip between the northbound and southbound roads. Since the transmission was now totally obliterated, I'd have to put the car into neutral and roll backwards until I could get the momentum needed to crank the wheel, do a U-turn, and end up facing backwards on the wrong side of the highway. And that was only Step 1. Why this seemed like a better idea than just putting my flashers on and waiting for somebody with a working cell phone to come along, I can't remember.

Once I was turned around, Step 2 was to get moving again and, before any cars came, gain the momentum necessary to roll down into the grassy median and up the other side. Then I'd be on the highway headed the right way, downhill, at which point I could take the freeway exit at top speed and coast safely into Aberdeen, which I hoped was nearby, although I hadn't noticed it before.

It may have been the worst plan I came up with on the entire Roadtrip.

Amazingly, most of the scheme worked. I managed the U-turn without dying, and after a brief but terrifying moment of rolling the wrong way down the highway, I worked up enough speed to cross the two-lane road and plunge into the median. The Spacemobile careened down into the ditch and up the other side, with only minimal slamming of my body against the driver's door. And then I was out. I took the West Aberdeen exit on two wheels and maintained enough momentum to coast an entire mile into the wilderness, where the town—and my salvation—supposedly lay.

Or not.

There was nothing in Aberdeen. And when I say nothing, I don't mean a house or two and a stop sign. I mean *nothing*. Not even a building. Just some railroad tracks and a small bridge over a filthy creek. Now I wasn't just on some no-name highway in Montana—I was on a dirt road in a phantom town most of a mile away from some no-name highway in Montana. Oh, and it was 105 degrees, and I hadn't eaten since yesterday.

I unbuckled my seatbelt and punched the steering wheel.

"HOOONK!" said the Spacemobile. Apparently the short-circuited horn was still working.

"Shut up. *SHUT UP!*" I yelled, jumping out of the car and kicking the Spacemobile up and down its turquoise belly.

I scanned my surroundings. This part of Montana was mostly hills and few trees, and every inch was brown and baking in the August heat. I was a good distance from any populated roads, the Spacemobile and my cell phone were dead, and I had no hope of resuming any kind of Roadtrip, much less the forty-eight-day kind, until somebody found me. Who knew how long that would take? I hadn't seen a car all day. How could I contact anyone? No one knew to look for me here. No one even knew what state I was in. And even if they did, Montana is huge.

I shook my head to focus. Nobody would rescue me here, brooding, unless I helped myself. After some deliberation, I started walking down the railroad tracks. What was the old saying? "All railroad tracks eventually lead to civilization"? Or was that rivers? Maybe I thought I could find a mine cart and take it east until I met Johnny Green in the sewers of Evanston.

After a few miles I came across a little railroad switch house labeled with a sign: "West Aberdeen." Funny, I hadn't noticed a *Regular* Aberdeen, to necessitate a West one . . . but at least it was a building. I needed an outlet. I kicked the lock off the door of the switch house, figuring it was a victimless crime. There were no outlets. But there was a phone.

Well, *this* was a stroke of good luck. The phone could only make collect calls, so I called my dad in Minneapolis, who put me on hold and called the Minnesota AAA, who put him on hold and called the Billings, Montana, AAA, who put them on hold and called a tow-truck driver. I sat there on hold in my switch house sauna.

"Well what town are you near?" asked the AAA guy finally.

"West Aberdeen," I relayed back.

"Where's that?"

"I have no idea."

"Do you at least know what area code you're in?"

"No. But I'm ninety percent sure I'm in Montana."

After much more of this, a tow truck was finally dispatched. I gave the best directions I could and headed back to the Spacemobile to wait. And wait.

Two hours crept by. I huddled against the side of the van in the Spacemobile's bountiful shadow, drinking the last of my water and milk, starving and fanning myself with the loose pages of my two-foot road atlas.

Another hour passed. The sun rose to its apex, erasing my shade and firing down angry heat on charred Montana landscape. I retreated inside the sweat lodge van, careful to avoid the metal seat belts which were glowing white and imparted instant second-degree burns to the touch. I began to worry that my description of "where the gravel meets the railroad tracks near the town that doesn't exist" might not have been specific enough.

Four hours. I was starting to get dizzy, and resorted to drinking the dingy water out of the bottom of the cooler. I reasoned I had another couple of hours before I became dangerously dehydrated and had to start thinking about siphoning radiator fluid.

What was happening? I couldn't leave the Spacemobile, lest my rescuer show up, find it abandoned, and leave without me. But if someone didn't come soon . . .

I closed my eyes. A heavy, helpless feeling rolled over me. Exhausted and defeated, I fell asleep in the Spacemobile.

"Ah! There you are!" came the voice. I forced open my bleary eyes and drank in the picture of a man in navy coveralls, standing in front of the most beautiful flatbed tow truck I'd ever seen. Frank, his nametag read. My savior.

"I thought you meant the *other* Highway Ninety!" said Frank. "Why would you be a mile off a local highway when there's a perfectly good interstate two miles over?"

I pulled myself out of the Spacemobile's teal belly and slid down into the gravel. I probably looked dead.

"It's a long story," I said.

But Frank just smiled. "We got a long ride."

Frank loaded the Spacemobile onto the back of the old flatbed, which was something of a feat, like loading an aircraft carrier onto a larger aircraft carrier. He had driven, I learned, the ninety-five miles down from Billings once already and searched for me all over before giving up and driving back, only to be called and yelled at by my mother who had learned that her son was marooned somewhere in southern Montana. Frank handed me a Gatorade from his cab, which apparently he'd brought for me all the way from Billings, and instantly became my new best friend.

"Sorry about making you drive down twice from Billings," I said, climbing into the cab with him.

"Oh, that's okay," said Frank. "I get paid whether I find you quickly or not!"

We headed to Billings, which Frank said was the closest place to get repairs. I was definitely in the West now. In New Jersey you can't even blow a tire without being able to coast into three auto shops.

The drive took two hours because the enormous flatbed could only go 50 miles an hour with my possession-packed Spacemobile on the back. I told Frank about my Roadtrip, and he regaled me with tales from his years as a wrecker driver, a mostly defunct profession which is part tow-truck driver, part ambulance, and part hearse.

"There was this one couple, I guess the guy fell asleep at the wheel, and they drove right off the road and through the metal guardrail cable on the side of the highway," Frank said. "The cable cut right through their car, literally sliced it right in two. Went right through the passengers, too. When we found the car, their legs were still in it, but I had to walk a good hundred feet into the brush to find their torsos."

"This other guy," Frank went on. "Oh, man! Had a head-on collision in his convertible with a semi-truck. Wasn't wearing a seatbelt. Splattered so much, we only found his shoes."

I ran my hand down to make sure I was buckled in.

"You've got some pretty good stories," I said. "How'd you get into this line of work?"

"Oh, you know, same way anybody gets into anything. I didn't always dream of being a tow-truck driver or anything, if that's what you mean," he chuckled to himself. "But sometimes the road you end up on turns out to be the right one."

The rig went over some particularly prominent railroad tracks and I watched out the back to make sure the Spacemobile didn't get bucked off the back.

"At first, my family wasn't sure about me being a driver. Neither was I. But it pays okay. And you know, it's the things I never expected that I like the most. Like being independent, out here on the road. Or the stories. I didn't know until I started doing it, but it really suits me."

We passed a deer-crossing sign, and Frank slapped his knee and laughed. "Oh, and that reminds me! This other guy in a convertible? Hit a steer that had wandered out onto the road, going ninety. Some of the parts," he chuckled again. "We never did figure out which one they came from, cow or guy."

We arrived in Billings, and Frank dropped me off at a repair shop, told me my AAA membership would cover the tow, and drove off with a wave and a smile.

That was the end of the good news.

Billings is a relaxed Montana city with about 100,000 people, not a lot going on, and an attitude of being perfectly fine with that. Upon knocking on the repair shop door and asking a few passers-by, I learned that since it was after 4 P.M. on Friday, everyone had gone home for the weekend. Nobody could look at the Spacemobile until Monday. It appeared I would be spending the weekend in Billings, as opposed to splashing happily in the mountain streams of Yellowstone.

Despondent, I did something I had so far not done on the Road-trip: I got a hotel. It was partly out of self-pity, and partly out of unwillingness to reduce myself to sleeping in the roasting hot Spac-emobile in a repair shop's front parking lot. Billings's Motel 6 was all the way across town, and I took a cab. I was too beat to do anything else. I didn't want to explore Billings. I'm sure it was a fine town, but I didn't want to be there. I left a quick message for my parents, who had escaped to our cabin for the weekend after they'd found out I was all right. Once again, I was on my own. I sat down on the edge of my Motel 6 bed and sulked.

What now? I only had a couple hundred dollars left. How could I pay for the Spacemobile? I didn't know what was wrong with it, but it was bad—Frank made that clucking and whistling noise when he looked at it, and this was a guy who used to pull charred arms from car wrecks. Even if I could get the car fixed, tackling the entire West in a week was already a tall order, and now I might have to kill three days in Montana.

I had started the trip with two goals: (1) To drive to all forty-eight contiguous states, doing something memorable in each, and (2) To do it in forty-eight days. As I had promised Sarah. As I had promised myself. Now these two things seemed at odds. If I stayed in Billings for three days, there was no way I could do both. Is finishing something in time worth sacrificing other goals in the meantime? What do you do when your goals collide?

And then there was the possibility that the Spacemobile wasn't repairable. Was there a chance I would never make it to forty-eight states at all?

I turned off the hotel light and went to sleep, even though it was only 8:30. Right then, no goals were being accomplished, and thinking about it was driving me insane.

Oh, and I was trapped in Billings, the groin of the Northwest.

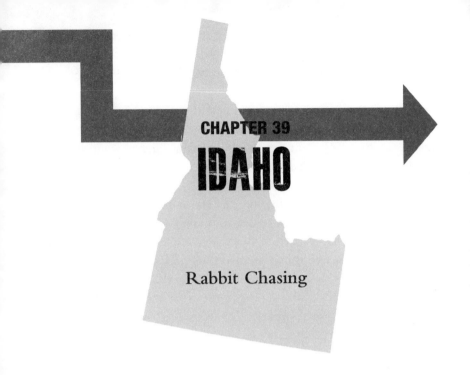

CHAPTER 39
IDAHO

Rabbit Chasing

I woke up the next morning with a new energy. A dark, competitive energy. This wasn't the first time two goals had clashed.

Freshman year of college, I showed up on campus and discovered that I had somehow talked my way onto the bottom of Northwestern's varsity baseball roster. Make no mistake, there was a big difference between me and all my square-jawed, piles-of-man-flesh teammates who came from around the country to collect their scholarships and tear baseballs in half. I was just a skinny lefty with a curveball. I was what you called a "preferred walk-on," but apparently the "preferred" part meant something, because when all the regular walk-ons came and went without making the team, I was still there. The coach made it quite clear that I was pitcher number eleven out of eleven, and that my role would consist primarily of ball-shagging and bench-warming. But it didn't matter. I had landed my dream of playing college baseball.

But I had another dream: experiencing college. And after three weeks of 5 A.M. lifting sessions followed by two hours of conditioning, four hours of class, five hours of practice, and then six hours at the library before I collapsed into bed while my hall-mates were emerging from their rooms to play beer-pong and GoldenEye all night, I realized that goal number two was stalling out before I could even fall asleep.

The solution was obvious: quit the team. It was apparent by this point that all the spots on the Major League ball-shagging rosters would be filled by guys with bigger biceps. All the free shwag was nice, and it was about to be Free Cleats Week, but baseball had stopped being fun for me.

But I couldn't quit. To me, another solution was just as obvious: I would simply work harder, and nail both goals. I'd reduce my sleep to DaVinci-style half-hour nap cycles, make my studying more efficient, and learn how to chug a Busch Lite and do pushups while cramming for a sociology final and playing New Tetris.

Miraculously, for a while at least, it worked. My performance in both areas suffered a bit, of course, but basically I was pulling it off. My grades weren't awful, my curveball was biting harder, and at least I had more friends than the guy in the single across the hall with a life-size poster of Moby on his door. I was living everyone's life at once. Of all the hard workers at a competitive school in the Protestant Midwest, I was the hardest working of them all. Life wasn't exactly fun, but I was pretty proud of myself.

There were times to take it easy. Those times were Thanksgiving break, and when I was dead. And then, there were times to push it. This was one of those times.

This was one of those times. I packed my things in my motel room in Billings. *I had tried to take it easy, tried to go with the flow. And where had it gotten me? To a coffee shop in Oklahoma? Going with the flow was for people too weak to control things. The world had tried to slam the door on my Roadtrip. Well, to hell with the world. I would do it anyway.*

Paul Jury

The baseball story did not have the ending I dreamt about. One afternoon, the head coach called me into his office and gave me the news that was no surprise to anybody. I was the eleventh pitcher out of eleven, after all. I thanked the coach for the opportunity, rubbed the bags under my eyes, went home, and slept for two days.

I had refused to cut either of my divergent goals. So one of them had to cut me. But it wasn't because they were divergent, I told myself. It was simply because I had been born with a fastball that was 5 miles per hour too slow. Something I couldn't control.

This time, I *had* control. It didn't matter if my arm was weak. My accelerator leg was strong. I would have both my dreams. This time, I wouldn't get cut.

I just had to figure out how.

I called a cab to take me back to the repair shop and was picked up by the same cabbie in a station wagon who'd transported me to the motel the night before. Apparently there's only one taxi in all of Billings, and he's it.

There the Blue Beast still stood, like a giant metal coffin. There had to be some way to resurrect it. The repair shop was closed, but the house next door shared a yard and a gate. I banged on the door, and found the owner of the shop.

I explained my dilemma. The owner was sympathetic—my story was more fun, he said, than the stories most folks had about why their cars were busted in Montana. He agreed to take a peek at the van, even on a Saturday. Billings might not be the most happening town, but the people sure were hospitable.

The owner poked around the Spacemobile's engine and underbelly, and came up with mixed news.

"Well," he said, scratching his sweaty head underneath his trucker hat. "Looks like it's the transmission, all right."

This was bad.

"But," he went on. "I can probably get it fixed for you by end of Monday."

This was good.

"It's gonna be around two thousand bucks."

This was very bad.

The owner stroked his goatee and regarded the Spacemobile like it was a terminal patient and we were discussing whether or not to pull the plug.

"What'd'ya wanna do?"

"Can you give me a minute to think about it?"

"Sure."

I grabbed a pen and a pad of Motel 6 letterhead from my bag and sat down in the shade of a tree. It was time for a plan. A zany plan. Hey, just because I'd decided to push it didn't mean I couldn't still be creative.

I sketched out and rejected many ridiculous plans that afternoon, including flying back to Minnesota to get the Imposter, scalping the Spacemobile for bus tickets, and one hare-brained scheme that involved renting a U-haul big enough to cram the Spacemobile inside of it, which would have cost about a billion dollars and violated several laws of physics. None of the plans involved hanging out at the Motel 6 in Billings all weekend.

At last, I came up with something that might work. I left the Spacemobile at the shop, turned on my freshly charged cell phone, and called every rental car company in the phonebook. The only way this plan was feasible was with a rental with unlimited miles, and the only company that would rent a car with unlimited miles to a twenty-three-year-old with an out-of-state ID and four speeding tickets on his record was Alamo. With the last pennies on my debit card, I booked a two-day rental, hung up, and pledged my lifelong devotion to the only rental car company named after a Mexican War defeat.

It was Saturday morning. If I could hit Idaho, Oregon, and Washington in two days—the longest I could afford a rental—I could get back to Billings by Monday noon, pick up the hopefully repaired

Spacemobile, be in Wyoming by dinner, and still have a chance to make it. Renting a car would destroy my budget, but so would booking a plane ticket or fixing the Spacemobile. Anyway, there was a chance the Spacemobile was under warranty—Lord knows the dealership in Minnesota had held onto it for long enough. If it wasn't . . . well, I'd cross that bridge when I came to it.

My atlas told me I had 2,000 miles to cover in just over forty-eight hours. It would be pushing it. But maybe the time for pushing it is when your goals are on the line.

I took the station-wagon cab up the Rimrocks, the cliff that divides Billings into its Valley and Heights areas. The sandstone rocks were tinged crimson, as if licked by the flames of an inferno, and I set my mind to the task ahead. It was time for a new game: How Many Miles Can You Put on a Rental Car in Two Days? Somehow, Forty-Eight States in Forty-Eight Days had turned into The Entire Northwest in Forty-Eight Hours, but at least it had the same numerical theme.

The cab dropped me off at Alamo, and I picked up the only car they had left. Yup, you guessed it. Another Ford Taurus.

Long live the Imposter.

I spurred my new beige Imposter all the way to Yellowstone by dusk. I found Old Faithful as the pink sky was beginning to fade behind the silhouettes of sparse birches and pines that guarded the geyser. Old Faithful had just finished erupting, and wouldn't again for another ninety minutes. I wanted to wait, in the otherworldly gloom, and talk to the other lingering spectators, to be that guy who pesters tourists about where they're from and what their stories were. But I had to keep moving. I didn't have time to wait for a geyser.

I plowed through the night across the corner of Wyoming and into Idaho, making it halfway across the state to Craters of the Moon before I couldn't stay awake anymore. The night was calm and perfect for sleeping outside, and I decided to sleep right on the hood of Imposter 2, after giving it a few minutes to cool down.

Craters of the Moon is a geological anomaly in the otherwise green Idaho prairie, an area where for a few miles the terrain consists entirely of black volcanic rock, often in crater shape. I opened my eyes right before dawn, as a deep purple sky was beginning to emerge behind the jagged black horizon. Warm air brushed my face. It felt like I was waking up on another world. I was probably the only person around for 100 miles.

I took a quick hike through the surreal landscape. But I couldn't stay. A fiery red and orange sunrise burned behind me as I got back into Imposter 2 and climbed into fifth gear. I didn't have time for a sunrise. I could watch it as I drove.

Four states in forty-eight hours. Then forty-eight states in forty-eight days. I didn't know what any of it had to do with my direction, but I didn't have time to think about it. I just needed to finish. People were expecting me to finish. *I* was expecting me to finish.

Daylight assumed full command of the sky as I flew across lower Idaho. If I was going to make it around the entire Northwest—an area the size of France and Germany put together—in two days, the No Speeding Rule would have to go. But this wasn't the Autobahn, and I had to be careful. It was only a year from my two tickets in twenty minutes in Iowa and Illinois. I'd never had much luck with speeding tickets. Especially in states that began with the letter *I*.

It was time to pull a move from my old bag of speeding tricks. It was time to go rabbit chasing.

Rabbit chasing is the art of finding a speeding car going your direction and simply following it, so that if anybody gets pulled over, it's them. It works pretty well, assuming the rabbit doesn't get nervous that you're following them and release an oil slick.

Driving through rural Idaho at 7 A.M. on a Sunday morning, it took me a while to find a rabbit. Heck, it took me a while to find another car, much less a speeding one. At last, a black Ford Mustang pulled onto my road from an adjoining highway and laid a patch of rubber as it tore off across the potato state. He must have been late for church.

My rabbit began to speed, and I began to follow. I think the speed limit was around 70; we were in the high 80s, and the rabbit showed no signs of slowing down. In fact, he was accelerating. Around curve after curve I chased him, and on each straightaway he emerged going even faster than the one before.

This continued for some time, the engine of the Imposter 2 now reaching a high, hypnotic hum. All around me the idyllic Idaho sky, blue like an infinite sapphire and lumpy with occasional bright white clouds, stretched away in all directions over verdant fields rising into distant auburn mountains. I hadn't checked my speed in a while, and coming around one last curve, I realized something was different. The straightaway was a long one—a several-mile empty stretch through flat farmland—and my rabbit opened it up. I was really cruising, but he was pulling away. Fast. I looked around and noticed that the mountains on either side of me were moving in an odd way. I looked ahead, and the road seemed to be converging with a strangely rapid sort of parallax. I looked at my speedometer. I was going 115 miles an hour.

Funny thing was, I wasn't even close to keeping up with my rabbit. He was pulling away now at an unmatchable pace across the central Idaho dragway. He must have been going 140. Possibly 150. He flew around a bend and I spotted him from the side—his car was almost a blur. I took my foot off the gas, set the cruise control at a modest 98 mph, and let my rabbit escape.

Pushing it was one thing, but having Frank the wrecker driver pull my maimed limbs from a smoldering wreck in Idaho was pushing it too far.

CHAPTER 40

OREGON

Damn Hippies

There are those who call Oregon a hippie state. Heck, even some of my college friends *from* Oregon did, and certainly anyone from Seattle or San Francisco. The image this paints for those of us from the rest of the country is a stereotype of unshaven, aging flower-children who live in vans and eschew the establishment and personal hygiene. It's these hippies who would give Oregon a bad name.

But I didn't see any of these hippies in Oregon. In fact, I didn't see much unusual at all, except that the state won't let you pump your own gas—an attendant has to come out and do it. But New Jersey does the same thing, and come to think of it, not having the freedom to pump your own gas seems distinctly *un*-hippie. The only other culturally unique thing I did was to buy knock-off Nike running shoes for $10 off the back of a truck, to finally replace the ones I'd lost in Florida. But you could argue that this reflects more on me than it does on Oregon; the guy selling the shoes was just being entrepreneurial.

Had all the hippies died out? No, more likely, what hippies there are in Oregon—and everywhere else—have simply evolved with the times. They still love peace, trees, and voting Democrat. They've simply traded their shitty vans for Toyota Priuses, their bra burning for liberal blogs, and their pot for better pot bought with medical marijuana cards. Hippies don't die. They just buy MacBooks.

But the smelly, tie-dyed, Man-hating hippie I was on safari for . . . doesn't exist anymore. Okay, maybe a few of them do. Mostly near Eugene.

I flew at a demon pace across Oregon. But speeding or no speeding, I was still determined to do something in every state. Even if it was only for a few minutes. I ate a quick meal at a terrible barbeque restaurant near La Pine that seemed suitable for my unshaven state of degraded cleanliness, and headed to Crater Lake. I figured I could multitask, taking in the sights while jogging around the lake's scenic rim. Yes, I was even going to keep training for my marathon during this madness.

Crater Lake is a huge glacial pool carved out of the top of an ancient mountain, where a volcano had blown out a conic indent that soon filled with crystal blue water. There's also a place in the lake where a second eruption caused a smaller mountain to rise and form an island. So basically it's a small mountain coming out of a lake in a valley . . . on top of another mountain. Very mirror-in-a-mirror.

The deep cerulean lake zipped by on my right as I hurtled around its rim, first in the Imposter 2, and then on my feet as I hopped out and ran, quickly putting a mile between myself and the car. Another day I would swim in that water. Another warmer, less-rushed day.

I was pulling it off. I could scarcely believe it: I was soaring across the Northwest, getting scenery like this, and was still on pace to make it back to Billings. My Type-A side was in blissful overdrive.

Unfortunately, I was about to experience another Sprint Mentality side effect. This time, a gastronomical one.

Have you ever started a run, and a short way into it you discover that the jostling has unsettled a mass of food you didn't even realize you were carrying? Not nausea. Unfortunately, I'm talking about the other direction. Apparently, the heavy load of greasy barbeque I was toting was not in the mood for jogging.

A mile and a half from Imposter 2, I was in trouble. The forces of gravity were working strongly, and Crater Lake wasn't exactly lined with porta-potties—or even their vividly named Oregonian cousins, Honey Buckets. Making it back to the car would involve another mile of jogging, and I didn't know if my system could handle that kind of turbulence. Even if I made it, there was still the thirty-minute drive to the nearest bathroom. The demands on my gastronomical fortitude would be immense, and failure would mean a disappointing disaster for my shorts and possibly the rental car's upholstery.

In tough times you have to make tough decisions. My tough decision involved a small hole, a pile of fallen leaves, and the cover of a pine tree a few yards off the Crater Lake rim road. I can't say I'm proud of this turn of events—the words "defacing a national monument" kept coming to mind—but you do what you have to. It was a huge tree, and I convinced myself it wouldn't mind one little donation of unsolicited fertilizer.

In the middle of my offering, a car drove by, the first I'd seen in hours. I froze, caught in the headlights of the driver's disgusted glare. There I was, unshaven and squatting against a pine tree, clutching a pile of leaves, wearing knock-off running shoes I'd purchased off the back of a truck.

"Damn hippies," the driver undoubtedly told his wife in the passenger seat. "Always giving Oregon a bad name."

CHAPTER 41

WASHINGTON

Revenge of the Sprint Mentality

If I'd been giving prizes, Washington might have received the Favorite State of the Roadtrip Award. Not because it was necessarily the most scenic, or because I had the best experience there, but because I left wanting more.

I soared across northern Oregon and southern Washington into the Yakima Valley, where desert, mountain, and river collide. Crisp highways snaked between mountains on one side and rivers on the other. It was some of the most splendid scenery I'd encountered. Or at least it seemed that way, as I blew through at 90 miles an hour.

I stopped in Desert Aire to visit my aunt and uncle, skidding into their driveway on two wheels. We had a nice dinner together while their articulate pet parrot, Goomby, squawked things like "Braaack! Daryl goes to church!" Then, after an hour, I announced that I had to go. Every store in Billings closed exactly at 5 P.M., I explained, and if I didn't have the rental car back the next day, I'd have to pay $100 for another day, and would not be able to get the Spacemobile back until Tuesday, setting my trip one more day behind schedule.

My aunt and uncle regarded me in a 60 percent amused, 10 percent disappointed, 30 percent confused kind of way. I felt simultaneously guilty and grateful for their hospitality. I wished I could have stayed longer and taught Goomby some biker lingo. I could have learned from my aunt and uncle. They were good Christian folks, motor-homing it around the country and the world, helping wherever they felt they were needed. They'd lived on an Indian reservation, in the African bush, and in Las Vegas, which was probably the most dangerous of the three. And I was their crazy nephew, flooring it around the country on his crazy mission, helping only himself. But I think they at least appreciated that I had driven all the way out from Montana just to have dinner with them.

I raced northeast toward the national parks at the tip-top of Washington, where my high-school friend Katie was working at an environmental camp. There were no highway patrol on those Washington roads—they were all off guarding the Oregon border, keeping the hippies out. I was invincible. Imposter 2's engine hummed the high pitch of progress.

It was now Day Forty-Four. If I kept up this pace, I could get the Spacemobile and still have three days to make it down to Los Angeles and around to Four Corners and have a shot at Forty-Eight Days. I would have to nix Seattle—there was no way I could get there and back on schedule without the aid of a time machine. But all three of the people I knew in Seattle were coincidentally away this weekend anyway, I told myself. I was sad that my once-touted Miami–Seattle leg now included neither Miami nor Seattle. But you have to skip a few things if you want to reach your goals.

I met Katie at a bar in the mountains about thirty miles from the Canadian border. The walls were logs, and there was a full bear-skin hanging on the wall next to the jukebox, supposedly shot by the guy who'd built the place. Now *this* was a mountain bar.

After half a case of beers with moose on the labels, we walked to where Katie was staying, and four hours later she kicked me from her bunk as her alarm went off. It was still dark outside.

"You're insane," said Katie, as I hauled myself out of bed and dressed, rubbed the bags out of my eyes, and said goodbye.

In one eighteen-hour binge of hellish driving, I'd covered Oregon, Washington, and Idaho. In one day, I'd logged 1,100 miles, including stops at Crater Lake, Desert Aire, and Mountain Man Pete's Saloon for Manly Lumberjacks. I was exhausted, but I was doing it. Life wasn't exactly fun, but I was proud of myself.

I catapulted across the skinny top part of Idaho, and dug my foot into the accelerator.

It was only 600 miles to Billings.

I could make it.

And then I saw the flashing red and blue lights in my rearview.

I've never had much luck, with speeding. Especially in states that begin with the letter *I*.

In a tiny town in upper Idaho, I got my fifth speeding ticket in three years.

So much for my driver's license.

So much for the Roadtrip.

It was a nitpicky ticket—a speed-trap coming into a tiny town where the limit suddenly drops 10 mph and a squad car is waiting there to snag you if you don't promptly brake. But it was still a ticket. I had gone back to sprinting. And now I was in deep trouble.

The white-mustached cop had taken my license back to his squad car with him, along with those dreaded, familiar words: "I'll be right back with your ticket." How did this even work? If you were caught driving with a suspended license, I imagined the police simply arrested you and took you to the nearest jail. But what if your license was *about* to be suspended? Would I be arrested? Or would he simply tear up my license and roll my car into a ditch?

Childhood advice from my dad should have covered this. "Watch your speed coming into small towns," my dad would always say, along with, "Always look for the win-win situation," and, "If you drink the last of the apple juice again, I'll slit your goddamn throat." Dad was a fountain of wisdom.

After an abnormally long time, the cop meandered back up to Imposter 2. For a moment, he stood there.

"Seems you've got a few tickets on your record already." I waited for him to take out the handcuffs.

"Yes sir," I replied.

"You should think about slowing down."

"I have been, sir."

"Not hard enough, apparently," the cop said.

I sighed. Not hard enough indeed.

"I guess not."

The officer's radio squawked something about returning to head-quarters. The cop listened, then hastily handed me the ticket with, amazingly, my license.

"Your home state DMV will be in touch about this." And he walked away.

Huh? What did that mean? Five tickets meant my license was suspended—I had been quite meticulous in researching this on the Minnesota DMV's website before I left. Didn't he have the right records? Was there some kind of court period? Would another cop be along to arrest me, as soon as the Bonner County police cleared up whatever Monday morning fiasco they had going on at headquarters? Maybe a scruffy-looking kid was sleeping outside a day care center.

One thing was clear: it was only a matter of time before the Minnesota DMV came looking for my license. Would I be forty-six states in when the bureaucracy caught up, and they'd have a blockade waiting for me at a state line? I didn't want to go to jail. My resume was spotty enough already.

I looked at the clock. The ticket stop had eaten up more than a half hour. It was almost noon, and Billings was still 600 miles away. It was too late to return the rental car today, even if I wanted to keep going. And I no longer wanted to.

I was a fool to think I could make it. I had it all backwards—by stubbornly refusing to give up my silly, rushing-it goal of forty-eight days, I'd now killed my chance of reaching forty-eight states. I had refused to cut either of my divergent goals. So they had to cut me.

Not knowing what else to do, I sat in Imposter 2 on the side of the road in upper Idaho. I felt like crying. I'd failed at things before, but this one felt deeper. I'd tried so hard to conquer something inside myself, and come so close, but come up short.

I recalled another piece of advice my dad had given me. "You can't keep pushing and pushing the world," he said. "Because eventually, the world pushes back. And you're not stronger than the world." Well, I had pushed. And the world had pushed back.

And now what? Drive back to Minnesota and turn myself in? Fly to Chicago and tell Sarah she'd won by default? If I'd learned anything on this trip, it's that the best things happen when I followed the least-expected road. And so I stopped pushing, turned away from going forward, and headed up instead. Into Canada. Just for a while. Just to escape. Just so I could say I did forty-one-states, plus Canada, in . . . well, however long it took.

The border-patrol officer checked my ID, smiled his Canadian smile, and let me through his white gates. Apparently, Canada's pretty chill about people with recently suspended licenses.

I didn't know where I would go or what would happen. But it was no longer my call. So I did the only thing I could think of. I kept driving and driving, until I found a peaceful mountain stream—cold, gushing, and silver under the cool sunset that bounced dancing orange light off the flowing water.

I dove in.

Afterward, I sat on a rock, pulled out my laptop, and wrote about everything that had happened. The hilarious. The terrible. No matter what, it was a decent story. And despite everything else, just sharing it made me happy.

CHAPTER 42
WYOMING

Cowboy Country

I sat for a while by the mountain stream in British Columbia, then quietly got back into the Imposter 2 and returned to America. I had to get the car back to Billings and deemed it unproductive to be caught with a suspended license and stolen rental car in a foreign country. (Though if there was any prison where I stood a chance of getting jail-yard respect for my skinny-white-guy toughness, it was Canadian prison.)

I slept near a peaceful lake in northern Montana that night and rolled back into Billings the next morning. I figured I'd return Imposter 2 first, hoping my terminally ill bank account could survive at least the rental fee. My debit card swiped clean, and I signed for the three-day charge with a strange sense of detachment. I was screwed every which way at this point, I reasoned. *What was another $100?*

I walked the three miles down the Rimrocks and back to the repair shop. I still hadn't come up with a way to pay for the Spacemobile's new transmission, but I had to check on it. I could at least try to convince the repair shop staff to let me live in it, under a freeway overpass somewhere, until my driving record regenerated.

The owner wasn't around at the shop. Instead, a young brunette behind the counter smiled as I came in.

"Big blue Volkswagen, right? I think she's ready. Same card we got on file?"

Before I could even respond, she disappeared into the back. The girl was about my age, and cute. The kind of girl I might think to flirt with, if I didn't have a girlfriend, if I wasn't going to be in Billings for only five more minutes.

There was no one else in the shop. I spied the exit. What would I do if I couldn't pay for the Spacemobile? *Wash dishes*, my brain offered. What? This wasn't a restaurant. I wondered if the girl and her boss would put me to work changing oil or refilling tires to pay off the debt. I was going to spend the rest of my days as an auto mechanic in Montana. At least that would take care of my direction thing.

"Here you go," said the girl, coming back with the receipt and van keys. She smiled. "You're all set!"

Well, *this* was strange. I had checked my balance in South Dakota, where it was down to less than $500. Enough to cover the rental, and the gas I'd used since then, but certainly not the $1,945 repair charge on the yellow receipt the girl held out. Had there been a mistake? Should I say something? Instead I stumbled clumsily to the door, tossing a quick smile over my shoulder. I'm pretty sure she never picked up on my idea of flirting with her.

I jumped into the Spacemobile, cranked the engine, and felt the newly reassembled transmission engage and pull me forward. How many miles can you put on a rental car in just over two days? 2,043, according to the pink Alamo invoice I pulled out of my pants pocket and threw onto the dashboard. And how quickly, after getting your regular car back, can you get the heck out of Billings? Two minutes.

Why had nobody come after me about my license yet? And why had my debit card swiped clean for the Spacemobile? Random auto shops in Montana seemed like exactly the kind of thing the fraud censors should be protecting against.

Cautiously I piloted the Spacemobile south, taking advantage of this mysterious opportunity. I wanted to get a feel for how it was driving. Not bad. They'd even fixed the Tourette's horn, to the good fortune of the driver ahead of me. Of course, the engine was still shutting off randomly in the middle of the highway—no repairman in the world could fix that. Sadly, I was beginning to get used to it, the way a person with one leg gets used to hopping.

I dialed my parents.

"Um, so I got the Spacemobile back," I rambled into their message machine. "And survived the Northwest. Mostly." I searched for more words. "Um, would you let me know if the DMV calls? Or . . . the bank?"

I hung up, then immediately called back and left a better message explaining everything. They would find out anyway. I hoped they wouldn't be too disappointed.

I put the phone down and realized I didn't know where I was going. But I didn't care. I was content just to be going. I hit the Wyoming border, and this time the Spacemobile made it across. There was no border patrol waiting. I wasn't supposed to be driving, but it seemed like a victimless crime, so to hell with what I was supposed to do: I would just drive.

So I drove. I had no plan. And for the first time in my life, I didn't make one.

That evening I came across Cody, Wyoming. At 8,000 residents, the city was still in the top ten for population in the country's least-populated state. The whole town smelled faintly like manure, but somehow in a good way. And the sign at the town boundary read, "Welcome to Cody, Rodeo Capital of the World!" It was a fairly brazen proclamation, but there probably aren't a lot of places outside of Wyoming vying for the title. Another sign followed: "Cody Rodeo Night: Tonight!" I had to admit, Cody was certainly backing up its talk.

If there was anywhere in America to roam around like an outlaw, this was it.

This was frontier country, a place where only a century or two ago people came to flee the east and toe the boundary of the unexplored. "Frontier" seemed a strange concept—besides the potential glory of getting a mountain named after you, why would anyone want to live in a frontier? The very word, by definition, means sleeping in weird places and freezing and being alone. But the frontiersmen didn't come west for room service. They came to do their own thing, in a place where nobody had made the rules yet. They came to be free.

I followed several thousand cowboy-hatted, boot-wearing fans into the well-lit Cody rodeo stadium that night. I knew that people in Wyoming didn't dress that way all the time (well, some of them did), but that didn't make me any less conspicuous, trudging through the turnstile in my stinky black shorts, Tevas, and baseball cap. Nobody seemed to care. If there's one place nobody judges you for your attire, it's a rodeo.

As I shuffled to my seat, I recalled that I *did* know someone in Wyoming. My old college friend Philip was rumored to be in the area somewhere, though he hadn't responded to my pre-trip e-mail barrage. I sent off a text message as I sat in the rodeo, and momentarily experienced the full range of what it meant to be a modern American.

The event began with a gunshot and a surge of beasts and boys, and lasted for nearly two hours of rural, rowdy, random fun. I had no idea what was going on as a cowboy tried to rope a steer that was chasing a clown around a barrel. Maybe nobody really understands what's going on at a rodeo.

I watched as cowboys performed various feats of cow-related agility on the dirt stage in front of thousands of adoring fans. Here, finally, were the rugged adventurers I'd dreamed about. But something was out of place: the cowboys tipped their hats and bowed to the crowd, who'd driven here in minivans with DVD players in the headrests. These men were heroes from another era, transported to a time where their skills were no longer needed, except as a spectacle. Sure, there are a few places where cows still need to be moved, but most of that is done these days by truck and robotic sheep dog. The closest thing to a frontier we have anymore is someplace where you can't get WiFi.

Yet the fans still cheered. Cowboys might be walking celebrations of a dead day, but we still name football teams after them, still make movies about them. Not because of their ability to rope a steer in an age of genetically engineered factory cows, but because of what they stand for. Like the bikers of Sturgis, there will always be a place in this country for anyone who rides free.

The next morning I awoke to a text from my buddy Philip and drove to a funky barbeque place outside Cody to meet him. The waitress gave me a curious look as I strolled in, bearded, grubby, and wearing a Cody Rodeo Night button on my Minnesota Vikings T-shirt.

"Table for one?" she asked.

"I'm here meeting a friend," I said.

"Sure you are." She led me to a small booth.

I glanced around the country restaurant. This was the kind of place where the staff knew each customer's name, and vice versa. The menu was two sides of a stained sheet of paper that seemed like it consisted of randomly selected items from a 900-page cookbook. An old woman daintily sampled her poached egg at the counter to my left, while the trucker next to her destroyed a rack of ribs.

"Don't get the pot roast," said Philip, startling me with a pat on the shoulder. "I heard it's made from the losing horse from last night's barrel race."

Philip slid easily into the booth across from me and grinned. He hadn't changed a bit since college, except that his curly hair had become even longer and was bordering on white afro territory.

Philip had been our dorm's resident philosophy major, and he was widely regarded by our friends as the only person with a degree more useless than mine. But Philip also carried a tall, athletic frame and had played on the club baseball team with me after I'd been cut from varsity. The club team proved to be a much more fitting and tolerable way to balance baseball and the other parts of college: I was used to 9 P.M. curfews before 7 A.M. Saturday pre-games, but as we stepped off the bus at our first club road tournament our president announced, "Okay, 9 A.M. game tomorrow! Be there by 8:45 . . . and if you're drinking heavily tonight, try to drink some water so you're not too hung over. All right, see ya, I'm going to the bar."

Philip was the ultimate triple nonthreat: club-level baseball talent, a vast knowledge of Hobbes and Kierkegaard, and a Thoreauvian environmentalist side. He was the classic, twenty-first-century unemployable Renaissance man that our nation's liberal-arts programs are so good at cranking out.

And his reason for being in Wyoming?

"Greatest job ever," Philip said. "So you know the fire towers they have scattered around national parks? Well, they don't have enough rangers to cover them all, so they hire random civilians to sit up in various towers all day, to radio in at the first sign of smoke. Easiest gig in the universe—I read for twelve hours a day, get paid by the hour, and look around with binoculars every once in a while."

"It's like my own personal reading loft, above the treetops," said Philip. "It's perfect for me while I figure out what I want to do about grad school."

"You just read? That's it?"

"Well, I take the occasional nap," he admitted. "But listen, I want to hear about *you*! I read half of *Moby Dick* today. I need some real people stories."

Philip had been following my blog, but the latest chapter hadn't been posted yet. I told Philip about the ticket, the license, everything. He found it hilarious that I had been cut from my speed quest by the great state of Idaho.

"So how are you holding up?" he asked finally.

"Strangely," I replied, "I'm fine. Though part of me feels like I was supposed to finish the Roadtrip in time."

Philip waved me off. "You weren't *supposed* to do anything," he said. "I hate to say it man, but I think you overestimate how much the rest of the world cares what you're doing."

"Thanks," I said.

"No, I'm just saying. The only one forcing you to do anything is you."

I nodded. The waitress brought me my breakfast skillet.

"There's one thing I still don't understand, though," I said, scooping up a forkful of hash browns. "I get it. I need to relax. But I tried to relax, in Oklahoma and other places. And nothing happened. What about all those people who just go with the flow their entire lives and end up sitting at home, unemployed, doing nothing? Am I just supposed to sit there and wait for the world to provide for me?"

Philip gazed at me thoughtfully for a moment. Then his eyes drifted around the restaurant, where two ranch hands were trying to extend their lunch hour with a poker game. "You know, I've been taking this Aikido class since I've been out here," he said. "On my nontower days, of course. Japanese self-defense. Pretty sweet stuff."

I wondered where he was headed with this.

"So the first day I come in," Philip said. "And the seventy-eight-year-old sensei is there, this little old man, weighs like ninety pounds, tops. He looks around at all of us. Tells us that self-defense is not about being big and strong, because there will always be someone bigger and stronger out there. No, self-defense is about understanding how energy works, and getting it to work to your advantage, and to your opponent's disadvantage."

I went back to my hash browns. Philosophy majors weren't always the best storytellers.

Philip continued. "The sensei scans the room, and his eyes settle on me, the biggest dude in the class. 'You're like big wave,' this little old man says to me. 'If I take you head on, I get smashed. But if I understand your power, and let it flow past me, you go on crashing to shore, and I'm still here. Now. Charge at me.' I glanced around at the other Aikido students. Was this guy serious? I was like triple his weight. Obviously, he was way better at Aikido than me, but he was, like . . . old. Fragile. I didn't want to hurt the little bugger."

Philip was in full story mode. "But the sensei just looked at me. 'Charge at me! Attack with all your strength. Unless, of course, you are frightened.' Well, that did it of course. Heck, I figured, I'd signed my release, I couldn't get sued. I rushed the little guy."

"The next thing I knew, I was upside down, flying across the room. I landed in the corner, against the wall, with my shoulder and neck jammed into the ground. I guess I must have really run at him fast, because he threw me almost all the way into the aerobics studio."

Philip had my attention again, and the attention of the trucker-hat-wearing guy in the next booth.

Philip continued. "'A lot of fighters,' the sensei said, as he sat on my chest, 'attack and attack and wear themselves out. Of course, the answer is not to *never* attack, or else the best you can hope for is a draw. The answer,' this ninety-pound old man told us, 'is to flow with the energy. To dodge and block and defend, and wait patiently for the moment of opportunity, when your opponent gives you an opening. And *then* . . . you strike. With all your strength.'"

Philip's fist shot across the table and stopped an inch in front of my spoonful of eggs. The guy in the next booth startled and dropped his fork.

Philip smiled, grabbed a piece of egg off my spoon, and withdrew his hand.

"Wow," I said at last. "Thank you so very much for clearing that up for me."

Philip shrugged and popped my food into his mouth. "You wanna know what I think?" he said, chewing. "I think something up there is trying to balance you out."

"God's trying to balance me out?"

"Religious folks call it God. Atheists call it coincidence. I call it the universe. Makes it seem more cosmic and awesome that way."

"The universe," I said.

"A lot of people are afraid to push it at all, and never leave their parents' house and their dad's business. So it's good to push it sometimes. Think of all the cool stuff that you never would have done if you hadn't pushed it. Like go to college. Or do this road trip."

"But if you push it too far . . ." Philip went on, "you end up like those ex-cons in Arkansas."

"So?"

"So maybe your default is you attack too much."

The waitress came back and stood over me.

"You ready for your check?"

I looked at Philip. He only had a water. A man after my own heart.

"So the universe wanted me to get cut from Idaho." I said after she'd retreated.

"And baseball, in college," Philip said. "I know you, man. You won't quit on your own, so somebody else has to do it for you. But wasn't leaving baseball exactly what you needed? You joined a fraternity. You joined club ball, which is the only reason you're sitting in this restaurant with me right now. You joined the creative-writing program, which I swear is the only class I've ever heard you talk about."

Philip sat up and stared straight at me, across the table, serious for once.

"And that's the thing I don't get," he said. "This blog, all those plays, everything. You're a writer, man. And you're a planner. How did you never have a plan that involved writing?"

I paused for a long moment. "I did. I guess I was just afraid of failing at it."

Philip grinned.

"You weren't afraid to try to drive a broke-ass van to all forty-eight states," he said. "And that's a *way* stupider plan that trying to be a writer."

Philip and I wished each other good luck, and I drove down the deserted Highway 120 through Meeteetse (population: 321, or 64 people for every 'e') to Thermopolis. Everywhere I went in Wyoming I came across strangely named towns. I guess people had to do *something* to amuse themselves out here, besides going to rodeos.

Thermopolis (Latin for "Hot Town," as in "Hot town, summer in the city," as the song may or may not go) is located right on top of Hot Springs State Park, which boasts the largest natural hot springs in the United States. This exciting fact glosses over one thing: hot springs are hot because of underground sulfur reactions. And sulfur stinks. Thus, the pros and cons of living in a hot-springs city: although your town has endless, free, naturally occurring Jacuzzi water, it smells like a year-round egg fart.

I stopped to think things over at one of the town's public natural spas. I know the "spa" part of that might sound expensive, but trust me, the "public" and "natural" parts offset things a bit. This was no froufrou Beverly Hills spa. We're talking an old-style, dirty-tile spa, like they probably had in ancient Rome. But it was just my speed. I paid my fifty cents and locked myself into my stall with my enormous off-white bathtub, let it fill up with warm groundwater, and plunged myself in.

I held my breath—to lose myself under the hot, silent, earthy water, and also to escape the sulfur smell.

I had failed in my quest for forty-eight days. But I was still alive.

If the universe would let me, I might as well try to finish the other forty-eight quest. Casually. On my own timetable. As the Roadtrip should be done.

And if I couldn't . . . well, I'd still be alive then, too.

For the first time in a month and a half, I shaved. I also did the trip's first laundry, at a Laundromat outside of town. Being a rugged adventurer was one thing, but socking everyone I met in the face with a stink-fist and a visual of a bearded pedophile was another. Everything wasn't just about me.

I hoisted my bloated dirty clothes bag out from the trunk and carried it inside. The thing was practically gurgling gas out of whatever fermentation process was occurring inside, and I earned several horrified looks as I spread the contents out over a few folding tables. Most of the items I washed; a few of them I threw away. This might sound wasteful, but the truth was half my clothes were from junior high, and anyone who knows me would agree that 90 percent of my wardrobe is always five years overdue for the trash heap.

Things were starting to make sense as I left Thermopolis. One mission was gone. But a more important mission might still be possible. However long it took me.

There was just one person who wasn't going to like this.

It took me until late into the night to be able to call Sarah. Reception was surprisingly decent in Wyoming, contrary to the claims of my Verizon map, but I couldn't find an electrical outlet to save my life. I finally gave up and found a payphone outside a gas station near the Utah border. I dusted off my old Chicago calling card.

"Hi," Sarah stated neutrally.

"Hi," I replied, briefly taken aback by her tone. She wasn't anxious, or mad that I hadn't called her in a week. Just distant. "I'm sorry I haven't called in so long. A lot of things have happened."

"I know," Sarah said. "I read about it."

I hesitated, not knowing how to broach this. "Tomorrow's forty-eight days," I said.

"I know."

"And I'm still in Wyoming. I still have six states left. If I even have a license."

"I know."

I took a deep breath. "I want to finish the trip. No matter how long it takes. No matter if I have to walk. I want to keep experiencing things. Forty-eight days doesn't matter to me anymore. But I know it matters to you. That's why I've been putting off this call."

I held my breath, waiting. At last, she spoke.

"You know, I've talked to all my girlfriends about this, because I couldn't talk to you. You don't want to hear what they've said. I know you're going to keep doing this. I know what I should do. What everyone wants me to do."

I steadied myself for the response I had steeled myself against.

"But I can't do it."

This was the opposite of what I'd expected. Sarah went on.

"I love you, Paul. Despite everything. And against all logic, that's what's making me stick in there anyway. The ball is still in your court."

"I don't want the ball to be in my court," I said.

"But it is. And it always has been."

Sarah sighed, like a person worn out from fighting a battle she knew she could never win.

"Just please try to understand. As long as this is the adventure you're choosing, it's going to keep burning. As long as you're off looking for something, I'll know it's not me."

What could I say to that?

"I'm so sorry, Sarah."

"I know."

We hung up. It was the most painful nonbreakup I'd ever experienced.

I was parked outside a phone booth near a tiny town called Mountain View. Even the town names had stopped being funny.

Perhaps not everything *made sense,* I thought, as I finally left Wyoming.

CHAPTER 43

UTAH

Cougar Junk

I wound down through Salt Lake City to Zion National Park, in southwestern Utah, and for a day, I just camped. Well, camped in the Spacemobile anyway, which is closer to a luxury RV than a tent. My first horrible night in the Imposter seemed so long ago. At this point, like a feral child, I would need a while to get used to a bed again.

People tend to picture Utah as rusty and dry, filled with desert and weird, salty lakes. But it's actually a pretty gorgeous state. By all logic, it should be—it shares the same mountains with its neighbor Colorado, a state that people picture as filled with green peaks, bubbling streams, and tanned natives with athletic calves.

Zion is like a green, inverted Grand Canyon, which I'd seen during our childhood tours of Arizona. Instead of a gaping chasm dropping down below you, Zion's majestic, Ponderosa-pine-laden mountain walls rise up on either side of you, cupping you in nature's hands. I hadn't planned it this way, but I was really glad I was seeing the West at the end of the trip. The East has a lot of things going for it, but in terms of raw natural splendor, it simply can't measure up.

I felt like a bandit, holed up in my sketchy van in the mountains with my spoiled license, hiking to look for waterfalls by day, curtaining myself off to type my demented thoughts into my laptop by night. I kind of liked it. I considered staying in Zion forever, but decided I would probably miss HBO.

That evening, my friend Sean and his family arrived in Zion. This was Sean from the Maine musical, and he'd been living in Minneapolis since graduation, waiting tables and taking accompanist gigs and piano students to keep his music career going. He and his family were on their annual trip out west, and I sat up late with Sean and his two younger brothers, Mark and Nicholas, after their parents had passed out exhausted from a day of driving and having to separate three rowdy boys in the back seat.

Our conversation went directly to the most profound subjects.

"This morning I saw a sign that said 'Beware of Cougars,'" piped up twelve-year-old Nicholas as the four of us roasted marshmallows under the warm, black Utah sky. My first mental image was of prurient older women prowling the wilderness for unsuspecting younger male campers, but Nicholas meant the animal. "Are there cougars around here?" he continued, his wide hazel eyes reflecting light from the fire.

"I heard that if a cougar attacks you, you're supposed to fight back," Sean answered.

"As opposed to bears," I added. "If a bear attacks you, you're supposed to curl up in a ball and play dead."

"Why, are there bears around?" asked Nicholas, alarmed.

"No," said Sean. "Just cougars."

A silence. Then Nicholas, timidly, asked, "How do you fight back against a cougar?"

"I heard that if a cougar has you pinned down, you're supposed to punch it in the nose and eyes and stuff." I answered. "And, if possible, kick it in the junk."

"The junk?" asked Nicholas.

"You know what he means," said Sean.

Nicholas was still confused. "Wait, cougars have junk?"

"Male cougars do," I said. "Obviously. I know if I was a cougar, and someone kicked me real hard in the junk, I'd probably stop attacking them."

"What if you get attacked by a female cougar?" Nicholas asked.

"I don't know," I said. "I only know about male cougars."

"What if you get attacked by a bear?" Nicholas asked.

"We told you, play dead," reminded Sean.

Nicholas persisted. "But couldn't you kick a bear in the junk? A male bear, I mean?"

"I think bears are tough enough to take being kicked in the junk," I replied. "It just makes them mad."

"Oh," said Nicholas. This seemed to make sense to him.

Sean had been deep in thought about something. "Do you think cougars ever learn to protect their junk, when they attack people?"

"I don't know if it happens that much," I said.

"But what if it did?" Sean went on. "What if you were a cougar, and you kept getting kicked in the junk, over and over again? Do you think you'd eventually learn to leave a leg crossed down there or something?"

"Maybe if it was a smart cougar," I said. "But then again if he was *real* smart, he'd probably stop attacking people. You know, because we have, like, guns and stuff."

"Or he could wear a jock strap," interjected Nicholas.

"I don't think cougars wear jock straps," I said.

Nicholas insisted. "One might if it was smart enough."

Sean punched his brother in the shoulder. "Where would a cougar get a jock strap? Mauling a baseball team?"

"I dunno. Maybe."

"Why would there be a baseball team in Zion National Park?" I asked.

"Maybe they're traveling to a tournament and wanted to do some sightseeing along the way," said Nicholas.

"Wait a minute," interjected Sean. "Isn't there a brand of jock straps *called* Cougar?"

There was a pause. There might be.

"If a cougar started wearing Cougar jock straps to keep from getting kicked in the junk," said Nicholas, at last, "is that what irony means?"

"You know, Nicholas," said Sean, "that's a very good question."

We sat for a long time in silence. Presently, Sean's dad emerged from the tent and stood by the fire.

"So, how many states do you have left?" he asked me.

"Just Nevada, California, and the Four Corner States, minus this one."

"You're close."

"Yeah," I said. "I hope so." I hadn't told them about the speeding-ticket thing. I didn't want them to think they were harboring a fugitive.

"You know, Mark's graduating this year," said Sean's dad, gesturing at his second son, who until now had been sitting reflectively by the fire, silent. "What would you tell him, now that you've done all this?"

I had no ideas what to say. I considered for a moment.

"Bring two sets of car keys."

But Sean's dad wouldn't let me dodge so easily. "I mean when he graduates."

I thought about it.

"If you know what you love," I said at last. "Go do it. And if you don't ... " Mark looked up. I got the feeling this category fit him better. "Go do something else. Anything else. But do something. See what else is out there."

I gestured around at the starry sky, the beat-up blue van, the friends I'd met up with in this stunning place. "Maybe you'll find out you like it. And if not ... at least you'll know."

Mark nodded, softly, and gazed into the fire. Sean's dad seemed satisfied with my answer. He patted Nicholas's head.

"Time to get some sleep, Nick."

Nicholas tossed his marshmallow stick into the fire and grabbed his flashlight.

"Dad, will a cougar stop attacking me if I kick it in the junk?"

"Who told you that?"

"Sean and Paul. They said unless he's wearing a cup."

"Why would you listen to Sean and Paul?"

"Because they're grownups."

Sean's dad shook his head. "Don't listen to them." He guided Nicholas back to the tent. "But yes. It might stop attacking you."

They disappeared into the darkness. Mark, Sean, and I sat quietly for a moment. I pulled out my cell phone.

"Look at this," I turned to Sean. "Still two bars. How far do you think we are from a city?"

"Who knows. A hundred miles?"

"Jeez," I paused. "Do you guys ever feel like there's a lot of pressure on us to do amazing things, because the world's so easy these days?"

"I dunno," said Sean. "I think it gives us freedom. Like everything cool has already been done, so why worry about it? The pressure's off."

He kicked a lose ember back into the fire with his waterproof boot. All was quiet again. "Hey," I said finally. "Your brother said we're grownups. Do you feel like a grownup?

"No," said Sean. "But maybe you never do. Maybe other people just start treating you like one, and that's what being an adult is."

"Jesus," I said. "God help us all."

Sean, Mark, and I got up and all took turns peeing out the fire. I headed back to the Spacemobile to sleep. Sean's family didn't need one more rowdy boy in their tent.

Perhaps the kid in you never dies, I thought. *He just starts paying property tax.*

There was nothing like old friends to bring him out again.

I said goodbye to Sean's family the next morning, after a breath-taking (and cougar-free) hike in Zion. It was perhaps the most beautiful place I'd seen so far, and it was a shame to leave it behind. But it could still be beautiful in memory.

Southwest Utah is basically all national parks, with few highways of any kind, so I was taking an incredibly strange, serpentine route up through Cedar City when my phone rang and my Roadtrip was given new life.

"I know your message told me not to," said my mother. "But I called the DMV. And they only have a record of four speeding tickets on your record."

"Right, four plus Idaho."

"No, four *including* Idaho," she said. It took a minute for me to realize what this meant. "That Minnesota ticket wasn't on there."

"But . . . how? I missed the deadline for the traffic school."

"They must have accepted it, after all," she said. "Or could be they lost the record. But fate stepped in for you. In the form of DMV bureaucracy, I guess."

"So . . . ."

"You're not going to get your license revoked," she paused. "Unless, of course, you get another ticket."

"Absolutely not," I said. "I'm through speeding."

"I'm glad to hear it," she said. "And some other good news. I figured out why you were able to pay for the Spacemobile."

"Was it under warranty?"

"No, dad's been yelling at the dealership on the phone about that all morning. I checked your bank account."

The privacy of having a family-connected account.

"Someone made a deposit."

"You guys didn't need to—"

"Not from us, you already owe us thirty grand. It was from Grandma. She's still connected to that account too, remember, from the money she loaned you for college."

My grandma.

"She's really been enjoying reading about your trip and wanted to help."

My dad chimed in, from another line, "She was just gonna spend the money on crap from the Home Shopping Channel anyway."

"Phil, hush!"

There it was. I could finish my trip after all. Thanks to my Midwestern grandmother, and a bit of pusher karma.

I drove on, a warm glow enveloping the whole van. The Spacemobile had cost me something I thought I wanted, but things would be okay. My Roadtrip had finally hit its stride, with five states left to go. Four, as I hit Nevada.

I looked down at the hood of the Spacemobile. Hadn't I wanted it to get me into adventures? I patted the dashboard.

"I forgive you, you stupid blue beast. I don't hate you. I only hate what you do sometimes."

The van purred, deep and guttural, like an obese kitten.

It occurred to me that I'd just had a disturbing insight into parenting.

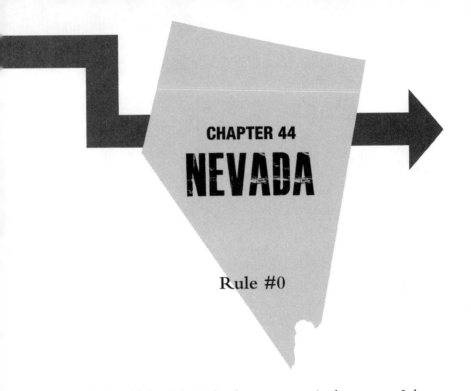

CHAPTER 44

NEVADA

Rule #0

Nevada should, by all logic, be the worst state in the country. It has no water and unbearable temperatures. It hardly has any naturally occurring resources, except silver, and who uses silver nowadays—runners-up at the Olympics? I don't even think grass grows in Nevada, unless it's watered daily by a casino.

Nevertheless, Nevada is not the worst state in the union. I won't say Nevada is the *best* state, but it certainly climbs up from the basement placement it deserves. Nevada surpasses its potential because somebody, once upon a time, understood.

"Look, people," this person probably once declared at a meeting of folks unfortunate enough to be put in charge of establishing Nevada as a state. "This place blows. We're not going to convince anybody to live here unless we do something drastic!"

"What could possibly be drastic enough to make people want to live in a state where there aren't any plants?" the resident naysayer of the group would have responded. He would have been a real curmudgeon of a fellow.

But our heroic Nevadan leader would have stood stoically for a moment, a brilliant idea burgeoning. "Simple," he would have pronounced at last. "We'll just make everything legal."

Thus, Nevada was born.

Nevada is a great place to visit. I'm not sure whether it's a great place to live or not, unless you like peeling burning strips of car upholstery off your back, but it's a fine place to drop by. You can gamble, drink publicly, patronize prostitutes . . . basically all the same stuff people do everywhere else, except that in the Silver State it's all legal.

I was surprised, then, that I managed to find something illegal to do in Nevada.

I drove all day and into the evening on a sparse spider web of tiny highways that took me west, then north, then south again. I got lost, then found, then lost again. But I didn't care. I had a bowl of cereal for lunch and a couple PBJs for dinner. I'd never again find the sandwich attractive, but I'd sort of gotten used to it, the way an orphan gets used to gruel.

Night came, and then midnight, and still I marched on down the streetlightless corridor of rural Nevada highway. I just felt like driving. Hurtling through the dark wasn't as frightening as it once had been. I'd given up the "No driving at night" rule—in fact, I'd given up all the rules. Why was I still making rules on a trip that was supposed to be breaking them? I only had four states left, and from that point on, the only rule I would follow would be Rule #0, which was not a rule at all: "Do whatever feels like an adventure." Right then, driving all night through perhaps the most desolate place in America seemed like an adventure.

I had no idea there could be a place so civilizationless, in our country of more than 300 million people. An important characteristic of a desert state is that everyone lives close together, in a couple of big metro areas. They have to: that's where the pipes bring the water.

Thus, 99 percent of people in Nevada live either near Las Vegas or near Reno. The rest of the state is empty.

And I mean *empty*.

So empty, in fact, that if you're driving a car with poor enough gas mileage, there are rural roads where you almost can't make it between gas stations on a tank of gas. This problem is exacerbated when the gas stations that do exist don't have credit-card swipers and aren't open half the time. Oh, and when you're traveling in the middle of the night.

I coasted into one of these places, on fumes, at midnight. I hesitate to even call the place a gas station—it was just somebody's abandoned house, with a gravel patch out back where a single old-fashioned pump jutted out of a chunk of cement. Not a light was on anywhere.

Besides speeding, relieving myself on trees and countless incidents of trespassing, stealing gas was the first actual law-breaking I'd done on the trip. I wriggled my way into the machine shed through a partly broken door, figured out how to turn the pump on, and filled up the Spacemobile. This, I didn't feel so bad about: who knew if anyone was going to show up again and open up shop? If you have the only gas pump in half a state, you have to expect *somebody*'s going to steal gas once in a while.

I consulted my atlas, and realized my problems weren't over. The route I was taking to Death Valley bordered a mysterious blank gray area on one side, and a whole lot of nothing on the other. There weren't any towns big enough to be dots. Where could I get gas again? Vegas, of course, but Vegas was 290 miles away, 40 miles farther than I estimated the Spacemobile could make it on a full tank of gas. I assumed there must be other stations along my way, but what did I know about gas stations in rural Nevada? Maybe it would be another deserted place like this one, with a better lock on the machine shed.

And so I did the second actual law-breaking of my trip, and this one I *did* feel a little bad about.

Near the pump was a full two-gallon gas can. It was no doubt left there for people who ran out of gas nearby and weren't nefarious enough to steal gas like I had done. That gas can undoubtedly was an act of good faith by the station owner, and it had probably saved multiple people from being stranded out in the middle of the desert, like a jug of water planted in the Sahara.

What could I do? I'd already played the "stranded in the desert" game once, and I wasn't looking forward to a rematch.

I stole the gas can.

I started to pull away.

I stopped.

I didn't know who ran the gas pump by day, but my progress couldn't come at their expense. Or at the expense of anyone else who might get stranded—and stay stranded—in the middle of the Nevada desert because I stole their lifeline.

I turned around, drove back, hopped out of the van, and left my last $60 in cash under a rock by the pump. I was already $80,000 in debt. What was a little more? I hoped it would be more than enough to cover my gas, and for the owner of the store to buy another gas can and keep from losing his faith in humanity.

I drove away and revised Rule #0: Do whatever feels like an adventure—as long as you don't stifle anybody else's adventure along the way.

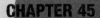

CHAPTER 45

CALIFORNIA

Letting Go

I entered California through Death Valley. This route was a fool-ish move from the beginning, trusting the world's least-reliable car through the country's most inhospitable chunk of land. I'd heard rumors about Death Valley: triple-digit temperatures even on cloudy days, no natural water for hundreds of miles . . . this was not the place you wanted your Spacemobile to break down.

Yet the van made shockingly efficient work of the sprawling des-ert. The Spacemobile might have been trying to convince me that it didn't belong on the scrap heap. Or else it simply wanted to get through Death Valley as quickly as possible. But mostly, my swift safe passage left me with the sense that Death Valley was simply not meet-ing the hype.

In covered-wagon days, I can only imagine how often the omi-nous stretch across eastern California lived up to its name. But Death Valley, probably *because* of its name and reputation, has gotten a lot of aid over the years. There are water-safety stops every two miles, and far more rest stops than a deserted stretch of county highway should have. I honestly felt overprotected, the way every airplane flight has twenty minutes' worth of safety instructions, despite the fact that many more people die every year of bee stings. My life had been in far greater danger in Montana.

Legend has it that Mark Twain once said that "America is built on a tilt, and everything loose slides to California." If he'd lived another fifty years, Twain might have amended his quote and admitted that some of it gets hung up in Las Vegas. But it's hard to sit at the Venice Beach boardwalk and not grant some truth to his words.

Yet there are other reasons people come to California, besides eccentricity and moral slipperiness. For one thing, people come to California to be free. The forty-niners came to be free of the struggles of life in the east, and to seek their fortunes. Early Hollywood came to shoot its films in every kind of terrain—deserts, mountains, and oceans—within easy access, all year round. And ever since, people have flocked to California to chase their dreams, to flee the nine-to-five, to be free from the "normal" lives that are so often expected elsewhere. California was where the Dustbowlers finally settled, their hard work and sacrifices ripening into the most populated American state.

Americans have always been about moving places to get free—that's how they became Americans in the first place. And even if there aren't any more frontiers in America these days, a lot of people see California as the closest thing we've got.

Maybe Twain was too hard on California. Or maybe Twain, a master of the English language if there ever was one, understood that "loose" and "free" are basically synonyms. Maybe Mark Twain meant both. Twain was a pretty sharp guy.

In any case, JD and I saw all sides of California freedom the afternoon we reconvened at a beachfront café overlooking the famed Venice boardwalk and the smorgasbord of humanity that traversed it. It was the first time JD and I had seen each other since the Amish General Store in Kidron, and now we were in Venice—a juxtaposition akin to leaving a monastery to join the circus. In L.A., the girl who brings you your food might be an actress or an immigrant, and the guy pacing up and down on the boardwalk yelling obscenities might be a crazy vagrant or a Hollywood agent on Bluetooth. L.A. was a place where everyone was following his own road, and JD wasn't the only person who had "slid" to California. One-eighth of America's population lived here. No matter what you were here for, it was hard to feel alone.

JD showed me around the city: the famous, the posh, the dangerous. If New York is a vertical city, L.A. is a horizontal one, sprawling for seventy temperate miles of freeways and palm tree suburbia. It was all new to a kid who'd moved there from Amish country, and JD was excited for his fresh start. This time, L.A. didn't seem so bad to me. Perhaps L.A. wasn't a place of strange, terrible things. Just new ones.

Some film-school friends let me sleep on a couch next to one where JD was crashing while he searched for an apartment. In the morning I said goodbye. But I'd come too far merely to see the ocean, turn around, and go back. So I did the most California thing I could think of.

The surfboard I rented from one of the beach-rental shops seemed a lot bigger and foamier than the ones I'd seen in *Point Break*, but the guy behind the counter told me it would be perfect for a beginner. I'd done a lot of things for the first time over the past seven weeks. Surfing was about to be one more.

Except that I couldn't even get to the surfing part. All those big waves are great when you can ride them in, but they're the same big waves you have to fight through to get out. The three-foot lake whitecaps I'd played in growing up in Minnesota hadn't prepared me to be smashed in the face by iron walls of Pacific saltwater that dragged me back the ten feet I'd progressed since the previous wave. Having a buoyant surfboard made things even worse, like walking into a windstorm with a parachute on. I would kick and crawl and fight as hard as I could, only to be pushed back again. After a dozen repetitions of this, I was exhausted, and hadn't even made it past the break. Nothing makes you feel as powerless as an angry ocean.

Finally a more experienced surfer came along, stopped, and watched me swallow another pint of seawater and scream at nature.

"Dude," he drawled. "You're doing it wrong."

Obviously.

"The break's gonna roll you back every time if you try to go right through it. You gotta go under."

He showed me. A huge wave broke right in front of us, and the guy calmly pushed the tip of his board through the surface and dove down a foot as the furious water rushed over the top of him. He emerged again, right where he'd left off, and proceeded paddling.

"You gotta relax," he offered as I tried to imitate, pushing my surfboard roughly under the next wave. I thrashed, slipped off, and caught my board right in the face.

"Don't worry about making progress when you're in the thick of it," my new mentor said. "Just dive, and chill out. Save your energy."

"Then how the hell am I supposed to get way out there?" I asked, frustrated, pointing out at the halcyon destination waters past the break.

"Wait for it to be calm. *Then* paddle."

We both dove under the next massive wave. It went better this time. Abruptly, we seemed to be at the end of a set of waves, and everything was flat. We paddled. In a minute, we were out past the break.

"See? Nothing to it," he said. "By the way, what the hell are you doing out here? The swell's huge right now, you're gonna get killed."

"I'm on a road trip," I said. "I've never been in this ocean before."

"Really, no way," he said sarcastically, sitting up on his board. "Well, it's not my fault if you drown, okay?"

"Fair enough," I said. I followed him, and sat up on my board in the suddenly calm water. I glanced around. No other waves seemed to be coming. "What do we do now?"

"We wait," he said. He held out his hand. "I'm Roger."

"Paul," I said, leaning out to shake his hand and almost falling in. "Thanks for teaching me."

"No worries," Roger said. "I just couldn't bear to watch you in there."

"Are you like a pro surfer or something?"

Roger snorted. "Ha! Yeah, right. I work at a health club. Evening shift. Gives me as much time as I want to surf. Isn't that what everyone's after?"

Before I could respond, Roger saw something and lay back down on his board.

"Get ready. Here comes."

I clumsily flopped chest-down on my board, and mimicked Roger as he paddled around to face the shore, abruptly aware that I wasn't really ready for this part.

Roger began kicking, slowly at first, to gain momentum. I kicked, along with him, my alarm rising along with the giant wall of water that was building behind us.

"Now what?" I shouted over the increasing roar of the wave.

Roger looked at me. "Now you paddle. With all your strength."

And he did. The wave rose underneath us, and Roger immediately hopped up on his board and zipped off down the foamy slope, cutting in and out of the wave like a surgeon. I kicked with everything I had and felt the wave starting to grab me.

Okay, I told myself. I'd practiced this part on shore, and once watched a surf documentary while drunk at 3 A.M. *Wait for the wave to fully take you, and then push up with your arms and get your feet under you. Nothing to it.*

The wave started to break around me. The ocean dropped away eight feet below. I began to panic.

"Abort! Abort!" Something in me screamed. "Tuck into a ball! Fetal position!"

No. Something new in me replied. *Just let go.*

My arms were trembling, but slowly they pushed me up. My board shook this way and that on the rushing wave.

Balance.

I got my knees under me. And then my feet. Stubbornly, I forced my legs to stand. They were shaking. But they did it anyway.

I was up. I was surfing.

And then I was falling.

The second I stood up, the nose of my board tilted downward, because clearly I had no idea where to stand on a surfboard. My chest collided with the board, and then I was upside down as the wave caught my fins and legs and flipped me forward, the board flying over the top of me. I plummeted straight down, and collided head first with the water.

For a moment, there was nothing. Only darkness behind my closed eyelids, and silence, as the fluid sea engulfed me and pushed me down, headfirst, into the depths. I could hear the muted crash of the different parts of the wave hitting the surface, like elongated thuds of one continuous heartbeat. And then the current grabbed me, and I was flipping end over end like a sock in a washing machine.

I wanted to kick and flail and claw my way to the surface. But something in me resisted. *Wait.* It said. *The wave is still there. Hold your breath and be patient. Wait for your opportunity.*

I waited. At last there was stillness. I kicked to the surface, screaming and laughing and gasping all at the same time. My board was on shore somewhere—I hadn't correctly leashed it to my foot.

I treaded water and started to swim back into shore, an idiotic grin spreading all over my face. That was probably enough surfing for today.

I passed Roger, on his way back out to catch another wave. He shook his head.

"Dude, you're a moron."

I returned the surfboard and cleaned up at one of the outdoor showers that speckled the shoreline. There are countries where people don't even have enough water to drink, and we have beach showers to wash the sand off your surfboard? I would never complain about having to eat sandwiches again. Of course, some pinnacle of evolution had jammed a wad of chewing gum into the shower nozzle, and the water shot out at a strange, sporadic angle, but I guess we can't have it all.

I dried off and walked to the end of the Venice Pier and stared out at the endless water. This was it. The end of contiguous America. I'd come a long way since I'd stared out at the Atlantic from the end of Long Island only five weeks earlier.

There was no going back.

I got in the Spacemobile, left Los Angeles, and was soon back in the desert of eastern California. It was a straight shot east to Four Corners, and the end of the Roadtrip. I was going to make it.

There was just one more thing I had to do.

Do whatever feels like an adventure, I thought. *As long as you don't stifle anybody else's adventure along the way.*

I finally understood what everyone on my trip had been secretly trying to tell me. Wyoming Philip. Georgia Luke. The crazy Gettysburg tour guide. If you love something, you can't be afraid to go after it.

And if you don't love something, you can't be afraid to let it go.

I picked up the phone and dialed Sarah. *Fear forward.*

"Why did you go to my family reunion with me?" I asked.

"Because you invited me."

"Yeah, but why did you agree to go? You didn't have to."

"Honestly?"

"Yeah."

"I went because we were going to break up if I didn't go."

"Not for the adventure?"

"What do you mean, adventure? It was a family reunion! What is it with you and your adventures?"

"And the editing-room floor," I said. "And Niagara Falls. And letting me go on this trip at all. You did these things for me."

"Why else would I do them? Who *likes* sleeping in weird places and freezing and being alone?"

Who indeed?

For her, Wisconsin had been a chance to spend time together. But more, it was a necessary step toward a goal: securing a relationship. A goal that everything I did seemed designed to destroy.

I pulled the van over onto the shoulder. On both sides of the road giant steel windmills whirled in rows.

I already knew the answer to my next question. I suppose I had known for some time.

"What about all those colored states we were going to see together? I thought we were going to have an adventure together someday."

"That was *your* adventure, Paul. I guess I had a different one in mind."

I suddenly realized I wasn't the only one with a list. I needed someone who was ready to experience things as much as I was. That was my ten. But Sarah needed someone who was ready to love her as much as she deserved to be loved. That was her ten.

"Maybe we're not perfect for each other," I said.

"I never said I was perfect," Sarah said. "And I never said you needed to be perfect, either."

"I did."

That was the difference between us. I looked in the rearview mirror. A basically perfect sunset hugged the mountains. You can settle for nine out of ten. As long as ten isn't the deal breaker.

In the middle of a wind turbine field in eastern California, Sarah and I broke up. This time for good.

All this time I'd been out gallivanting around the country, Sarah'd been waiting to start her own adventure. An adventure of love. An adventure of knowing someone better than you know yourself, and starting a life together. An adventure she couldn't have with me, because that was one adventure I wasn't ready to have yet.

In order for two people to be together, their adventures had to match.

"Tell The Chairman I said goodbye," I said.

"I'll tell Mister you said it."

I paused. "I loved you, Sarah."

"Goodbye, Paul," she said.

I hung up the phone. All around me, the windmills churned like clocks, blowing the past away. I looked again in the rearview. The sunset reminded me of Sarah's painting. We had carried each other's burdens long enough. It was time to unload, and drive away. I didn't cry. Not yet. I just put the car into gear and pulled back onto the highway, leaving beauty behind.

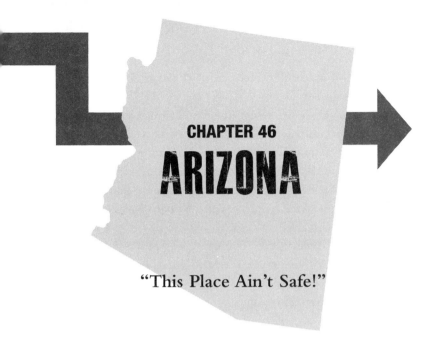

CHAPTER 46

ARIZONA

"This Place Ain't Safe!"

I drove like a zombie for 300 miles across California into Arizona. The Spacemobile was a lonely place, and not only because driving across eastern California and western Arizona in the dark is like driving across Mars (with Conoco stations).

I made it all the way to a convenience store near the Navajo reservation that occupies the entire northeast corner of Arizona before I stopped. With a pang of guilt, I realized I'd driven blindly through the state with perhaps the greatest scenery of all. From the haunted mountain ghost-town of Bisbee to the 1,000-foot Spider Rock jutting like a stone pedestal out of Canyon de Chelly, from Indian cliff dwellings to Petrified Forest to that tremendous canyon carved out of the earth by nature from a time humans never knew, Arizona laughs at other places' attempts to compete with its landmarks. I knew these spots because I'd been to them all, during annual trips to visit my grandparents in Sun City—trips that made me appreciate all there was to see in this country in the first place. And I knew I'd be back.

Paul Jury

I just wasn't in the mood to browse gift-shop bottle openers shaped like Montezuma's head.

The convenience store where I stopped for gas was nothing special. In fact, it was notably sub-special. The two teenage girls working inside looked like they'd rather be doing anything else as a slightly older teenage guy, the only other person in the store, teased them.

I pulled the Spacemobile away from the pump and parked next to an SUV in front of the store, next to a bank of payphones. My cell phone, almost poetically, had died at the end of my call with Sarah, and I needed to make a call. The deed was done, but it couldn't become official until, as with all breakups, I told my mom.

"Mom, I broke up with Sarah."

"Oh, no. . . . How did it go?"

"Not so good."

"Did she cry?"

"You know, she didn't."

"Did you cry?"

"Of course I did. After. You know I can't take that stuff."

From where I stood, I could see through the front window of the store, where the guy inside was making a real ass of himself. I guessed there wasn't a lot to do in this particular corner of Arizona on a weekday night.

"How much of it was the long-distance thing?" my mom asked.

"Some of it . . . though some of it was also that I needed to be free. I'm twenty-three, you know? I've only dated a couple of people. I don't want to spend the rest of my life wondering what else is out there, glancing over my shoulder and wondering if every other girl might be a potential adventure I was missing."

"I suspect Sarah wouldn't want that, either."

Inside the store, an argument had broken out between one of the girls behind the counter and the guy. I tried not to notice.

"But mostly, I realized I wasn't ready to give her what she needed. I feel horrible that I made her feel helpless for so long. I didn't know."

"Nobody likes feeling helpless," my mom said.

The argument in the store was getting worse. The second girl was on the phone.

"Did you love her?"

"You know, the entire time we were dating, I tried to force myself not to. Like I knew the end was coming. But I guess maybe I did."

"Did you *say* you loved her?"

"I tried to force myself not to do that, either. Like, if I said it, then it would come true, and I'd be attached, and it'd hurt more." I paused, distracted by one of the girls, now screaming at the guy. "Is that a cowardly thing to do?"

"Sort of."

A girl threw a plastic ashtray at the guy's head. He ducked, and continued to taunt them.

"Did she say she loved you?"

"A couple of times. I never knew what to say back."

"I bet that was kind of awkward."

"You're telling me. I'd always have to pretend I didn't hear it, or say, 'I really *like* you,' or 'I love *spending time* with you.' Girls hate that."

"Yeah, they do," Mom agreed.

Suddenly, a pickup truck roared up to the store and slammed on the brakes behind me. A second guy, who was around 20, jumped out, ran past me into the store, and punched the first guy in the face. The girls screamed. The two guys began wrestling in the store, trying to hit each other, but mostly just pulling each other's clothes and spinning around in a circle.

In my brief sojourn as a bouncer, I'd seen worse fights. For about half a second, I wondered if I should intervene, then quickly realized I had absolutely nothing to gain from this. And my calling card didn't have much left on it. I tried my best to continue the conversation.

"Anyway, uh, I also didn't say 'I love you' because I wanted to save it. For when I really knew I felt it."

The fighters in the store fell through a Little Debbie snack cakes display shelf. The girls screamed again.

"That's fair."

Fighter #1 ran out the door to the SUV parked next to the Spacemobile, trying to make a getaway. But Fighter #2 was right on his heels and tackled him against the door of the truck about twenty feet from me. The two began rolling around on the gas-stained pavement, panting and swinging at each other. I was now glad I hadn't intervened.

"But I didn't know when I would feel it. And every time it came up, we'd end up arguing, and both end up hurt."

Fighter #1 jumped into his vehicle and started the engine, but Fighter #2 kept landing blows through the open window. The SUV rolled backwards and began making a slow circle around the parking lot, the driver still being punched by the assailant he was unable to shake off. In my brief sojourn as a bouncer . . . I'd never seen a fight like this.

"Well, they say a relationship should be a recreational activity," my mom said. "It's no good if you're fighting all the time."

The mobile brawl passed about five feet from the Spacemobile. I changed my mind again and wished I'd somehow been able to stop the fight, back before it involved a moving car. I snuggled up closer to the payphone.

"Did she ask you to call, those nights?"

"Um . . . what?" I said, wondering if the Spacemobile was about to have a breakdown that *wasn't* caused by terrible German engineering.

"Did she make you call her, all those nights you drove around looking for outlets?"

"No. But I'd feel guilty if I didn't." I was honestly surprised I was still able to keep up this conversation.

"She never asked a thing that wasn't reasonable. It stinks that this is how I thank her."

Finally the driver slammed on his brakes and Fighter #2 fell off the car. The driver backed up, and then surged forward again, trying to run his assailant over. He stopped just short of crashing through the front window of the store.

"Hopefully she'll understand someday," my mom said.

Fighter #2 ducked safely behind a cement wall by the ice machine, about ten feet from me, swearing and taunting. At least now I knew where to charge up my phone. The driver began peeling angry donuts around the lot, narrowly missing gas pumps and the Spacemobile.

"Right?" my mom pursued, as the driver finally burned off with a squeal of tires, furiously honking his horn and flashing his lights.

"Yeah," I recovered. "I hope I will, too."

Fighter #2 did a crazed little victory dance, and then stalked over in my direction, toward his car.

"You will," said my mom.

The pugilist stomped past, casting a wild glare in my direction. "You better get out of here, fool! This place ain't safe!"

I covered the mouthpiece of the phone as the guy stared at me. I nodded. "Yeah . . . I think I'll probably take off."

The fighter charged off as I uncovered the phone. "Ma, I should go. This might not have been the best gas station to stop at."

"Okay," she said. "Well, I'm glad we got to talk. Hope you feel better."

"Yeah," I replied, as the crazed guy nearby continued to trounce wildly around the parking lot, cursing to himself and spitting. "I'll be fine. Love ya."

"Love you too. Bye."

I got back into the Spacemobile, which was still somehow untouched. I made haste down the road, leaving the fights behind.

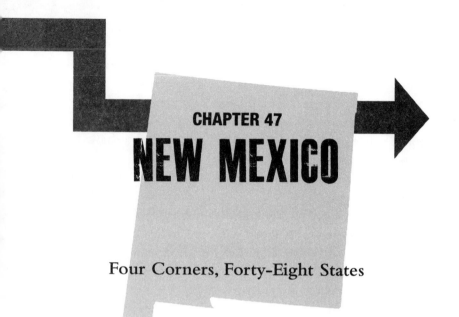

CHAPTER 47

NEW MEXICO

Four Corners, Forty-Eight States

I awoke the next morning at dawn in the boiling womb of the Spac-emobile, parked along the side of a desert near the border of Arizona and Utah. The new sun blinded my blinking eyes, but as I opened the sliding door and climbed out into the world, the morning breeze cooled my sticky skin. I was aimed at Four Corners. It was a good day to complete my mission.

But not, of course, without a little more trouble.

I swung north into Utah to hit Monument Valley, home of ran-domly jutting skyscraper rocks that rise from the flat horizon into top hats and thumbed gloves. It's the same type of painted stone that stretches all the way across New Mexico, where I'd visited Albuquer-que and Gila National Forest as a kid. New Mexico, not surprisingly, has the same kind of stunning desert scenery as its sister Arizona, only somehow Arizona came out of the deal with more cool gorges.

Monument Valley was a 180-degree different kind of beauty than the green carpet of forest in New England or the pure white beaches of Pensacola. I felt so fortunate that I'd gotten to see it all. Then again, it wasn't such an inaccessible amount of good luck that others couldn't do the same thing. All it took was $3,000 scraped together from simple jobs, two parents trusting enough to let me borrow cars for two months, one generous grandmother, and a really crazy idea. And, most importantly, being born into a country and a time where a trip like this was possible.

Less than 100 miles from Four Corners, the Spacemobile decided to drop its transmission again, almost as a statement. I wasn't even mad—heck, I'd almost been expecting it. I was in no hurry this time. I pulled the powerless van to the side of the highway, got out, and snapped probably the most iconic picture the Roadtrip could possibly have mustered: the pitch highway in the foreground, the auburn monoliths of Monument Valley in the background, and the hood-open, disabled Spacemobile in the middle.

Thankfully, the universe was on my side this time. There's cell reception in southeastern Utah—despite there being exactly three people there—and Highway 163, where I had broken down, is one of the only roads. It only took AAA forty-five minutes to find me.

Eagle, the Native American driver, smiled as I climbed into the passenger seat of his newly burdened flatbed. "Where do you wanna take the car? Probably the best place is over to Farmington, in New Mexico—"

"No!" I shouted, startling him. "No," I repeated, more calmly. "I can't go to New Mexico yet. It's complicated." Eagle probably thought I had killed somebody in New Mexico, but he didn't ask questions. This wasn't his first desert-country tow.

I had a plan for Four Corners, one final silly plan, and it didn't involve getting towed to Farmington first. Eagle didn't bother me about it. We had a pleasant drive up to another repair shop he knew, in Blanding, Utah.

The mechanic in Blanding told me the transmission would likely be covered by the warranty from the repair shop in Billings, who hadn't done a quality-enough job sewing it back together, though in their defense they probably didn't think I'd immediately turn around and drive the thing 5,000 miles across the entire West. The mechanic also told me he figured he could have the van fixed in a couple of hours. It was a slow day, he said. I was surprised by the implication that he ever had a *fast* day, since his shop in Blanding was about a billion miles from anywhere. I was on the road again by that afternoon.

This secret, wacky plan of mine involved getting to Four Corners without crossing into New Mexico or Colorado first. This plan was problematic, because the only way to access Four Corners by road is by Highway 168, which cuts across the corner of New Mexico and fires off a tiny frontage road (aptly named 4 Corners Road) to the site. So I did something that's pretty much impossible to do in most other parts of the country: I drove off Highway 168 a few miles early, still in Arizona, and simply drove across the desert.

It seemed oddly appropriate that the last few miles of my Road-trip would be carried out not on a road at all but dodging rocks and cacti in the Arizona desert. The only manmade things in sight were occasional oil pumps—those tall mechanical contraptions that rise and fall like piano hammers in the desert—which gave the whole scene a notably Mad Max feel.

More than once I had to drive wildly out of the way to avoid some dry creek bed or rock formation. More than once, I got incredibly lost and had to reorient myself using the shadows of the late-afternoon sun. Think it's easy to lose your way driving across America on back roads? Try driving across it *off* the back roads.

But I didn't mind. Every second, I expected the Spacemobile to bottom out and die for good. But it didn't. And finally I saw flags in the distance.

A few people turned and watched as a rocking Volkswagen kicked up dust and rolled into Four Corners that afternoon. They gawked as the van came to a stop between two bushes, and a sole bedraggled traveler hopped out and marched to a symbolic metal axis carved into the concrete in the middle of nowhere. They probably wondered what the heck the story was, as this random drifter jumped into the air from Arizona and landed simultaneously in New Mexico and Colorado, one foot in each state, with a triumphant war cry that startled all nearby tourists.

They probably didn't know that I had done it.

I had combed the entire country to finish my Roadtrip by driving through the raw desert, all so I could hopscotch directly from forty-six states to forty-eight. It was a ridiculous plan only a pusher could have executed, and only a nonpusher could have enjoyed.

I looked at my cell phone. It had been fifty-two days since this ridiculous trip had begun. I had failed in my symmetric quest to reach forty-eight states in forty-eight days.

But I didn't feel even 1 percent less proud.

CHAPTER 48

COLORADO

The Odds

Four Corners had been my pot of gold. Of all the scenic destinations in the United States, the one I had most looked forward to was simply a place where four states met in the dirt. And now, of course, came the disappointment: Four Corners really is just this engraved compass rose in a slab of cement in the middle of the desert, with a few tacky gift shops around. Reality can never quite live up to your dreams. But that doesn't mean it isn't worth celebrating.

There wasn't much else for me to do in New Mexico. I'd been to the state before, and frankly, completing my Roadtrip there seemed like a tough thing to top. I took 168 up into Colorado, past the ironic brown "Welcome to Colorful Colorado" sign set against a plain brown backdrop of rock and dead-looking, drought-season plants. I snapped a picture, the final entry in the giant forty-eight-state "Welcome To" sign collage I was making.

I climbed back into the Spacemobile. As I reached the mountains, Colorado returned to more of what I'd expected: emerald peaks, guys on mountain bikes, girls in tank tops and cut-off shorts. Colorado's tiny towns were bumpier and had more "chain your tires" signs, but they still adhered to the same basic formula as forty-seven other states' towns, despite regional differences. In the Southwest, there were more hacienda roofs and fewer trees. In the South, the gas stations were more likely to mention Jesus on their signs. On the East Coast, the towns seemed connected into one giant, continuous small town. But they all felt like home to me now.

South of Denver, I called my dad. It took a few rings before he let me interrupt the preseason Vikings game he was watching.

"Dad," I said. "I'm moving to Los Angeles. I'm going to try to be a writer."

"I thought you hated Los Angeles."

"No," I replied. "I was just afraid of it."

I heard my dad shift the phone to hear better.

"It's okay to be afraid," he said. "As long as you do it anyway."

I was trying to get to the northern Denver suburbs to meet my friend Greg. As always, navigation was tough without interstates.

"And hey," my dad added. "The odds are probably best in L.A."

"Tell Grandma I'm sorry. I know she'd rather see me married in Minnesota."

"Oh, I think she just wants you to be happy. She'll get over it. Just don't miss Christmas or she might stab you."

"Of course."

I was pretty sure I'd turned onto the wrong highway, but I didn't care.

"So what made you decide?" my dad said.

"You know, it's weird," I said. "There wasn't any one thing, any one moment. But when I think back, the signs were there all along."

The Spacemobile was also starting to make weird noises. I took a deep breath. One more question.

"You're not mad?" I asked. "That I'm not coming back to Minnesota to work for your company?"

"Don't be ridiculous," said my dad. "I knew you weren't coming back the second you left."

I'd never been much for fate. I preferred to rely on statistics, and probability. Like the probability that, because the Spacemobile broke down exactly every 2,000 miles, I'd better call AAA and upgrade to their premium membership, which included five free annual tows instead of two. And thus, it didn't seem like some supreme intervention of the universe when, less than twenty-four hours later, the Spacemobile symbolically broke down one more time near Denver.

My tow driver—Carl this time, I think (honestly, all their names were starting to blur together)—dropped me off at the Volkswagen dealership in downtown Boulder. I called Greg to see where I could meet him, once he was done with work and the mechanics were done sewing another dead car part onto my van.

I stepped outside the dealership to get better reception.

"Hey Greg, I'm here finally—I had no idea this was such a big area," I said.

"Yeah, it's huge," returned his filtered voice. "There're like a couple million people in greater Denver."

"I'm probably nowhere near you, then. I'm in Boulder—they had to tow me all the way up here because it was the nearest dealership. But I can cab back. Where do want to meet?"

"Actually, I'm in Boulder too," said Greg. "I work here."

Something caught my eye, and I moved toward the edge of the parking lot.

"If your car's not ready, I can swing by and pick you up. I'm about to leave—"

"Wait a minute, Greg—you work at a car dealership, right?"

"Yeah."

"A Ford dealership?"

"Yeah..."

"John Townsend Ford? In downtown Boulder . . ."

"Yeah . . . ?" he sounded puzzled. "How do you know that?"

"Right next to a Volkswagen dealership. Are you by any chance wearing a pinstripe shirt, and standing next to a window in your office?"

Greg turned and looked out his window. There I was, staring at him the whole time, about thirty feet away.

Greg and I sat under the stars on his back porch that night, drunkenly contemplating the mysteries of the universe.

He told me of his training to become a pro skier, of his car-selling job in the meantime, and how last night his roommate had thrown up into the map pocket on the back of the driver's seat in Greg's car after a long night at the bars. I was glad they were still making time to party.

My friend had grown up in Michigan and was now living in a city far away across the country, chasing what he loved. It was a bond we would soon share.

"So many people just stay where they grew up, forever," I said, reaching into the box of Coors and tapping the Rockies for a sixth time. "But what are the odds that we're born into the exact state, the exact *city*, where we're supposed to end up?"

"Or that the first girl you date is the one you're supposed to be with," said Greg.

"Or that the first job you have is the one you're supposed to keep."

Greg thought about it for a minute. "It depends, I suppose. On whether or not you believe in fate."

The Colorado stars glowed over the mountain silhouettes in the distance. Greg got up and tried to pee off the porch, and nearly fell into the bushes.

"So you're gonna be a writer, huh?" he said, sitting back down. "You better write about my stupid roommate puking last night. I swear to God, a map pocket has to be the *worst* place to clean vomit out of."

"I'll try," I said.

"What if you can't get paid for writing for a while?" he asked.

I shrugged. "I can always try to find a job writing textbooks or something."

Greg sat back down. "How does it feel to finally know your direction?"

"Good," I said. "Though part of me is annoyed that I wasted an entire year in crappy jobs and uncertainty, figuring it all out."

Greg just looked at me. "Dude. You haven't wasted a thing."

That next night I slept my final night of the Roadtrip in the Spacemobile, on the shoulder of a highway on-ramp somewhere in central Nebraska, nestled snugly between two semis. The Spacemobile *had* once been a German delivery truck, after all, before they put in more seats and took out all reliable engine components. It really was an awful vehicle. But it had taught me some important lessons.

I don't think the truckers minded the relatively tiny turquoise van in their midst. Deep in their road-trip hearts, I think they understood that this car—and its driver—was just one of the guys.

CALIFORNIA 2

The Next Adventure

The Roadtrip wasn't quite over. There was still the small matter of packing up all my things in Minnesota and driving back across the country again to Los Angeles. For some people, a 2,000-mile drive across three time zones would be enough to be called its own Roadtrip, but for me it felt like a cool-down. Somehow I still hadn't driven the Spacemobile into the ground, and my parents magnanimously told me I could bring it with me to California until I did. They called it a belated graduation present. I think they just wanted to be rid of the damn thing.

I ran my marathon, up and down the hills and through the rain of Rhode Island, where my brothers cheered me on in a race to downtown Providence that *didn't* get sidetracked by Connecticut cops. My all-terrain training served me well, landing me in 247th place out of about 2,000 people. But I didn't sprint. That temptation will always be with me, I guess, but a marathon's no fun if you push it the whole time, and the scenery's better if you slow down. And maybe the 88th percentile is still pretty good.

I spent my last week in Minnesota canoeing in the Boundary Waters with Charlie. He was my best friend, after all, and it would be the last time I saw him for a while. Charlie had grown out of smuggling marijuana in Cheez-It boxes, but we did bring a water bladder full of whiskey into our canoe. Some things you never grow out of.

One morning as Charlie packed up the tent and I trudged through the woods trying to find where I'd hung our bear bag, I was hit with the same feeling I'd had one afternoon in the Upper Peninsula of Michigan, right before college. The blank slate. I gazed out at the sunrise over a thousand connected lakes of my home state, and I had no idea what lay ahead for me in California. I knew what lay behind me, but none of that seemed to matter. I felt a disconnect from time. There was only the present.

I carried that feeling with me as I left my parents' home in Minneapolis for the last time. My future stood ahead of me, unwritten. The only difference now was that since the last time I'd left home, my past had added another chapter to me. Maybe several chapters.

My dad came with me as far as Denver, where I dropped him off to visit some clients before he flew back home. I don't know whether he did it to keep me company or to keep me out of trouble. Maybe he did it for a little Roadtrip adventure of his own as he underwent a transition of a different kind, as his oldest son headed off into the world. I welcomed the company. It was comforting to know that even as I moved on into the dark, I could still carry the lights of home with me. I left Denver down Highway 40 toward Salt Lake City, a beautiful route my dad had taken so many times before. Maybe I was following him just a little bit, after all.

I drove through the Rockies of Colorado and Utah, two of my favorite states from the Roadtrip, and swung up to drive through southern Idaho again, this time *not* at 115 mph. My parents had scraped together a little extra money for me, for a first month's rent in L.A. and hotels on the way there, but I couldn't keep myself from checking out deserted side roads and sheltered freeway underpasses and thinking, *Ooh, I bet that would be a pretty good place to sleep!* With my ability to subsist off nothing but trail mix and milk for months at a time, I figured that in the worst case, if things didn't work out in L.A., I'd make a pretty terrific homeless person.

I crossed the final item off my "Things to Do in America" list when I hit the Redwoods of northern California. Nothing makes you feel insignificant like standing next to a 200-foot-tall tree that's been rooted there for 2,000 years, watching insignificant things like you come and go.

The forest-lined corridor at the mouth of Highway 1 at Leggett marked the final leg of the final leg. The Spacemobile would not let it pass uneventfully.

I had determined to ride the scenic Pacific Coast Highway all the way down the coast. It's not the fastest or safest way to get to L.A., but I figured if I could only pick one road to drive, I might as well choose the one that's most memorable. The Spacemobile was not pleased about my choice. Either it had wanted to die peacefully in Billings or it was upset that the Roadtrip was coming to an end, but whatever the reason, my trip south on the scenic Pacific Coast Highway was one mechanical disaster after another. Navigating the PCH, with its precipitous roads and hairpin turns, is an amazing but challenging drive in any car; attempting it in the Spacemobile was like dancing a ballet in ski boots.

In San Francisco, one of the tires went flat and I had to be towed again. The tire hadn't caught a nail or anything—it had simply decided to give up and die.

Near Monterey, the muffler's back end started dragging, kicking up sparks behind the van like an inverted bumper car until I was able to reattach the thing with some duct tape and a consequently ruined driving glove.

Then in Santa Barbara, the other end of the muffler came loose, which was a far more dangerous situation. I now had a long piece of metal jutting forward and grazing the concrete, ready to hit a pothole and spring the van up into a front flip in an automotive pole vault. So I did the only thing a reasonable person would do in such a spot: I simply pulled off the muffler entirely, threw it in the rear of the van on top of the desk, dresser, and queen-sized mattress that were already back there, and kept driving. I figured with a car as roguish as the Spacemobile, a muffler is kind of an optional piece of equipment anyway. Maybe I could put it to use, like put a wig on it and use it to get in the carpool lane. I could hear the conversation:

COP: Excuse me sir, you can't use the carpool lane with onl—Is that your muffler in your passenger seat?

ME: Wha—! Dude, that's my girlfriend!

Random note: If my girlfriend was a muffler, her name would be Muffleen.

These are the kinds of thoughts that bubble up when you're crawling slowly down the Pacific Coast Highway, wondering what part of your car will fall off next.

But I didn't care. L.A. would wait for me. In the meantime, the highway was beautiful. Have you ever driven somewhere, and *really* didn't care how long it took to get there? Only when you stop worrying about your destination do you really appreciate where you are.

Smoke began seeping from the hood as I finally entered L.A. County. I don't think anything was even wrong with the engine—the Spacemobile just wanted to add a final piece of flair to my dramatic entrance. Tourists turned and stared at the smoking van with Minnesota plates as I passed through Santa Monica and noticed the Route 66 marker at the end of the pier. That stupid road had led me from Chicago to Los Angeles after all.

And that was how I limped into Redondo Beach, my new home: cracked windshield, no bumper, stalling, smoking engine, broken emergency break, and the filthy muffler in the back, kept off my furniture by the spread-out pages of a torn, dog-eared two-foot-tall road atlas. Maybe the Spacemobile was telling me it was time for my journey to end. Or maybe it was just a terrible, terrible car.

Part of me wished the Roadtrip wasn't over—that I could drive around forever. But it was time for the next adventure. And with forty-eight states, 19,000 miles, five cop stops, four tows, three cars, one girlfriend, and twenty-three years behind me, I was no longer afraid to drive into the darkness.

The next morning we roused the Spacemobile to help us pick up a ping-pong table for my new house with JD and two other college friends. That magnificent blue beast fit the entire damn thing inside.

THE PLAN

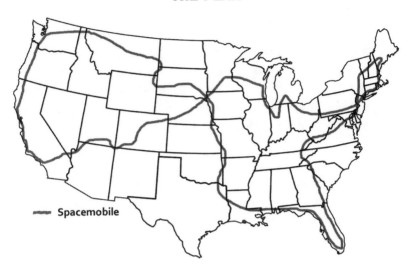

THE RESULT

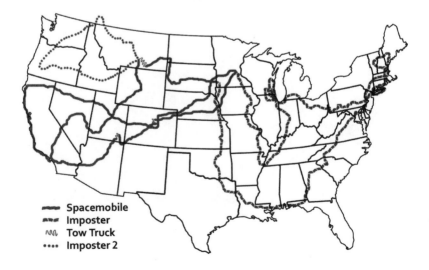